The Conservatoire Américain

A History

Kendra Preston Leonard

THE SCARECROW PRESS, INC.
Lanham, Maryland • Toronto • Plymouth, UK
2007

SCARECROW PRESS, INC.

Published in the United States of America
by Scarecrow Press, Inc.
A wholly owned subsidiary of
The Rowman & Littlefield Publishing Group, Inc.
4501 Forbes Boulevard, Suite 200, Lanham, Maryland 20706
www.scarecrowpress.com

Estover Road
Plymouth PL6 7PY
United Kingdom

British Library Cataloguing in Publication Information Available

Library of Congress Cataloging-in-Publication Data

Leonard, Kendra Preston.
  The Conservatoire américain : a history / Kendra Preston Leonard.
    p. cm.
  Includes bibliographical references (p.   ) and index.
  ISBN-13: 978-0-8108-5732-2 (pbk. : alk. paper)
  ISBN-10: 0-8108-5732-4 (pbk. : alk. paper)
  1. Conservatoire américain—History. I. Title.

MT5.F66C66 2007
780.71'14437—dc22   2006026100

To Karen and Winston Leonard,
to Anita Wiegand,
and to the memory of Lucia Ward

Contents

Acknowledgments

There are many people who have assisted me in the creation of this book. I would like to thank Pierre Boyer; Thérèse Casadesus Rawson; Diana Vilas Gladden; Joe Kerr; and Debra Takakjian, all with the Fontainebleau Associations; the Office du Conservateur du Chateau, Palais de Fontainebleau; and the Bibliothèque Municipale de Fontainebleau.

I am grateful to Elizabeth Austin; Walter Bailey; John G. Doll; Jay Gottlieb; James Harrison; Charles Kaufman; Jean-Pierre Marty; Emile Naoumoff; Jean O'Hara; Elizabeth Saylor; and the late Mrs. H. P. (Elsie) Watson for providing me with archival materials and interviews.

Thanks also to Linda Carmona; Jessie Fillerup; Karin Pendle; Karl Rufener; Carl Serpa; Beth Snodgrass; and Robert Zierolf; and to Dorel Abbott; John Abbott; Perry Bartsch; Marion Bleyler; Mr. and Mrs. Hiram Cody; Mr. and Mrs. Charles Cole; Joan Clark; Lorene Dover; Ursula Harris; Dr. and Mrs. Drew Litzenberger; Virginia Mallard; Matilda Mauldin; Mr. and Mrs. Maloy Rash Jr.; Mr. and Mrs. Clay Whittaker; Anita Wiegand; and Karen and Winston Leonard.

I am indebted to Renée Camus of Scarecrow Press, who has been a champion for this book. I would also like to thank the book's anonymous reviewers for their generosity of time and assistance.

Research for this book was supported by grants from the National Coalition of Independent Scholars; the Peabody Conservatory of Music Alumni Career Development Fund; and the University of Cincinnati University Research Council. The Fontainebleau Associations also supported my research through two residencies at the Conservatoire.

Introduction

In the years preceding the First World War, American music students seeking advanced study typically traveled to Germany to enroll at the conservatories—known as *Hochschule*—there. Few American universities or colleges offered professional-level programs for training serious composers or performers until the late years of the nineteenth century (Yale, which granted its first degree in music in 1890, is one example) and early years of the twentieth century. The majority of those schools that did attempt to educate musicians did so for the purposes of creating music instructors for primary and secondary schools and private teaching. Although a few institutions were founded around the turn of the century for professionals—Juilliard opened in 1905 with the aim of keeping Americans in America for their studies—many students still felt that the best place for them to obtain their education was in Europe. Based on the assumption that Germanic models of composition and approaches to precise execution in performance were the best any nation had to offer, a significant number of American composers and instrumentalists attended school in Germany and Austria following their initial studies in the United States. America's best-known nineteenth-century composers, including John Knowles Paine, George Chadwick, Arthur Foote, Amy Beach, Sidney Homer, and Edward MacDowell, all benefited from German or Austrian educations that exposed them to repertoire, interpretations, and techniques lacking in American music schools of the day. These schools emphasized clarity of form and a strong allegiance to tonality, and introduced Americans to abstract and programmatic conceptualizations, with most American composers choosing to work in the latter camp.

Instrumentalists also went abroad for their advanced studies; pianist Amy Fay's celebrated memoir of her time as a student of Franz Liszt is but one account of an American musician receiving training in Europe.[1] Female instrumentalists were especially drawn to study in Germany and Austria, where, following the model of Clara Schumann and other professional women, female concert artists were both comfortably situated as normal members of society and positively received in the concert hall as serious artists. The students who made this trek and enrolled in the *Hochschule* in those countries were serious practitioners who had exhausted their domestic resources for coaching and pedagogy and were, without exception, less interested in pursuing the more traditional path of becoming an educator than in attaining the career of a soloist. Pianist Julie Rive-King, violinists Camille Urso and Maud Powell, and cellist Elsa Reugger all left the United States to pursue further training in Germany and Austria, having found that the societal limitations placed on women in the United States hampered their abilities to reach their full potential.

With the entry of the United States into the Great War, however, much civil interaction between America and Germany ceased. Reactionary musicians refused to play works by German composers; orchestras began to replace German musicians with those from France, Belgium, and Russia; and it was decidedly impolitic—and often logistically impossible—for anyone to go to Germany, for educational reasons or any other purpose. The practice of American composers and performers pursuing study at Leipzig came to a halt, and Americans began staying at home for advanced musical training. However, this loss of continental training opportunities was felt among students across the country, who found that, with few exceptions, the education provided by music schools in the United States still could not compare with the more rigorous and demanding courses they had taken abroad. At the end of the war, students began exploring their options in regard to international education and found that France, grateful for the assistance provided by American forces during the war, was a welcoming place for young musicians. While Americans could not generally enroll at the Paris Conservatory due to its severe admittance restrictions, there were other opportunities for advanced instruction.

Although France had not been the top destination for American musicians prior to the war, it had a long and distinguished history of excellence in music education. Children in France were required to learn an instrument and take intensive courses in music history, analysis, and ear-training from a young age, resulting in a significant percentage of citizens with absolute pitch. Dance and music were part of the traditional elementary and secondary school curricula, and students with exceptional abilities were channeled into regional conservatories at an early age for accelerated training. From these regional conservatories, students were prepared for auditions at the national conservatories, the most prestigious of which was the Conservatoire National Supérieur de Musique et de Danse de Paris, known as the Paris Conservatoire. Here, students worked with a master teacher and an assistant who oversaw practice sessions, participating in daily master classes, rehearsals, and performances. As they reached the end of their studies, students competed for a number of prizes in their areas; only a first prize, or *Premier Prix*, guaranteed graduation and full recognition in the professional musical community. Prior to the war, alumni included Hector Berlioz, Georges Bizet, Gustave Charpentier, Alfred Cortot, Claude Debussy, Paul Dukas, Marcel Dupré, Jacques Ibert, Édouard Lalo, Maurice Ravel, Camille Saint-Saëns, and Pablo de Sarasate.

The Paris Conservatoire might have been the perfect place for Americans seeking to study abroad following the war, were it not for its limiting admissions policies. The Paris Conservatoire did not, at that time, admit any students over twenty-six, nor—with a few exceptions—any foreigners. There was, however, a solution. In fact, the French had gone so far as to establish a conservatory specifically for American music students, a school born out of wartime musical exchange. This institution, known as the Conservatoire Américain, boasted a faculty and courses drawn directly from the Paris Conservatory and provided three months of intensive study during the summer months at the Palais de Fontainebleau, located just outside of Paris.

Over the course of its existence, the Conservatoire has been host to the world's top musicians both as students and faculty. Composers and performers including Aaron Copland, Virgil Thomson, David Diamond, Elliott Carter, Bathia Churgin, Quincy Jones, Idil Biret, June Anderson, Emile Naoumoff, and Pamela Frank all studied at the school during the course of their careers. The faculty roster has boasted Robert and Gaby Casadesus, Nadia Boulanger, Maurice Ravel, and Yehudi Menuhin among those providing instruction. While there has been copious scholarship about these individuals— Boulanger and her students in particular—there has not previously been a full accounting of the Conservatoire's history as an individual entity that stands as one of the foremost institutions for training American musicians in the twentieth century. *The Conservatoire Américain: A History* charts this history through the use of archival documents, letters, school publications, diaries, and interviews with pivotal figures in the school's past.

The Conservatoire Américain: A History is divided into seven chronological sections. In addition, three first-person interludes testify to the experiences of students and faculty at turning points in the Conservatoire's history: from the summer before the outbreak of the Second World War, to the return of the school to its home at the Palais de Fontainebleau following the war, to the last years of Nadia Boulanger's life and tenure as director, to the school's struggles for relevance in a post-Boulanger musical world. The prologue details the founding of the Conservatoire and the goals of its creators to develop a school where Franco-American relations, high levels of musicianship, and equal opportunities for professional women could be fostered. It includes the definitive statement of these goals set forth by cofounder Francis Casadesus at the time of the school's opening in 1921 and describes the faculty and students recruited by the Conservatoire to fulfill these aims.

"The Institution without Precedent" chronicles the Conservatoire's first "golden age": the period prior to the Second World War during which the school taught record numbers of students and attracted stellar performers as faculty members and clinicians. This section also discusses the extramusical educations students received in social behavior, European culture, and class structures. "Exile and War" provides an account of the school's existence in the United States during the war, a time when it was kept alive by a handful of dedicated instructors in America and supporters in France. Secret rooms, borrowed pianos, and a fervent desire to maintain the Conservatoire's standards in a time of great privation all contributed to this period and gave it a bit of a cloak-and-dagger history.

"La Belle Dame Sans Merci" takes its name from the Keats poem of the same name, in which a knight finds that the lady who has promised him love has, in fact, enslaved her admirers. The section deals with Nadia Boulanger's rise to power within the Conservatoire and her controversial tenure as its director, during which she was viewed both as a teacher of near-mythical abilities and as one who was seen as manipulative and damaging in her relations with students. By including widely varying viewpoints from her students, this section seeks to demythologize Boulanger by assessing her actions on behalf of the Conservatoire in an objective light. "Après elle le deluge" refers to Louis XV's comment that following his reign, French society would fall into a state of collapse; the years following Boulanger's death epitomize this precisely. This section discusses the problems the Conservatoire experienced following Boulanger's death. This was a period marked by instability in the school's mission and direction, as well as a continuous flux in leadership. "The Frog Rodeo"—a term used by administrators and students alike to describe the chaotic French and American collaboration that tries to keep things organized at the school—describes the Conservatoire's most recent incarnation as a mostly well-intentioned but not always well-executed program. Finally, the epilogue offers an assessment of the Conservatoire today.

Note

1. Amy Fay, *Music-Study in Germany: The Classic Memoir of the Romantic Era, with a New Introduction by Francis Dillon* (New York: Dover Publications, 1991).

~

A Note on
Bibliographic Abbreviations

Source materials for this book were found in many places. These included the Conservatoire Américain's archives in the Palais de Fontainebleau and in the school's other holdings in Fontainebleau; the Bibliothèque Municipale de Fontainebleau; the Conservatoire Américain's archival storage areas in New York; the personal holdings of administrators of the Conservatoire Américain; the private archives of Diana Vilas Gladden in New Haven, Connecticut, which encompass the personal materials of several late administrators and students of the school; and original materials (such as interview transcripts) held by the author. In order to accurately reflect the locations of these materials, notes and other citations often include the following abbreviations:

CA/F—Conservatoire Américain Archives, Palais de Fontainebleau and Conservatoire Américain properties, Fontainebleau, France
CA/NY—Conservatoire Américain Archives, New York
CA/GA—Conservatoire Américain Archive, Gladden Archives, New Haven, Conn.
BMF—Bibliothèque Municipale de Fontainebleau, Fontainebleau, France

~

Francis Casadesus's Manifesto and the Founding of the Conservatoire Américain (1918–1920)

On June 26, 1921, the Conservatoire Américain opened its doors in the Palais de Fontainebleau to some ninety American music students. After years of German domination of American higher education in music, a musical reversal was upon Europe. France, grateful for American assistance during the Great War, was prepared to offer to its allies an entirely new and engaging prospect: a summertime conservatory created expressly for American musicians wishing to acquire the performance techniques, analytical methods, and interpretative skills taught at the illustrious Paris Conservatoire. The vision was a revolutionary one, led by French and American musicians sharing a common goal of promoting intercultural musical exchange and higher learning.

The Conservatoire had its genesis in the military-music enthusiasms of General John "Black Jack" Pershing, the commander of the Allied Expeditionary Forces in World War I. An avid supporter of military bands, Pershing was the creator of the famed "Pershing's Own" virtuoso army band. After hearing European military bands, he became concerned about the proficiency of American ensembles, and sought to imbue the skills of his bandmasters with a little European flair, requesting the creation of a training program for them in 1918. The men chosen to create and direct this school for American military bandleaders, located at the Loire chateau of Chaumont, were conductors Walter Damrosch and Francis Casadesus. Damrosch, born in Germany in 1862 but by this time an American citizen, was at that time the much-admired director of the New York Philharmonic and well known in Europe. Eager to spread classical music across the wide plains of his adopted country, Damrosch was an influential supporter of new orchestras and music schools throughout the United States, and was an exceptional educator, creating the first radio and television programs in classical music for children. Parisian-born Casadesus was likewise a highly regarded musician: a man of immense energy and talent, he was born in 1870 to a large and influential musical family, and he and his siblings began their musical education at a young age. Casadesus studied with César Franck at the Paris Conservatoire, where he received equal training as a composer, conductor, and pianist. He conducted the Opéra and Opéra Comique orchestras, toured as a conductor in Russia, and wrote extensively for French music journals.[1] Together, Damrosch and Casadesus represented a synthesis of American and French approaches to musical education and training: in short, they were perfect choices for Pershing's multinational project. Working in concert, they ably outlined a program for the bandmasters' school, at which American soldiers would receive thorough training by the very best musicians France had to offer. The Americans would gain the continental musical education no longer available to them in Germany, and French musicians would be able to display their prowess, cultural sophistication, and generosity at a time when the other major musical power of western Europe was politically and economically unable to perform. Casadesus and Damrosch began their project by readily acknowledging the objectives and intents of the nations involved, and aimed high, hoping to create an institution that would meet the demands and goals of both.

All of the teachers at the bandmasters' school were to be either high-profile graduates or active and well-known professors from the renowned Paris Conservatoire. Classes would likewise be patterned after those at the Conservatoire, and the repertoire would be predominantly French. French technique and interpretation also figured heavily into the course planning for the Americans' summer school, and students were expected to acquire and retain French approaches to both performance skills and analytical abilities. This school for Army bandmasters, named the École Américaine du Chef de Musique, opened for the first time in the summer of 1919. Its goals were straightforward: to train army musicians, as instructed by Casadesus and Damrosch, in the areas of theory, counterpoint, harmony, and solfège— areas of study often brushed aside by American bands. In addition to classroom instruction, students were given individual lessons and participated in master classes designed to strengthen their instrumental performance skills and provide them with the rudiments of conducting large and small ensembles, preparing them for leading their peers in concert. Students learned to seek the "grande ligne," a French musical philosophy which holds that melody above all creates form and structure; and were introduced to the French ideal of "bon gout"—the good taste necessary to interpret and perform any piece of music appropriately within the French aesthetics of subtlety, shading, and lyricism.

Although the bandmasters' school was not intended to be permanent, Casadesus and Damrosch soon found that support ran high for the continuation of a summertime "American Conservatory" in France, one that would expand on the initial idea of the bandmasters' academy and develop into a more fully realized conservatory open to civilians. In addition to continuing to promote what Damrosch termed French-American "artistic solidarity," this proposed school also would give France all of the advantages enjoyed by Germany's year-round conservatory programs in Leipzig, Düsseldorf, and Cologne: professors from the Paris Conservatoire would continue to teach, and American students would have an outlet for European study similar to what they had enjoyed in Germany prior to the start of hostilities. Having only recently emerged from the long, emotionally and economically devastating Great War, the idea of France outperforming the German musical system of traditional and summer conservatory programs—a system of which the Germans were very proud and which, prior to the war, had attracted vast numbers of American students in search of advanced musical training—was irresistible for the French. Indeed, the wartime "Comité-Franco-Américain," a society of young French musicians that included Nadia and Lili Boulanger, had sought to provide comforts in the form of morale-boosting events and newsletters for troops drawn from the cultural life of both countries. Members of this committee, which included American patron and composer Blair Fairchild, were highly enthusiastic about Damrosch's and Casadesus's plans, and while they were not directly involved in the founding or development of the Conservatoire Américain, the fact that the committee had existed during the war further encouraged the men to pursue their course of action. Damrosch, with his eye on the further education of even the most polished American musicians, began to see the potentials of sending his New York Philharmonic players for extra schooling while the orchestra enjoyed its summer hiatus. With the war over, the French often were eager to show their appreciation for the American war effort, and Casadesus and Damrosch had no trouble establishing several committees both in France and the United States to help with the financial requirements of such a school, as well as with publicity and the recruitment of students and faculty.[2] The partnership of Damrosch and Casadesus in this expanded endeavor could not be bettered: Damrosch had access to American dollars and publicity, as well as the ears of his society patrons in New York; Casadesus presented the initial idea to con-tinue the bandmasters' school on a more elevated plane and had the reputa-tion and contacts within France needed to succeed at finding domestic spon-sors and enthusiastic professors for the faculty. Since the philosophical elements of the school's mission had essentially been settled with the open-ing of the bandmasters' school—now simply expanded to include civilians—the difficulties would come in the form of financing the operation and in the logistics of actually opening and maintaining a school that hoped to attract hundreds of young Americans to France for upward of three months.

To begin his part of the Conservatoire's founding, Casadesus wrote that he simply "began an inquiry in America on the subject of the founding of an 'École des Hautes Études Musicales de France.'" The response to his let-ter was enormous, and an outpouring of encouragement and support came from all quarters: musical, governmental, and commercial. "My initial let-ter," Casadesus wrote, "produced interest [from] a large number of important people."[3] With these "important people" including composer Camille Saint-Saëns and music publisher Jacques Durand, both of whom fully endorsed his idea, Casadesus began researching the logistics of his idea: the precise goals of such a school, the location, the capital. Among those interested in help-ing with the project was Maurice Fragnaud, the Sous-Préfet (equivalent to lieutenant governor) of Fontainebleau, a bedroom community of the na-tion's capital. Fragnaud made Casadesus an offer: abandon the Loire and drafty halls of Chaumont and establish the new school closer to Paris, in Fontainebleau.

Fragnaud's offer of his town and its chateau for the new school's home was a smart one. A lifelong music lover, Fragnaud found himself in charge of the municipality of Fontainebleau at a time when the little village's prox-imity to Paris—just forty miles southeast of the capital—might have caused it to be overlooked in government dispensation of restoration funding and in both domestic and international assistance. While Fontainebleau was considered a posh suburb of the capital and home to an impressive former royal residence, its streets remained unpaved and its railway station was in disrepair following the end of the war. By bringing to his town a conserva-tory boasting famous musicians from both sides of the Atlantic as adminis-trators and faculty, as well as by delivering the society patronage that would surely accompany such artists and their endeavors, Fragnaud wisely reck-oned that Fontainebleau could only be bettered by the experience. Count-ing on the influx of cash that students and professors would likely spend in Fontainebleau, Fragnaud also correctly predicted that the presence of a con-servatory would assist its economy. For American musicians, Fragnaud further reasoned, a serious summer music school in France would prove irre-sistible for both accomplished performers and amateurs, especially at a time when composers and performers balked at the traditional idea of studying in Germany. With all of these aspects in mind, he arranged for the newly es-tablished Conservatoire Américain to be granted the use of the vast Louis XV wing of the Palais de Fontainebleau. This pairing of school and chateau would become an important aspect of the Conservatoire's identity as it de-veloped, creating an association that inextricably linked the fortunes of the school to its relationship with the Palais. As a location for a music school hoping to emphasize the artistic heritage of France and to impress its Amer-ican pupils, it was matchless.

The location of the school in the Palais, in addition to being logistically impeccable, also provided a glamour and sophistication unrivaled by other European conservatories. For the wealthy patrons backing the school, the idea of students attending classes in one of France's grandest chateaux was an extraordinary status symbol. The school's staff began using images of the Palais in promotional materials even before the first students reveled in the extravagance of living and studying within its tawny walls. Astute adminis-tration by the Conservatoire's publicity arm continued the association of the music school with the town and the Palais that originated with Fragnaud's decision to host the school, and eventually alumni, having been enchanted by their surroundings, also contributed to the sense of grandeur coupled with the Conservatoire Américain.

Initially built as a hunting lodge in the 1400s, the Palais de Fontainebleau fell in and out of favor with French royalty for many years until Louis XV re-turned to the vast treasures of the chateau, commissioning new works for it. Shortly after Napoleon's rise to power, the emperor took the chateau as his residence, filling it with even more valuable art and adding a theater while restoring parts of the building that had fallen into disrepair. Home to price-less paintings, furniture, antiquities, frescos, silk and damask wall hangings, sculpture, and other fine and decorative arts, the Palais de Fontainebleau is a worthy rival to Versailles.

The surrounding forest was landscaped for the pleasure of royal riders and hunters. Two celebrated gardens, the Jardin de Diane and the Jardin Anglais, were carefully planned, one to re-create a shaded glen with leafy trees, pea-cocks, and a quiet fountain displaying a whimsical sculpture, the other an ex-hibit of color and design. In the eighteenth century a glass pavilion was built in the center of the Etang des Carpes (Carp Pond), which itself is bordered by a terrace of the chateau and long lines of trees. Most famous of all is the centerpiece of the Palais, the Horseshoe Staircase that descends from the entrance of the castle into the White Horse Courtyard. Between the chateau and the grounds, the new music school had found a very luxurious place to call home, one with more than enough room for faculty and student lodgings, practice rooms, classrooms and studios, and concert venues.

While Casadesus and Fragnaud worked in France to secure the conservatory a location, Damrosch was at work across the Atlantic. Impressed by the strength of the initial French reactions to the proposal, Damrosch threw his energy into the idea of a summer school for Americans in France, calling on his own patrons and colleagues in the United States to contribute financial and material resources and to raise publicity for the school. Damrosch proved an excellent fund-raiser for the school, contributing significantly to the coffers of the fledgling conservatory. He worked in New York with charitable groups including the American Friends of French Musicians (a relief agency that had raised money during the war for enlisted musicians and their families), courted countless individual patrons, and mounted an extensive and costly advertising campaign prior to the school's opening in 1921. Networking within his New York social circle, Damrosch urged society figures to support and become personally involved with the project, among them Harry Harkness Flagler, the president of the Symphony Society of New York and a prominent philanthropist especially interested in American arts and music, having endowed the New York Symphony Orchestra with the funds needed to make its first European tour with Damrosch; Charlotte Sanford, president of the New York Schubert Club and an early patron of the bandmasters' school; Mr. and Mrs. Blair Fairchild, both musicians themselves; and Mabel Tuttle, the president of L'Alliance Franco-Américaine. Damrosch promoted the new school heavily within the orchestral world as well, asking Leopold Stokowski and other luminaries of the concert hall to endorse the project. Such endorsements, in turn, fueled more contributions and donations, and naturally led to high rates of interest and application among potential enrollees.

Once a location was secured and the necessary financial backing was coming in from both French and American patrons, Casadesus was ready to announce publicly what he had achieved thus far, as well as articulate the long-term goals he and Damrosch had decided on for the school as it progressed beyond the bandmasters' academy. In August 1919, Casadesus issued a statement, in English, describing the path he had taken to that point, and his ultimate ambitions for the Conservatoire. (For the sake of authenticity, it is presented here in its original form; clarifying indicia in brackets are the author's.)

After having spent seven months at Chaumont, teaching instrumentation to the A.E.F. [Air Expeditionary Force] Bandmasters and Musicians School, created through Mr. Walter Damrosch, by General Pershing, and having seen the wonderful influence that Americans and French have over one another, having also learned to love and esteem the citizens from free America, I have judged it necessary to continue in a practical way such natural, pure, and agreeable relations.

With this aim in view, I immediately thought of putting, during the summer vacation, the courses of the Paris National Conservatory of Music, at the disposal of American students wishing to study in France and perfect their musical education here. Several American friends persuaded me not to do so, as Paris has too many attractions and the young students would find too many temptations.

But recently I have met at the home of some American friends a very kind man in the person of Mr. Fragnaud, Sous-Préfet of Fontainebleau. This gentleman, a great lover of music active and generous, was pursuing the same object and, we decided to transfer this school to Fontainebleau, in this way the American families would send their Children to France would be reassured [as to the stability of location]. This school would open each year beginning in July 1920 and would consist of the primary courses of the Paris Conservatory of music, these courses would be put to the disposal of American students of both sexes having already received a very complete musical instructions in the Conservatories and Music schools of America.

After much effort we have obtained those same eminent Conservatory professors come to give their courses during the summer at Fontainebleau, these courses would be held either in the beautiful Chateau of that town one of the most beautiful in France which would be given over to the American students by the Ministry of Fine Arts or in a new building built for this purpose, thus allowing them to perfect themselves in the different branches of Musical Art and to obtain by competition the different awards, equivalent to those awarded French Students at the Paris Conservatoire.

The municipality of Fontainebleau understanding that it was their duty to take the first step and despite the heavy and cruel burdens of the war they have voted unanimously the sum of 100,000 Francs for the creation of this summer school, this sum would be added to by French donations besides the municipality not wishing American students to be imposed upon by unscrupulous individuals has decided to see to their room and board.

The high school of Fontainebleau will be able to receive 200 American students of both sexes, the women students will find lodging in the Chateau (about 80), the men students will find lodgings in the College dormitories which are not occupied during the summer and also in private families who will place some rooms at the disposal of the municipality to lodge American students.

The Principal of the School will be an American so as to offer the students the guarantee of an absolutely impartial justice in case of any complaint or claim.

  [. . .] Signed, Francis Casadesus[4]

After publishing this statement, Casadesus was congratulated warmly for his idea by yet more "important people" on both sides of the Atlantic, and the Conservatoire Américain was hailed as one of the brightest inspirations in recent musical life.[5]

During the months following the publication of Casadesus's manifesto, Maurice Fragnaud continued to promote the music school strongly as a highly viable commercial enterprise for the town of Fontainebleau, convincing his local government as well as state ministries to invest significantly in the project in addition to the loan of the chateau for the Conservatoire's base of operations.[6] Taking a gamble on the "institution created without precedent in France,"[7] the Municipality of Fontainebleau not only provided 100,000 francs—a significant sum, especially in the postwar economy—to help Casadesus develop the school, but allocated another 25,000 francs for "necessary musical materials," leaving the bulk of planning to his discretion. Fragnaud served as a liaison with the offices of the Palais de Fontainebleau, further negotiating space and materials for the school's use, resulting in the chateau providing an impressive amount of space for the enterprise and basic furnishings for many rooms.

Casadesus and his French colleagues worked quickly to finalize the details of the school's opening summer. The session was to last from June 15 to October 1, although school music teachers could attend a shortened session, enabling them to return to the United States in advance of school openings. Whereas Casadesus and a few assistants had been the only faculty at the bandmasters' school, the roster for the Conservatoire boasted a number of impressive names. Isidor Philipp, one of the most prominent professors of piano at the Paris Conservatoire, agreed to head the Conservatoire's piano department; Camille Decreus and Paul Silva-Herard also joined to teach piano; and rising stars Robert (Francis's nephew) and Gaby Casadesus filled out the department. Composer and organist Charles-Marie Widor would lead the organ class. Violinist Maurice Hewitt, cellist Andre Hekking, and harpist Marcel Grandjany were hired for the strings department. Andre Bloch headed up the composition department, and Nadia Boulanger was hired as the professor of harmony. Arrangements were made for gas and water to be turned on in the chateau, and a final budget for the entire operation, the council promised, would be forthcoming.[8]

On November 29, 1920, Casadesus and Fragnaud convened a meeting to officially mark the creation of the school.[9] Those present at the convocation included Paul Seguin, the Commissaire de Gouvernement; Gaston Menier Senateur, the President de Conseil General de Seine et Marne (the area in which Fontainebleau is located in the Île de France); the mayor of Fontainebleau; Isidor Philipp; Jacques Durand, music publisher and President de la Chambre Syndicate des Editeurs de Musique, along with five other music editors and their assistants; the directors and heads of piano manufacturers Maisons Pleyel and Erard; composer Camille Decreus; several municipal councilors of Fontainebleau; Albert Bray, architect and conservator of the Palais de Fontainebleau; and Paul Leon, Director of the School of Beaux Arts that was also being established in the Palais de Fontainebleau for students of painting, sculpture, and architecture. It is clear from the notes of this meeting that all involved were excited about their "inspired creation," and ready to work to make it a grand success. The school received its formal name, L'École des Hautes Études Musicales de France, and a shorter, more specific appellation, the Conservatoire Américain.

In his manifesto, Casadesus makes clear his intentions for the Conservatoire Américain: superior American musicians—those "having already received a very complete musical instructions in the Conservatories and Music schools [sic]"—would be studying with the most superior French musicians. Students were to be evaluated at the time of application on a scale similar to that used by the Paris Conservatoire, which had opened in 1783 and quickly had become one of, if not the, most prestigious school for musical training in the world. Initially, the Conservatoire was open only to students of French background, although in the late nineteenth century this restriction was lifted, and today the school actively recruits students from other nations. Entrance to the Paris Conservatoire was exceptionally difficult. Students had to pass a rigorous set of exams and auditions in order to be considered, and they had to fall within the narrow age requirement prescribed by the school. Once admitted, students studied with a principal teacher and an assistant, who oversaw practicing and technique lessons. Juries measured the progress of the students, who were obliged to compete for the highly desirable performance, solfège, composition, and other prizes awarded yearly by the Conservatoire. To become a world-class performer in France, it was necessary to study at the Paris Conservatoire and receive such an award; no substitutions would do in a young musician's training.[10]

As a graduate, Casadesus would have been intimately familiar with these procedures. Indeed, he repeatedly mentions the Paris Conservatoire as his model: students would sit for placement exams upon arrival, and competitions for the much-desired *Premier Prix* would be held in composition, harmony, and all instruments. Of the twenty courses offered the first year, including composition, counterpoint and fugue, conducting, organ, piano, violin, cello, harp, and voice, seventeen were slated to have *Premier Prix* competitions at the end of the summer.

There was an additional goal, though, that reached beyond levels of instruction and attainment: equality in treatment between male and female students. It is apparent from the manifesto that equality of the sexes was to be a goal of the school. From the turn of the century and through the prewar years, female performers had been gaining social acceptance. Paris Conservatoire piano professor Marguerite Long, well known to Casadesus from his days there, as well as to the rest of his administrative council, had become very highly regarded as a piano virtuoso, and her student Gaby Casadesus was one of the first faculty members hired. The conditions set forth by the manifesto—that specific lodgings were set aside for female students—indicate a willingness if not eagerness to be inclusive of women at the school and to cultivate their talents on the same basis as that of male students. This progressive stance was one that was liberating for American students, many of whom were restricted at home in regard to advanced studies and were rarely encouraged to pursue serious concert careers.

However, not all of Casadesus's intentions survived beyond the school's first year. While it maintained high levels of training and held competitions for the *Premier Prix*, the Conservatoire almost immediately jettisoned one of its loftiest goals in its initial appeal for students: that of highly selective vetting of prospective students. A far cry from the detailed screening forms of the Paris Conservatoire, applications for admission to the Conservatoire Américain's first session requested simply the applicant's name, the course he or she wished to take, and letters of recommendation. These letters tended to be from clergy, bank managers, and personal or family friends rather than professional musicians or professors. They make for interesting reading, providing a window on the lives of the students and their musical situations, but are clearly not the kinds of materials on which prospective professionals should be judged for admittance to an elite music school. Composer Aaron Copland, who was the first student to enroll, provided a recommendation letter in which his teacher remarks that his student always pays on time, but says nothing about young Aaron's talent or dedication to a life in music.[11] Franco-American society figure Mabel Tuttle, having taken on a formal role in the Conservatoire's stateside administration as a sort of admissions officer, collected applications in New York, commenting on the suitability of each applicant in pencil on the application or with a typewritten statement. The exact criteria she used for accepting students are unknown, but by and large it appears that students from her own social rank or a similar background were acceptable, while individuals from groups outside of the East Coast's white establishment were more suspect. In general, though, with a good bank balance and positive character references, almost everyone who applied for the 1921 session was admitted. The exclusions from this open-door policy were dictated by the firm social restrictions of the period: for many years after the school's opening all of the class photographs show a uniformly white student body, though it is hard to say empirically whether this is the result of manipulations within the admissions process or the effect of the divisions of race and class within the United States. Applications from black students were indeed rare. Notes on Josephine Baker's niece's application denote her relationship to the famous entertainer and to her race, and the word "pass?" is lightly penciled in.[12] No records exist of her acceptance or attendance, and the episode further queries the school's—or perhaps simply Tuttle's—admission policies in regard to religion and race during this early period. While some Jewish students—like Copland—were accepted, a tacit quota seems to have been adhered to so as to limit the numbers of those admitted. More than a few students with potentially Jewish surnames had their applications marked with "Jewish?" in pencil, presumably by Tuttle or an assistant, and unsigned correspondence indicates the perceived need to keep Jewish students under a certain limit.[13]

For those applicants deemed suitable to attend its inaugural session, however, the experience was a unique one. Upon acceptance, female students were assigned a room in the Palais; men were given the information necessary to make living arrangements in town. The first students of the Conservatoire Américain ranged from highly skilled professionals to amateur beginners.[14] Aaron Copland is the most widely known of the class of '21; the class also included composer Zo Elliott and organist Stanley Avery. Other students who enrolled that year were aspiring soloists; music-school teachers; and several young women who may have been quite serious and accomplished musicians, but whose parents were more interested in their acquisition of French taste and clothes than in musical skills, attested to by their letters to the administration enquiring about the possibilities of Paris shopping trips, French lessons, and other nonmusical activities.[15] Many women were very serious musicians indeed: violinist Barbara Lull had already made her Carnegie Hall debut when she attended, and Emilie Rose Kay was recommended by her private teacher, who also mentioned that, if accepted, she would be bringing her Stradivarius.[16] Students came from thirty-eight states. Some were more experienced than others, having finished their formal higher education in the

United States and begun careers—Avery attended when he was forty-two years old and already established as a professional choirmaster and organist. Others, like Copland, were in their early twenties and not yet recognized professionally. Still others were hardly out of childhood, the forerunners of the prodigies yet to attend. Because of the social mores of the day, few female students came unaccompanied: mothers traveled with daughters and lived with them in the chateau or in rented lodgings. Some students and their mothers took classes together, the older women brushing up their skills as their daughters acquired their own. In New York, Tuttle arranged for students to travel together in groups on the *France* from the United States in early June, where they would be met in Paris and escorted to Fontainebleau. After a week at sea, students disembarked in Cherbourg and made their way to Paris and the Gare de Lyon station, where they boarded trains for Fontainebleau.

Casadesus and Damrosch had laid the foundations for a potential paradigm shift in the music world. By offering elite training to American musicians in France, they were effectively declaring the period of German-dominated American instruction to be over. If their vision succeeded, young American composers, instrumentalists, singers, and conductors would spend the twentieth century absorbing French repertoire, style, and musical language, along with a dose of culture and arts outside of music alone. It was a bold experiment in wresting musical control away from one part of the world and bringing it to another, and had the potential to change musical thought and pedagogy in unforeseen ways as the lessons of the Conservatoire were disseminated throughout the United States by alumni. As students arrived at the small Fontainebleau train station, this new experiment was about to become a reality.

Notes

1. Gaby Casadesus, *Mes noces musicales* (Paris: Buchet/Chastel, 1989).
2. Historically, the Americans involved with the opening of the Conservatoire Américain were lauded with most of the credit for doing so. Damrosch himself claimed sole credit in 1932 for its creation, casting its then director, Charles-Marie Widor; head of the piano department, Isidor Philipp; Casadesus; and Fragnaud in very secondary roles. *Fontainebleau Alumni Bulletin*, May 1932, 9.
3. Report of the Conseil d'Administration, November 29, 1920, BMF.
4. Document of Francis Casadesus, August 8, 1919, BMF.
5. Report of the Conseil d'Administration, November 29, 1920, CA/F.
6. Report of the Conseil d'Administration and financial statements, May 20, 1921, CA/F.

7. Report of the Conseil d'Administration, November 29, 1920, CA/F.

8. In fact it did not appear until late May, just a month before the school was to open, marking a lack of financial preparedness that would haunt the school even to the present day.

9. The meeting of November 29, 1920, marked the first official convocation held with a view to establishing a school in the Fontainebleau area. Maurice Fragnaud and Francis Casadesus had held private and informal meetings, referred to in Casadesus's manifesto (see below), prior to this larger gathering. The notes for those less formal discussions, if any were taken, are no longer extant.

10. Charles Timbrell, *French Pianism* (Portland, Ore.: Amadeus Press, 1999), 26–32.

11. Application dossiers of 1921, CA/F, BMF.

12. Notes of Mabel Tuttle and admissions dossiers, undated 1920s, CA/F.

13. Application dossiers of the Conservatoire Américain, undated 1921–1930s, CA/F, BMF.

14. Application dossiers of 1921, CA/F, BMF.

15. As attested to in some cover letters from parents; one mother inquires about the shopping in Paris, CA/F.

16. Application dossiers of 1921, CA/F, BMF.

PART I

THE INSTITUTION
WITHOUT PRECEDENT

CHAPTER ONE

~

The Institution without Precedent (1921–1928)

The town of Fontainebleau celebrated the opening of the Conservatoire Américain in 1921 with great ceremony. The streets from the train station to the center of town were lined with French and American flags and with welcome banners. Thousands of Fontainebleau's citizens greeted the American music students upon their arrival from Paris. Camille Saint-Saëns, the school's honorary president, gave the inaugural address on the morning of June 26 at the school's official opening. He thanked Maurice Fragnaud and, in ornate language appropriate for his nineteenth-century manners, addressed those gathered for the opening about the internationality of composers and about the influence traveling had on composers who had done so widely during their careers—Bach, Gluck, Mozart, Meyerbeer. "Overall, young ones," he proclaimed, "do not search for originality, but let your own personality form naturally. He who searches for originality arrives only at the bizarre and the mad. [. . .] France welcomes you with open arms [and] the intimate union between France and America assures the triumph of peace without which the arts could not flourish."[1]

Saint-Saëns went on to discuss contemporary music, taking time to decry much new music for his interpretation of its deliberate disrespect for melody and rhythm. The current compositional atmosphere, he told the students, faculty, and crowd of townspeople, was warlike, but clearly the forces of melody and lyricism would win. Although Saint-Saëns's opening-day declamation may have been dismissed by some in the audience or seen today as the ideological rant of an aging composer, his cri de coeur on the battle lines

of new music set the stage, however subtly, for the ideologies of the composition faculty at the school. Composition at the Conservatoire was taught as
strictly as any other Paris Conservatoire subject, resulting in extremely well
trained musicians. However, a conflict developed over the inclusion and acceptance of certain compositional approaches and techniques. Although his
tenure as honorary director of the "American Conservatory" was short-lived,
Saint-Saëns's remarks had a long life, as echoed, however consciously, in the
approaches of the composition faculty, who, as it will be seen, studiously
avoided including avant-garde or emerging compositional techniques in
their work with their American students but who at the same time emphasized that students find their own voices.

To further celebrate the opening day, faculty organist Charles-Marie
Widor gave an afternoon recital at the town hall featuring the works of
Saint-Saëns as well as his own and selections from Bach. After a banquet
lunch at the Palais, Damrosch and Fragnaud gave speeches, and uniformed
soldiers performed band music throughout the afternoon in a nod to the
Conservatoire's military origins at Chaumont. Saint-Saëns appeared again at
an evening concert in the Galerie Henri III, along with Widor, Gustave
Charpentier, and the Harvard Vocal Ensemble. A second lavish banquet
took place during intermission, and the band again struck up to play works
by the composers in the audience.

As night settled over the chateau, fireworks illuminated the luminaria-
ringed carp pond. Near the island in the center of the carp pond stood a float
bearing the French and American flags, lit by floodlights. Students and faculty signed a book marking the opening of the venture, and Saint-Saëns included a bit of doggerel:

De Fontaine-belle-eau les carpes
Entendant l'arpège des harpes
Enlès dont les pianos
le soumettent des eaus

[In Fontainebleau (fountain of beautiful water) the carps
listen to the arpeggios of the harps
while the Enlès pianos sink
submitting to the drink][2]

The celebratory mood of the Conservatoire's grand opening lasted on, but
lessons, classes, and rehearsals began immediately. One class each in composition, counterpoint and fugue, harmony, conducting, organ, piano, violin,

cello, chromatic harp, pedal harp, and harpischord were given, along with three classes in voice and an instrumental ensemble class. Finding that the range of student abilities was wider than anticipated, piano professor Isidor Philipp and violin professor Maurice Hewitt partitioned the piano and violin classes into higher and lower divisions, allowing them to spend more time working with students at the appropriate levels and speeds. Aaron Copland described his daily living situation at Fontainebleau and his choice of courses in a letter home to his parents:

Fontainebleau, June 25th, 1921
Dear Ma and Pa,
   At last I am in Fontainebleau! Everything has turned out splendidly. There was an autobus at the station to meet us, and we had dinner at the Palace. It certainly is a marvelous place, all surrounded by forests and woods. The conservatory rooms are on the ground floor, the girls live upstairs, and the boys live with French families around the town. I am living in a room by myself which I like *very* much. It is as big as our parlor, with 3 windows bigger than ours, is nicely furnished, has running water, and the nicest old lady to take care of me, who speaks French only, so that I am forced to learn by talking to her. I have already hired a piano (at about $5.00 a month.) The house is on a very quiet street, about a 10 minute walk from the Palace, where we eat all our meals. The dinner was very good, so I don't think we'll have any trouble on that point. My trunk is going to be sent here tonight. You have no idea how good it is to feel that I am settled, at last.
   [. . .] I have been playing on one of the baby grands at the Palace all afternoon, and enjoyed myself immensely, after not having a piano for over 2 weeks. I have decided to study piano here also for 220 francs, (about $20) a month extra. If I don't think I'm getting my money's worth, I'll quit after a month. The piano teacher, Isidor Philipp, is very famous, and known all over Europe and America, and I think is certainly worth the money.[3]

Indeed it was. The French council, with the general approval of the American committee, had chosen its professors for the Conservatoire with great care. As Casadesus and Damrosch had planned, the majority were drawn from the ranks of the Paris Conservatoire. The council was prescient in insisting that its professors come from that august institution, as its reputation only grew when its alumni—including Robert and Gaby Casadesus— toured throughout North America in the 1920s and 1930s. Professors at the new school were instructed to work hard, and most gave two private lessons per student each week in addition to almost daily master classes and other group sessions throughout the 1920s. Professors were excited about the school, and evidently dedicated to its success, offering regular concerts and working and socializing with students as part of an effort to enrich their individual experiences as much as possible.

The Conservatoire was equally determined to keep its faculty well compensated and happy to be in Fontainebleau for the summer. As the value of the franc fell in the mid-to-late 1920s, professors were paid in dollars, an extra incentive to keep them on the faculty. Though there was a hiring freeze on new faculty owing to a limited budget in that area, the faculty received a raise of thirty percent in 1926, and in 1927 the work of the faculty was further rewarded when all received a raise of 40,000 francs, to make a total of 200,000 francs per summer. The Conservatoire was also eager to add to its faculty to meet student needs and in order to entice more applicants. Following the 1927 session, healthy finances enabled the hiring of a new oboe teacher to teach part-time at 6,000 francs annually, and at the end of that year the bank balance showed 630,000 francs in the combined account of the Conservatoire and the École des Beaux-Arts. Later that year, two additional professors were contracted, pianist Helda Rosewald and soprano Félia Litvinne, who, because she originally was from Russia, was obliged to take out French citizenship in order to teach at the Conservatoire Américain.[4]

Piano classes were the most populous, perhaps owing to the stature of the faculty. In addition to Isidor Philipp, a venerable figure in the piano world, two early and influential members of the Conservatoire faculty were Paris Conservatoire pianists Robert and Gaby Casadesus. Gabrielle Casadesus, née L'Hôte, was born in 1901 in Marseille and had begun her piano studies as a small child. At the Paris Conservatoire, study with Marguerite Long and Louis Diémer led to her *Premier Prix* at age seventeen. Like Gaby, Robert studied with Diémer at the Paris Conservatoire, where he trained also as a composer with Xavier Leroux. Both Gaby and Robert were already well known by the 1920s and were regarded as some of the top artists of the time. They married on July 16, 1921, in Paris and went immediately to Fontainebleau, where Robert was to be Philipp's assistant in the piano department. There they campaigned together for the inclusion of more French repertoire and especially for recent French repertoire in the piano students' assignments, lessons, and concerts. The Casadesuses performed much new repertoire by their countrymen themselves, especially that of their close colleague Maurice Ravel, gently bucking the tradition of Philipp's adherence to Saint-Saëns's claim that new music was bizarre and undeserving of serious consideration.[5] Students often benefited greatly from studying with Robert and Gaby in concert: the former working with a student on interpretation

The Institution without Precedent (1921–1928) ～ 7

and musical understanding; the latter taking students through her own daily technique and assigning exercises designed to create the French touch at the keyboard. Pianists of all levels and backgrounds flourished at the Conservatoire, many of them returning to Fontainebleau for additional summers of study in order to further their skills for their own teaching careers or to prepare for professional recitals.

The classes in harmony, counterpoint, and composition were especially thorough, as students of Nadia Boulanger discovered. Boulanger, at age thirty-four, was already on the faculty of the Paris Conservatoire when she began teaching at the Conservatoire Américain in 1921. Though she had taught privately since she was sixteen, and had tutored her younger sister Lili to great acclaim, Boulanger had just one year of formal experience as a teacher of harmony, counterpoint, accompaniment, and history at the École Normale de Musique when she was hired by the Conservatoire Américain as a harmony professor. However, her previous experience and innate gifts as a teacher bore out, and she soon accumulated a huge following among the composition and harmony students who attended during the school's first decade, among them Copland, Virgil Thomson, Colin McPhee, David Dushkin, George Antheil, Louise Talma, and Herbert Elwell.

By 1927 Boulanger had sixty-six students, fifteen more than André Bloch, the official professor of composition. In fact, she impressed her students to the degree that many stayed on in Paris after the Conservatoire Américain had closed for the year and continued their studies with her. Boulanger retained the severity of Paris Conservatoire standards and, as Saint-Saëns's opening address might have predicted for the composition faculty, she reined in too much experimentation by her students, especially those lacking the requisite groundwork and schooling. Her students studied music ranging from Renaissance counterpoint and masses to the fugues of Bach and Beethoven, from works by Schütze to those of Hindemith and Stravinsky, and classes could spend an entire summer on a monothematic canon of works chosen by Boulanger: rhythm in Stravinsky, organic structure in Renaissance masses, Debussy's harmonic language and its influences. Although despised by Saint-Saëns, Debussy had become commonplace in the performance and analysis repertoires of Fontainebleau students, but few other contemporary composers were accorded such status, and for many years the twentieth century ended for Boulanger's students with *La mer* and the *Prélude à l'Après-midi d'un faune*.

The composition course ended the summer with Paris Conservatoire–style evaluations and led to the standard competitions for *Premier Grand Prix*, *Seconde Grand Prix*, and *Mentions honorables*. The rules of the competition in 1924 are indicative of the level of study and proficiency assumed of the students:

> Pupils cannot take part in this competition unless they have given ample satisfaction in a *preliminary test-competition*. This *Test-competition* comprises the writing of a *fugue in four parts* (on a given theme) besides a *chorus in eight parts*. The installment of each candidate will take place at the Palais of Fontainebleau. The competitors will be rigorously isolated and have to compose one of the following works *according to their choice*
>
> 1. A *cantata for three voices and orchestra;*
> 2. A *sonata for violin and piano or violoncello and piano;*
> 3. *The first movement of a String quartet.*[6]

Although only a select few students ever achieved a *Premier Prix*, the levels required by the composition and the composition-related courses attracted publisher Jacques Durand to concerts, and he sat in the front row at every twice-a-week concert selecting new talent to publish, choosing, in 1921, Copland as his first protégé.[7] The young composer's *Cat & Mouse* for piano was premiered in Fontainebleau and published by Durand. Five years later, the composition class of 1926 was deemed talented enough to merit a broadcast of their works on national radio from the Eiffel Tower, aided by the student vocal ensemble.

The highly visible success of the composition program at the Conservatoire, along with the equally traceable results shown by pianists coming through Philipp's department, gave the school much-needed credit in its first years in becoming more solidly established as a permanent fixture of the French and American musical landscapes. While not every student thrived in the tough atmosphere of Boulanger's classes, the Conservatoire could, after just a few years of operations, point to students whose Fontainebleau experiences had clearly benefited them in terms of their professional development and opportunities. For the school's administration, such successes were sweet returns on the initial hard work Casadesus and Damrosch had done in laying the groundwork for their "summertime conservatory" and ensured that patrons both French and American, private and public, would continue to support the school as it grew out of infancy.

For performers, the Conservatoire's three-month summer course consisted of intensive rehearsals and coaching, master classes, and public performances. Students who played large or fragile instruments rented them from music stores in Paris in order to avoid the cost and trouble of transport. Practice rooms were located in the chateau and, in order to accommodate motivated students, some rooms were divided into smaller practice areas and a partition was built in 1927 to help control the prodigious noise of the organ. Repertoire for instrumentalists—like pianists—consisted primarily of French works dating from Couperin through Ravel and those by standard common practice–period composers including Bach, Mozart, and Beethoven.

All performers—pianists, singers, and instrumentalists—were strongly encouraged, if not actually required, to present premieres of their colleagues' newly composed works. Steinway, Erard, Pleyel, and Chickering offered prizes and scholarships for pianists for their performances given during the school's session: prizes were often scholarships or cash, intended to encourage students to return to Fontainebleau. Concerts were numerous, with twenty-five or more each year by the students and many more by faculty and visiting artists. Small, two-or three-day festivals were held in which a large number of works by a selected composer were presented. Fauré, Debussy, and Ravel were accorded this honor along with Rameau and a number of other French Renaissance and Baroque composers.[8] The head of the Société de Musicologie proposed a series of historical concerts, and while period instruments do not seem to have been used, there was a lasting vogue of giving concerts of Renaissance and early Baroque music. All of the French-music festivals—whether centering on early music or contemporary composers— were of special use to the faculty, who used them to help students understand the French musical aesthetic of transparency, continuity, and line. Pianists demonstrated their newfound *souplesse* and pedaling techniques while drawing out the long, sensuous lines of Debussy's preludes or miniatures by Fauré. Thus American students learned the technique and the repertoire of their adopted land hand in hand, leading to expert understanding of French compositional approaches and performance practice in American performers of this period.

All students participated in the school's vocal ensemble either as singers or keyboard accompanists, deepening their knowledge of music history and the foundations for the more modern music they performed at their recitals. Concerts were held in the tapestry-hung Jeu de Paume—once the king's tennis court—and in the Salle des Colonnes, an impressive but acoustically untenable salon noted for its gilt and marble.[9] In its inaugural year, 25 concerts were given by the students of the Conservatoire Américain, presenting 105 French works and 20 non-French pieces. Works performed included those by Francis Casadesus, Chabrier, Chausson, Debussy, Dukas, Fauré, Franck, Ravel, Roussel, Saint-Saëns, Widor, Granados, Paganini, Rachmaninoff, Rubinstein, and Lili Boulanger; and select students performed in Paris on September 23 in celebration of the first year of the Conservatoire Américain.

Faculty also presented recitals, and guest artists made frequent appearances, usually combining a concert date with a master class or coaching sessions. Especially noted by students were those performances presented by harpist Grandjany, Robert and Gaby Casadesus, and the Society of Ancient Instruments (including members of the Casadesus family), which was held in the Chapel of St. Saturnin. Other prominent performers of the first decade of the Conservatoire included child piano prodigy and later staunch Conservatoire supporter Beveridge Webster, the Quarles Trio, pianists Marian Hahn and Clara Rabinowitch, flutist Quinto Maganini, singers Victor Prahl and Charles Pemmac, and Philadelphia Symphony Orchestra violinist Max Polikoff. The number of concerts and other public events both in Fontainebleau and in New York—billed as alumni recitals—emphasized the new school's rosters of faculty and student talent, and enabled potential supporters and students to take part in the Conservatoire Américain experience before committing funds or a summer to the school.

In addition to all of the musical exposure given its students, the Conservatoire also presented readings and discussions of French literature, and noted writers were brought in for informal classes with interested students. Social events were often hung on the framework of a reading or discussion, and were held both in the Palais and at professors' homes, including Boulanger's and the Casadesuses'.[10] Students became fully immersed in French culture and life, and their education ranged from the poetry of Paul Valéry to cheese tastings and from the art hanging in the Palais to impromptu but enthusiastically given French lessons.

The first years of the Conservatoire's existence were not without difficulties. In fact, there were considerable problems with the school's expectations and abilities to reach its target audience, especially in its first years. At a meeting in December 1921, Francis Casadesus lamented the lack of preparation done by the Palais staff to ready the building for its charges. Even more disappointing to the faculty was the state of the Americans' solfège, theory, and dictation skills, which they found often insufficient for the levels of instruction they had hoped to provide. Of the composition students in the class of 1921, not one was judged worthy of a *Premier Prix*, though two honorable mentions were given. In the organ class, two *Premier Prix* were awarded, with another two in the top piano class and seven in voice. No violinists were deemed sufficiently superior, nor were any cellists, harpists, or students of harmony, counterpoint, and fugue. Several *Seconde Prix* were issued, along with some half-hearted honorable mentions. The students' ignorance in music history was another disappointment, and techniques were not as high as had been expected. As Stanley Avery frankly recalled of the first group of students, "We were really a more or less hit-or-miss crowd and there were some in the nearly 100 students who hardly knew what it was all about. Their approach and lack of receptivity must have astonished the scholarly professors who were put over us." Although Avery felt that, "the majority [of students] came in earnest and were equipped to take the splendid instruction furnished," there was sufficient concern to merit discussion among the administration and faculty.[11] Finally, Casadesus noted the need for increased administrative staff and funding.[12]

Casadesus and Damrosch immediately set about making improvements on both sides of the Atlantic for the following summers. Clearly, acceptance standards would have to be more stringent in order to ensure higher quality students. Looking back at their original plans for admittance requirements, Damrosch prepared formal and fairly strict entrance exams including sections on theory and history for students to take as part of the application process. Those who passed would then be assigned a series of etudes to prepare for an audition in New York. If an applicant was approved at this audition, he or she was then to receive another set of etudes to prepare for assessment in Fontainebleau. However, in choosing to accept only the students with the most potential as professional musicians, the Conservatoire would inevitably lose much of its capacity for income—namely, accepting less gifted or only moderately talented students from wealthier families. In order to alleviate this necessity, the Comtesse Montesquieu Fezensac á Bourron, the Comtesse Beneditti, Blair Fairchild, and others granted annual scholarships of 5,000 francs to be given to more capable but less wealthy students so that the school might be less dependent on accepting less advanced students in order to pay the bills. More fund-raising was also undertaken in the United States in order to publicize the school and attract more advanced students.

Unfortunately for faculty and the more advanced students, the uneven mix of student talents remained. Despite additional financial assistance from donors and the overall strengthening of the Conservatoire's assets, there was never quite enough for an endowment, and this progressive plan for stricter auditions and admissions was never implemented due to the continued need for tuition from amateurs. While they may not have been the most proficient students, those in this category did pay full tuition, almost without exception. As a result, a weak compromise was made by the administration, which realized that its goal of staying solvent was not entirely compatible with its goal of limiting admission to only the best and most proficient. Instead of limiting enrollment, guidelines for students' behavior and scholarly obligations were drawn up and accepted students were required to sign contracts, in which they agreed to attend all classes and complete assigned homework. This measure, meant to convince students of the seriousness of their studies and their participation in Conservatoire events, had mixed results; each session had its inevitable group of less sincere students, generally outweighed by those who were prepared to work and threw themselves into the Fontainebleau experience with gusto.

Because of the perceived levels of student performance and participation, some faculty and council members suggested ending the competitive trials for prizes at the end of each session, arguing that the students simply weren't prepared for the trials of such competitions. They proposed, instead, that students sit for an exam that would lead to a diploma rather than to a true *Premier* or *Seconde Prix*. This specific plan was meant to ease the concerns by faculty that awarding students whom they believed to be undeserving of these prizes would devalue the prizes themselves. The implication that the competitions of the Conservatoire Américain were not as rigorous as those of the Paris Conservatoire, and that this was an injustice to both schools was one strongly believed by the faculty, dashing Casadesus's hopes of creating a system of awards equal to those of his alma mater.[13] The practice of competing for the illustrious French prizes would thus slowly be phased out, although competition and prizes in composition remained and a competition for the *Premier Prix* was offered sporadically in piano and strings. By 1926, however, most students were awarded diplomas or certificates either for "excellence in execution" or "fitness for teaching." Even with this change, the administration asked professors that the certificates be signed by them individually and not by the Conservatoire itself, which did not want to take responsibility for a student's level of competence or to damage its fledgling reputation by institutionally endorsing students they did not feel worthy of that distinction.[14] Diplomas from this period are large, elaborately engraved documents, portraying two nudes, one holding a score and a baton, the other a sculpture of a winged victor. The nudes, representing muses, sit in a wreath of oak leaves and acorns which is further ornamented by theater masks, the scroll of an instrument, a palette, and architectural straight edge and T-squares. The diplomas often bear the signature of a student's private lesson teacher alone, though a few are signed by instrumental department faculty and some by the director.

Despite the hand-wringing over unsatisfactory students and standards of education and performance, though, the Conservatoire's most pressing concern during the decade was its solvency. Although the city of Fontainebleau and Damrosch's fund-raising had produced enough cash to start the project, there was still not enough capital to create an endowment of any kind on which the school could depend. During the initial year, the enormous cost of opening such an institution drained its coffers and caused repeated problems. In 1923 the hiring of fifty-two pianos created a financial strain, compounded by set-up costs of 50,000 francs that year, and it was believed that more money was needed for the director's salary. That same year, the Conservatoire was joined legally with the École des Beaux-Arts, its architectural-training sister-school at the Palais, in order to strengthen the influence of both institutions and their financial position as well. This did, indeed, help, and the finances of the schools became more secure as the decade progressed.

Money and support for the Conservatoire often arrived cloaked in various guises. In 1924, John D. Rockefeller gave 4,000,000 francs to the Palais de Fontainebleau for repairs. While Rockefeller's bequest does not specifically mention the Conservatoire Américain, he was aware of the school and "this did not go without influencing the donor."[15] The school's fortunes improved slowly, year by year: in 1925 a new organ was bought for 25,000 francs, indicating a strengthening of the school's financial situation. The illustrious Presser Foundation also made significant contributions to the school during this time. The following year donations of 17,000 francs were given to the school, adding to its solvency.

Logistical and cultural differences also threatened the school. By 1923, the Palais was engaged in a petty but heated dispute with the school's council over the allocation of funds for such student amenities as linens. The administration, realizing that the school's location in the chateau *was* salient in many respects and to many supporters, alternated between making conciliatory gestures to Palais staff and sending sniping internal memos about Palais conditions and employees. In addition to exasperating squabbling over linen costs, cultural differences caused friction between the school and its hosts. The Palais staff expressed its unhappiness about the free-wheeling and casual-minded Americans living in the chateau: young women could be seen sitting in the windows brushing their hair and, according to chateau staff, distracting the men stationed there for military drills. The women were also known to hang out their "unmentionable" laundry in their rooms, a grave error of judgment in the eyes of the Palais's keepers. Unaccustomed to such behavior, the Palais administration began a slow but steady push for the students to vacate the place as living quarters. The council of the Conservatoire responded by investigating the possibilities of lodging all of the students in town: contracting with a hotel, purchasing a house for the students, or forming a coalition among the town's hotels to board students individually or in small groups. None immediately proved satisfactory, due to the perceived need that the unchaperoned female students had to be supervised. The council stressed the need for the hiring of an older woman to do this. Francis

Casadesus pinned notices to the school bulletin board pleading for more re-strained behavior on the part of the students.[16] In the summer of 1922, sixty students moved into some of the 140 rooms allocated by the Palais, but the battle had not been won.

In October 1922 an article appeared in *Figaro* titled "Is the Palace of Fontainebleau a Fire Hazard?" Referring to the recent installation of elec-tricity in the wings inhabited by the students, the newspaper implied a grave danger, commonly echoed by many who had not yet accepted the new sys-tem of electricity as a safe one.[17] Conservatoire Américain council members protested, and the Office of the Conservator of the Palais de Fontainebleau assured the public that the new water, gas, electric, and telephone lines in the chateau were closely monitored. However, the problem wouldn't go away, and in December 1922 led to a rift between Damrosch and Francis Casadesus. Casadesus, who had received some letters of complaint from stu-dents about the living conditions at the Palais, decided that the Palais was right: students should be housed elsewhere. Stung by the suggestion, which would sever part of the enormously appealing link and the emerging symbol-ism of Conservatoire and chateau, Damrosch wrote to Fragnaud:

> I am more sorry than I can say that our friend, Casadesus, who in 1918 was so modest, self-sacrificing and idealistic, should now endeavor to ruin the insti-tution which you and he founded, by throwing doubt on the advisability of the American students living at the Palace. I have just written to him and urged him to treat the whole matter with a dignified silence and that if he persisted in his revengeful attitude he would lose the friendship and respect of the en-tire American committee. I [. . .] hope that you will be able successfully to re-fute his assertion and prove that, first—that the Palace is absolutely sanitary, second—that the American students in no way injure the property, and that the school has become one of the finest institutions demonstrating the inti-mate and cordial friendship between France and America.[18]

The American committee did, indeed, ask for Casadesus's resignation the same month, as was reported by American Secretary Francis Rogers to Frag-naud: "The following cable was sent to Mr Casadesus today: 'Earnestly re-quest you accept retirement and not endeavor further to injure future of School. Such efforts eventually will harm only you.'" Despite this, a month later (January 1923), the American office received in reply a telegram from Casadesus: "Minister Fine Arts appoints me Honorary Director with congrat-ulations and full pay."[19] As a concession to potential fire problems, the restau-rant in which the students ate was relocated to a site outside of the chateau grounds, but the majority of students lived in the Palais until the 1930s, mov-

ing in 1925 from the Louis XV wing to 150 rooms in the Pavillion Henri IV
in the rear of the chateau. Unfortunately, Francis Casadesus's reputation on
the American side of the Atlantic had suffered irreparable damage.[20] In 1923,
Max d'Ollone, a Prix de Rome–winning composer and former head of the
École Normale de Musique and of the Paris Conservatory, replaced Casadesus
as the acting director, although Casadesus maintained his title of honorary director. Later that year Charles-Marie Widor took over general direction of
the Conservatoire from Ollone, and pianist Camille Decreus was appointed
resident director the following year.

Notwithstanding the ubiquitous political machinations and the slow
adaptation of the French hosts to American standards and foibles, the 1920s
were good years for the Conservatoire. During this time the school established an enduring tradition and set high standards, despite the few weak students who, in the first years of the school's existence, had so dismayed the
faculty and overshadowed the majority who arrived ready and prepared to
work and learn. News of the kinds of instruction offered and of faculty expectations had spread with the return of earlier students to the United States,
and classes from the later 1920s included serious musicians and young professionals. Those who came to Fontainebleau without the intent of pursuing
musical careers were, nonetheless, enthusiastic, and many were earnest in
their studies, achieving acceptable levels of skill and knowledge that as-
suaged early administrative concerns. Copland may have described it once as
"a rather conventional school,"[21] but it was, in fact, rather exceptional, and
peopled with extraordinary musicians, both faculty and students. Ninety-four
students opened the 1923 session, in 1926 there were 143 (seventy-two in piano alone); in 1927 there were 128 students, and by 1928 it became necessary to limit the number of students in piano, owing to the program's burgeoning popularity. In 1924 the Conservatoire Américain was endorsed by
no less than the following: René Vivani, the former premier of France;
Robert Lansing, the former U.S. secretary of state; H. E. Jules Jusserand, the
French ambassador to the United States; and the highly regarded musicians
Frank Damrosch, Percy Grainger, Josef Hofmann, Benno Moiseiwitsch,
Pierre Monteux, Ignatz Paderewski, Olga Samaroff, Carlos Salzedo, Leopold
Stokowski, Efrem Zimbalist, and David Mannes.

Stories of the success of the Conservatoire Américain spread, and in 1925
the Italian government planned to start a "Conservatoire Américain d'Italie"
of its own at the Villa d'Este. In his notes to the council meeting that June,
Widor expressed his indignation over this "upstart" but hoped that its creation would spur the French government to contribute more aid to
Fontainebleau.[22] Outside agencies took notice of the school, including an

opera troupe that wanted to provide six scholarships for the Conservatoire in exchange for exclusive recruitment rights. Although Durand and some of his colleagues supported the plan and wanted to collaborate with the Metropolitan Opera Company in New York, it was opposed by Decreus and came to naught. However, the idea was part of a larger patronage system that was evolving within the confines of the school and through faculty-student relations. Durand continued to solicit compositions from students for publication, and in later years Nadia Boulanger steered her society benefactors to her students for commissions and performances. The attention paid by the public to the school was important advertising, although the school intensified its American advertising campaign in 1927, again hoping to attract a higher caliber of students.

The mixture of students' abilities and intentions changed little during these first years of the Conservatoire. Many returned year after year. Teachers spent two months at the school and then returned to their own classrooms, but the remainder of the students stayed on until the end of the session. Older students brought husbands, wives, and occasionally children, many of whom began lessons of their own at the chateau as they came of age. Young talents heard of the new school's exciting program, and teachers, too, flocked to study in Fontainebleau. Overall, the Conservatoire had become a serious institution of learning.

The Conservatoire's students enjoyed the social aspects of the environment as much as the training they received. Students were expected to arrive with some French and were charged with acquiring skills and refining talents under the strict eyes of the professors, but even the strictest masters recognized the need for their students to enjoy their time abroad.[23] Paris was a perennial favorite for day trips and weekends, and students flocked there on their days off to visit museums, hear concerts, meet other musicians, and to shop and indulge themselves in the restaurants the capital had to offer. Paris was a true temptation: Josephine Baker danced at the Théâtre des Champs-Elysées; Gertrude Stein and Alice B. Toklas frequented the English lending-library at Sylvia Beach's Shakespeare and Co. bookstore; George Balanchine was creating new works for the *Ballets Russes*; and the weekly travails of the exiled Yussupovs were entertainment headlines: the prince and his wife could themselves be observed by anyone with the trust fund needed to pay for meals in their restaurant. Closer to home, trips into the lushly landscaped forest were common, as was horseback riding. Dances and parties were held throughout the session and students frequently created their own diversions: in August 1927, Beaux-Arts and Conservatoire students worked together to hold a naming and christening of the cygnets born on the carp pond that year to the swans, already named Francis and Diana by an earlier generation of students. A newspaper account told the story of how students had constructed an elaborately decorated boat, chosen a "Queen of the Swans" from their midst, costumed her, and held a grand ceremony out in the pond, naming each of the six baby swans for the Conservatoire's professors. The students sang from Gluck's *Orfeo* and "La Marseillaise" to accompany the festivities.[24] In a similar fashion, the Conservatoire Américain concluded its seventh year with a spectacular celebration at its traditional end-of-session fête. The *Alumni Bulletin* of January 1928 reports that the fête took place in August at the side of the Carp Pond, where, in keeping with a royal tradition, a

> young carp with a gold and dated ring in its nose was used at the high point of the ceremony. Rameau['s] music from "Castor et Pollux" written in part at Fontainebleau, was employed and the costumes were of the same period as the music, Louis XIV and XV. The presiding lady impersonated the Duchess of Burgundy whose son, the little Dauphin and later Louis XV, gave the command for the depositing of the ringed carp in the Pond. The ceremony was concluded with a dinner and dance at the School Restaurant.
>
> The notable concerts were the programs of Paul Dukas, Arthur Honegger, the Festival of Old Music (Vivaldi, Bach, and Rameau), and the Saint-Saens program of M. Philipp—the recitals of Madeline Grey, Beveridge Webster, Marcel Dupré, Paul Bazelaire and the Philadelphia String Quartet.
>
> The demand for entrance to the Conservatoire is now attaining a point where early registration will have to be required. Former students who think of returning will do well to consider this point and not delay.[25]

The school had done well for its first years: it had established an excellent reputation, collected supporters and admirers, boasted an outstanding faculty, and was producing successful students, both male and female. By the end of the 1920s, Conservatoire Américain alumni were teaching at Hunter College (Louise Talma), performing at Town Hall (Barbara Lull), in Italy (Marie Montana, née Ruth Kellogg Waite), and with the American Opera Company (Edith Piper), working for NBC (Reynold H. Brooks), writing for *Modern Music* and composing prolifically (Copland), teaching and studying in Paris (Marie Neubeiser, Victor Prahl, and Ruth Ware), directing the Rutgers University School of Music (Robert M. Crawford), and making European concert tours (Rock Ferris and Abram Goldberg). As America's "summertime conservatory," the Conservatoire Américain was succeeding in its mission.

Notes

1. "Founding" Book (scrapbook of 1921), BMF.
2. "Founding" Book (scrapbook of 1921), BMF.
3. Aaron Copland and Vivian Perlis, *Copland 1900 through 1945* (New York: St. Martin's, 1984), 45–46.
4. Notes of the Conseil d'Administration, November 1927, CA/F.
5. Gaby Casadesus, *Mes noces musicales* (Paris: Buchet/Chastel, 1989).
6. Brochure for the Conservatoire Américain, 1923, BMF.
7. Gaby Casadesus, interview with author, July 20, 1999, possession of author.
8. Numerous concert programs from virtually every year attest to the composer-festivals held, CA/F.
9. The Jeu de Paume is one of only a handful of surviving early tennis courts. It was in usable condition for the sport throughout the twentieth century, but in the 1990s the Palais de Fontainebleau fully restored the Jeu de Paume to its original Louis XV condition and an early version of the game is played there today by a growing group of "real tennis" enthusiasts.
10. *Fontainebleau Alumni Bulletins*, 1920s–1990s, possession of author. Also a practice that continues to the present day.
11. Stanley Avery, "The First Years," *Fontainebleau Alumni Bulletin*, June 1947, 3.
12. Notes of the Conseil d'Administration, December 1921. Also: Livre des Éleves, begun 1921, end date unknown, both CA/F.
13. Notes of the Conseil d'Administration, October 1923, CA/F.
14. Notes of the Conseil d'Administration, October 1923, CA/F.
15. Notes of the Conservatoire Américain de Fontainebleau, undated, CA/F. Also: Interview with Emile Naoumoff, October 14, 2000, possession of author.
16. Avery, "The First Years," 4.
17. In fact, after Cornelia Vanderbilt had electrical wiring installed in her New York home, a small fire broke out. Though it was proved not to be the result of electrical problems, she had the entire wiring system torn out and reverted to the use of gas.
18. Letter, Walter Damrosch to Maurice Fragnaud, December 1922, CA/F.
19. Letter, Francis Rogers to Maurice Fragnaud, January 1923, CA/F.
20. As late as 1968 Conservatoire Américain staff in New York described him as "so inefficient and impossible that he was promptly replaced." Letter, Marie Brodeur to Martha Crawford, October 10, 1968, CA/NY.
21. Copland and Perlis, *Copland 1900 through 1945*, 47.
22. Notes of the Conseil d'Administration, June 1925, CA/F.
23. Letter, Francis Rogers to Maurice Fragnaud, January 19, 1924, CA/F.
24. *Echo de Paris*, August 11, 1927, CA/F.
25. G. Reynolds, *Fontainebleau Alumni Bulletin*, January 1929.

CHAPTER TWO

~

The Age of Opulence (1929–1939)

In October 1929, the American stock market crashed, plunging the United States into an economic depression. Despite this grave turn of events, enrollment at the Conservatoire Américain remained strong, with 160 students attending in 1929 and 150 in 1930. Tuition hovered around $300 for the three-month course, and discount transportation was available on several steamship lines. Clearly a significant part of the attraction was the social aspect of school life, coupled with the somewhat better European financial condition. Seeking an escape from the grim realities of home, students flocked to France, where the economic situation would not fully exhibit the effects of the American depression until nearly two years later.

The handbook for Fontainebleau students published in the May 1930 *Alumni Bulletin* addresses this interest in the social aspects of the Conservatoire experience, stating that "[d]inner clothes (Tuxedo) and evening gowns for the ladies can be worn about five to eight times during the season."[1] Formal dress was indeed required several times a summer at dinners, dances, and of course, concerts. "You may bring as much [baggage] as you like," the handbook advises, "by paying for over-weight." Students could send their trunks of music and clothes ahead, as long as they settled the fees with the "Major-Domo" upon arrival at the Conservatoire. Swimming, golfing, tennis, and riding were activities that participants could take up in their leisure time. The Samois Country-Club, open to the students, featured pools, tennis courts, rowing, yachting, and hunting and fishing. The Fontainebleau Golf-Club, normal admittance a thousand francs, also was open free of charge to the students of the Conservatoire. In addition there were "trips to Paris for theatres, opera, concerts, sight-seeing tours, clothes, etc." One student even brought her own horse to ride through the perfectly manicured Forêt de Fontainebleau and to take advantage of Fontainebleau's other famed horse country offerings.[2]

A bit prematurely, a tenth anniversary celebration was planned for the fourth of July in 1930, with Walter Damrosch in attendance. Concerts by and dinners with guest artists and alumni were scheduled to show off the best of the Conservatoire's alumni, students, and musical supporters. Reports from the next summer—1931—are filled with references to the "blaring phonograph at the Grand Café jumping blithely from cute little jazz tunes to the Bach D minor Fugue," the visit of the Sultan of Morocco, the nightly dressed-for-dinner processions on the Rue Grande, and elaborate costume parties. These parties and dances, patterned after the much-heralded fancy dress balls held in June in Paris, were the highlights of the social season among Fontainebleau students.[3] While the Parisian masquerades were enormous affairs held by members of the aristocracy who were known to have served three hundred lobsters at once, with their guests costumed as Louis XV shepherds, odalisques from the Arabian Nights, and safari guides complete with lion cubs, Fontainebleau students held their own balls at the chateau or at the student lodgings, constructing costumes in the style of the Renaissance, as chessmen, and as the ever-popular Louis XV himself.[4] For one ball, women were ferried across the Etang des Carpes in a giant fish-shaped boat, sitting in its open mouth as two of the male students paddled or poled it along.[5] Even Gaby Casadesus was impressed by the surroundings, and recounted that her bathroom in the chateau "was sumptuous, with an enormous bathtub with golden, swan-necked faucets."[6] The chateau served as the playground of the students and faculty alike, and Palais personnel expressed no reservations with the Conservatoire in showing off the national treasure when photographers were present to document the splendor.

Classical music figures were not the only guests of the Conservatoire. Native American dancers Chief Oskonon and Princess Spotted Elk, touring in Paris, were invited to demonstrate traditional tribal dances for the students at one ball in 1931. A later gala held by faculty pianist Camille Decreus and his wife featured a preparty program of folk songs sung by Nina Tarsova, and the "grand success" of the summer was the "Gold Rush of '49" costume dance, for which the dining hall was transformed into a road-house, complete with a bar and roulette wheel. The International Barn Dance a year later also was a memory of much delight, recounted in the *Alumni Bulletin*:

"A group from Boston opened the activities with a real square dance," and costumed partygoers included a bridal party and one student wrapped "in a steamer rug and spectacles as a German tourist."[7] Beaux Arts students dressed as cupids and flirted with the Conservatoire pupils.

The palace was not the only place where members of the Conservatoire community socialized. Informal gatherings were held at the homes of Fontainebleau residents. An elocution class given by Mrs. Francis Rogers, the wife of the New York General Secretary for the school, led to uproarious skits performed at an impromptu comedy revue. Teas were held, as were jazz evenings. A local American family named Townley opened their home to students for "psycho-philosophical discussions," where students read and debated "important developments in the fields of psychology, philosophy, and their allies."[8] That summer the Townleys' garden was the Fontainebleau equivalent of Paris's Left Bank. Bastille Day celebrations brought with them traditional dinner-dances, complete with copious amounts of free-flowing champagne, and one Bastille Day celebration brought traffic to a stop when the Conservatoire students joined residents to dance in the streets.[9]

Trips were popular too, combining social outings with education. Excursions to Vaux-le-Vicomte, Versailles, and Chartres were perennial favorites. Paris was always a prime destination, with something for everyone: Conservatoire professor Marcel Dupré's organ performances at Sacré Coeur, shopping at the chic Paris department stores, viewing the collections at the Louvre, and for the gourmets, dining: "from Turkish to Russian foods; from 'moules' on the terrace near the Paris Flea Market to the big cheese binge at Androuet's, to polish off the summer."[10]

The faculty also hosted parties for the students at which they could associate with guest performers and dignitaries, occasionally leading to commissions and performances for the students. Tenuous ties made over dessert frequently became opportunities for musicians who were invited to perform at a benefit or to compose on commissions sponsored by society figures. Back home in the United States, the aura of having hobnobbed with the elite of France tarnished no reputations. Nadia Boulanger began holding Sunday get-togethers at her summer home in Gargenville, where she held a banquet of French and Russian cuisines, followed by "good talk."[11] Robert and Gaby Casadesus hosted students at their home in Bois-le-Roi, a nearby village, where faculty pianist Jean Batalla also held parties at his house.[12]

Despite all of the parties and sports and trips to Paris, most students of the 1930s did come to the Conservatoire prepared to work. Due to the high expectations, strict study, and advanced levels of performance that the professors demanded, the reputation of the Conservatoire had grown steadily since its inception, and alumni were quick to promote it both in Europe and back home in the United States. In the French musical community the school enjoyed the continued endorsement of Charpentier, D'Indy, Ibert, and Ravel; in America a strong and determined propaganda machine was operated by the New York office of the school, headed by philanthropist Francis Rogers, society patron Mrs J. West Roosevelt, and others.[13] Alumni of the Conservatoire were also becoming well known, none more so than the first student himself, Aaron Copland.

A rising star, Copland had left France in 1924 after extended study with Boulanger both in Fontainebleau and Paris. By the early 1930s, his name had become known across America. His first New York premiere had featured Boulanger as the soloist of his *Organ Symphony*, conducted by Damrosch in January 1925. Since then his *Music for the Theater* (1925), *Piano Concerto* (1925), and *Piano Variations* (1930) had gained a measure of fame for the young composer. Copland was often called on by the school to speak about his experiences there, and he wrote about an equally visible Fontainebleau figure in the *Fontainebleau Alumni Bulletin* of May 1930:

[Boulanger's] mastery of the art is phenomenal and has been written about before this. I cannot believe that she owes it merely to her exhaustive conservatory training. She is anything but a pedant. One feels a living substance at the core of her knowledge. Whether she is correcting the merest counterpoint exercise or reading a new and difficult orchestral score at the piano, it is always there. When technical mastery is imbued with that living substance it takes on a new significance. It is because she loves music well that Nadia Boulanger is a master of her art and knows its most recondite secrets.

Her relation to the American composer is somewhat curious. I have never known her to take any special attitude to American music either in the sense of seeking for it some quick and easy road to an expression of national consciousness or in the sense of taking a condescending attitude towards an art that is still, more or less, in its infancy. It is a current European fashion to be conscious of Americans as Americans rather than as men. Particularly with regard to our music they are over anxious to discover the American note. Nadia Boulanger has never singled out an American composer as different, as such, from a French composer or a Spanish composer. She seeks rather the profound personality that can create great music and considers such a personality as beyond a question of territorial boundaries. In doing this she throws each pupil back on the strengths or weaknesses of his own individuality. She makes him the stronger by so doing. At the same time her faith in the future of America is striking. But her faith does not rest on a blind sympathy, but in testimony of the works she already knows.[14]

During this period, Boulanger was in the process of securing her place as the composition teacher of choice at Fontainebleau, although she remained listed in the brochures as secondary to André Bloch within the department until after the Second World War. There can be no doubt that she was an extraordinarily influential figure in the course of twentieth-century music, especially American music. During the 1930s, streams of American composers—encouraged by the positive reports from earlier pupils—passed through the Conservatoire Américain as both formal and informal students, including William Ames, Marc Blitzstein, Robert Russell Bennet, Theodore Chandler, Israel Citkowitz, David Diamond, Robert Delaney, Douglas Moore, Walter Piston, and Melville Smith.[15] Jacques Durand continued to publish works by Fontainebleau composers in France, and the influence of Boulanger, her patrons, supportive alumni, and other Conservatoire figures assisted the composers in mounting performances both in Europe and America.

Boulanger's attentions at Fontainebleau were naturally turned toward the more proficient and talented of her students, but she did not neglect the opportunities other students—both at Fontainebleau and within her Paris circle—afforded her. Working to promote both her best composition students and herself, Boulanger was keenly aware of the value of her non-professional and society students, many of whom were highly skilled amateurs and interested in promoting the arts through their positions in the social order. Like her friend the Princesse de Polignac, heiress to the Singer sewing machine fortune, many of her students were in positions to aid Boulanger financially in the promotion of her career as a conductor, and her students in gaining commissions and recognition. Just as Polignac had built a series of salon concerts around Boulanger's conducting and organ playing, socially connected students in the United States arranged concerts for her there, entertained and housed her, arranged for interviews with the press, and provided her with an unending flow of new students for her classes in Fontainebleau, while at the same time carefully following and supporting the careers of her protégés.[16]

The composition studio was not the only busy place in the Palais during these years. Isidor Philipp was refining his style of piano "technic" with his Fontainebleau classes. As the head of the piano department, Philipp maintained a strong hold over the students and professors alike. Choosing only the best students for his own personal attention, he nevertheless supervised the teaching of piano professors Camille Decreus, Poul Silva Herard, Jean Batalla, Nathalie Radisse, Hélène Chaumont, and Marcelle Herrenschmidt.[17] Philipp believed that the "varied and expressive tone" was the highest quality of a pianist, and strove to approximate the colors of the orchestra in all works. Pianists should be knowledgeable listeners to symphonic works, he decreed, and his students often studied orchestral scores at the piano. Careful analysis of a work went hand in hand with Boulanger's harmony classes, and this kind of study, coupled with the three things a pianist required: "first, technic; second, technic; third, technic," would bring superior artistry. Of the same mind-set as Saint-Saëns when it came to much "new" music, Philipp's tastes ran to Liszt, Czerny, Thalberg, Busoni, and Godowsky, the most technically—if not always musically—demanding composers. However, his teaching won him devoted students with considerable skills and polish.

The faculty's approaches to teaching American students continued to develop during the early 1930s. Organ professor Marcel Dupré set forth his ideals for pedagogy and learning in 1933, in a document that served as a plan for many of the teachers trying to uphold the French methods of instruction despite the difficulties in asking American students to make such an adjustment to their learning style. In his opinion, the trouble was not so much teaching the students in Fontainebleau, but making sure that the students retained what they had learned upon returning home. Dupré began his teaching guide by stating the more long-term concerns of the faculty:

> The problem of the Summer Course of Instruction at the Fontainebleau Conservatory reveals several points of view. Although it depends both on the teacher's psychology and the student's application during the course of study, it only concerns the student when he, or she, has returned to America. The method of teaching employed at Fontainebleau in two ways—private lessons and classes—satisfies the ideal in view.

He went on:

> The teacher who, during the tête-à-tête of the private lesson, can observe each student at close quarters and study his character is thus able to direct the class, which brings them all together in such a way that each benefits by it. Thanks to this little link between the class and the private lesson, time is gained and the student can acquire the maximum of what he can hope to acquire in only a few weeks.
>
> To say the truth the difficulty only begins when the student has left his teacher and returned home; for, if he does not want to have wasted his time, he must continue to carry out the methods indicated so that the rudiments obtained may bring forth fruit.

Dupré then listed three basic principles that he expected Conservatoire students to heed:

1. What matters is not the number of hours employed but the concentration used when working. The real musician works less with his limbs than his brain and when he does work, he does not waste a moment.

2. The preparation for his work is as important as the work itself. A thoroughly thought-out fingering, the comprehension of a part of a piece read mentally beforehand, the decision made about muscular movements to be affected, greatly help a virtuoso in the movement of his fingers which must always be carried on with the strictest mental discipline. As for the composer, before beginning to write, he must conceive the rough outline of his work, then gradually obtain a clearer vision of the details, their choice, the arrangement of the place they must fill and the importance they must occupy.

3. No one should rely simply on memory as to what the teacher has said. It is absolutely necessary to note down during the lessons every possible indication about the text, but clearly, carefully, and without scribbling. A respect for the printed work is an elementary and material form of respect for the work itself. It would be wise, in the evening, to sum up all that the teacher has said so that the different indications given may form a firm basis for working alone in the future.[18]

This description of how to approach practicing and lessons offers a glimpse of the methods American students were asked to master during their three months in Fontainebleau. Economy of time and effort; a detailed analytical understanding of the work to be studied; and an absolute respect for the instructor's guidance and interpretative suggestion were three powerful tools for students unaccustomed to such tactics.

Students were not only encouraged to heed Dupré's advice in terms of their primary instrument, but in terms of secondary areas of study as well. The idea of the dually talented and productive musician was still being promoted in the mid-1930s, and the ideal of the pianist-composer or violinist-composer was often embodied in the professors: Robert Casadesus was well-regarded as a composer and frequently performed his own works in recital and with orchestras. Boulanger and cellist Paul Bazelaire were also musical polymaths, a trait common to their generation.

Judging by the Livre des Éleves, the records kept of nearly every session beginning in 1925, both men and women were fully expected to take courses not only in their own instrument, but in composition or harmony as well. For women, many of whom came to Fontainebleau intending to study harmony alone in order to improve their teaching prospects, this was a departure from the modest expectations their previous training had provided, and under the tutelage of supportive instructors and in an environment where American professional limitations did not apply, they flourished, and far more women than men received multiple diplomas and honorable mentions.

The Livre contains lists of diplomas granted and the classification of each; it is from this document that the picture of the well-rounded musician becomes more complete, because the names of the same students occur again and again: in harmony, solfège, piano, organ, or in the study of a second instrument. Of these secondary areas, which included organ (for pianists), keyboard improvisation, accompaniment, vocal coaching, figured bass, and sight-reading, the two more academic subjects of harmony and solfège proved most popular.[19] Solfège was standard among women as an area second to instrumental performance, and teaching diplomas in it were awarded overwhelmingly to them. Women in general were more likely to try for both performance and teaching certificates, while male students sought performance diplomas alone, perhaps counting on that to see them into a teaching job should the need ever arise.

The early 1930s saw changes in the curriculum designed to promote practical primary and secondary study: new courses in music history, elementary French, stage deportment, lieder, and a sonata class were all added to the curriculum in 1933. Isidor Philipp began a class around the same time to help students combat stage-fright and to accustom themselves to playing from memory, which, although becoming more common, was still not the standard for European soloists.[20]

Outside of the practice room and away from the scores, there was a continuing problem of relations with the Palais, which reached a nadir in 1932 and 1933. Regarding the long-proposed acquisition of a student dormitory that would alleviate some tensions with the chateau, Damrosch wrote to Fragnaud in January of 1932 that

> [t]hese are terrible years for all institutions that serve higher ends, and until the incredible financial depression changes for the better, we cannot hope for anything like a proper registration for the Fontainebleau school. The people simply do not have the money, and for this reason Mr. Flagler and I have decided not to ask for any money from musical patrons for the dormitory at present. It would be useless.[21]

This was a major sticking point in dealing with the curator of the Palais, Albert Bray, who was adamant that the students move out as soon as possible. The original agreement was that the Palais would house the students "provisionally." The Conservatoire was to build a dormitory of its own by 1931, at which point students would no longer live in the chateau. The dormitory was never built, although the school began to shop for a hotel of its own, leasing the local François I Hotel in 1932. Land and funds were set aside for a dormitory later in 1932, but nothing came of the plans for the classically inspired building designed by a member of the Beaux Arts faculty.

Supporters of the chateau's keepers were vocal in the local and national press, rallying around the old suggestions that the Palais was unsafe for students and that the students were unsafe for the Palais. The next year found Widor asking the minister of education for assistance: "I appeal to your patriotism, sir," he begged, "with the support of the American Ambassador." For twelve years, he said, the Conservatoire had provided outstanding French propaganda—why, look at the Italians trying to start their own school at the Villa d'Este! Continuing the school was a matter of national interest, and those who persisted in calling the chateau unsafe for students were guilty of dangerous acts.[22]

Widor's calls for patriotism and for national propaganda echoed exactly what was happening in the consciousness of American music students: the Conservatoire had been in residence long enough to connect the school and the Palais firmly in cultural memory. Its brochures, bulletins, and promotional materials boasted fine engravings of the chateau, and the thought of the school being located elsewhere was near unthinkable. Musical memory pegged Ravel and Debussy with the Jeu de Paume, Boulanger with the Salle Pedagogique, and school fêtes with the Etang des Carpes and the gardens. Many believed that should the Conservatoire leave the Palais, the school would cease to be. This was not an extreme position, but an astute realization of the importance of locale in the minds of Conservatoire patrons and students alike.

It was not long before the French press took up the issue, and, not wanting to be accused of anti-Americanism, was critical of the curator, Bray, and his inflexible stance. Administrators of both the Conservatoire and the Beaux-Arts school cannily played to this when dealing with the press. The head of the Beaux-Arts division gave an interview to the *Musical Courier* in April 1932 in which he appealed to the pride of the French government:

We are keenly aware of the propaganda value of the Fontainebleau school for Americans and are ready to do all in our power to encourage such propaganda in the arts. [. . .] We know that Italy, Germany, and Austria have offered chateaux generously to American students, and maybe the French government may see its way to do the same thing.[23]

In New York, Francis Rogers responded that, in order to gain press attention, the French Conseil d'Administration was hurting its own cause by making the case seem more drastic than it actually was. Rogers, who was well spoken in French and in constant contact with the French Conseil, was not fully cognizant of the troubles with the Palais, but he forged ahead in the manner of a man accustomed to bluffing his way into victory. "Recent advises [sic] from your Paris correspondent," he wrote to the *Musical Courier*, "have been interpreted by some of your readers as meaning that the French government is likely to deprive the Fontainebleau School of Music of its right to function this summer in the famous old palace. [. . .] In the summer of 1933 (June 25 to September 25), all classes will be held in the palace, . . . and most of the female students of music and fine arts will be lodged again in the Louis XV wing."[24] To add insult to injury to the Palais's staff, though intended to help assuage the difficulties of the male students, who were previously asked to find lodgings in town, the Louis XV wing was opened to male occupancy for the first time in 1934, meaning that more students than ever resided within the Palais. One student wrote of that summer that:

One floor of the Palace dormitory-section was assigned to the male students, thus breaking a precedent of long standing. The students certainly liked it; their temporary guardians were satisfied that all was well; and even the Palace guards managed somehow to overcome that feeling fostered in them since the beginning of the American occupation, that they are the keepers of somebody's harem.[25]

Such conflicting views from the French and American administrations could not have helped clarify the matter nor speed it to a conclusion, but ultimately the government gave in and a truce was reached. Once again, it was couched in ambiguous terms: the Palais would house students until the Conservatoire had the means to house them elsewhere, and dedicated classroom space was set aside for the school.

The middle of the decade found the school at a turning point, stemming from the effects of the depression finally settling in over Europe and coinciding changes in faculty and directorship. In June 1934, Maurice Ravel was named general director of the Conservatoire Américain, replacing the retiring Charles-Marie Widor. Of his appointment, *Le Journal* in Paris wrote:

Such unanimous regret has been engendered by the departure of Charles-Marie Widor, who was able to give an impetus wholly unique to this school, and who gave it the benefit of his high competence, his great experience and his generous interest, that the nomination of Maurice Ravel to this post is news of a nature to cause rejoicing among all the friends of French music.

We do not doubt that our American friends will applaud this news unreservedly and that they will be grateful to the greatest French musician of today for having shown in so tangible a fashion the interest and sympathy he feels for young Americans. We ourselves have not less reason to be glad of a decision which will have the most fortunate repercussion for French art in America.

Everything that can contribute to concentrate the attention of the foreigner upon Maurice Ravel, upon his genius and his works, facilitates at the same time the approach to French thought and art. His style, clear, pure, logical, perfectly simple, limpid and direct, he inherits from the masters who brought French music to a point of perfection which astonished and delighted the greatest foreign musicians, Bach most of all.[26]

Hyperbole aside, both the French and American administrations were delighted that Ravel had accepted their offer of directorship. It was hoped that having such a distinguished name associated with the Conservatoire would bring to it additional prestige, better students, and, in the lean and hungry years of the mid-1930s, increased enrollment. Apparently, at least, the enrollment goals were met: student numbers did increase in the late 1930s, with the greatest gain coming between 1936 and 1937 when the school gained fifty-three students.

At the same time that Ravel was named as director, the school announced that Robert Casadesus would be returning in the coming summer to head the piano department in place of Isidor Philipp, who intended to retire.[27] Casadesus was warmly welcomed to the Conservatoire after an absence of ten years, which he and Gaby had spent touring both as soloists and in two-piano or four-hands partnership. Upon his return to Fontainebleau, Robert Casadesus found a school greatly suffering from the effects of economic depression, which hit France that year. The 1934 season yielded only sixteen pianists out a paltry total of thirty-three students, and in 1935, as the depression deepened, there were just eleven pianists out of a mere total of twenty-six. In fact, the *Alumni Bulletin* of March 1935 ran a special article on the first page assuring all that the school would indeed open as usual. To increase numbers, alumni were offered discounts on tuition.

Casadesus immediately began working to increase recruitment and to improve the standing of the Conservatoire's piano department. He played twice during the season in concerts in the Jeu de Paume. Departing in repertoire from Philipp's beloved Liszt, Casadesus chose to play more French and French-oriented repertoire as well as some German standards. His recitals in the old tennis court included de Séverac's *Le retour des muletiers*, Ravel's *Toccata*, Debussy's *Reflets dans l'eau*, Schumann's *Papillons*, and Beethoven and Chopin sonatas and scherzos. He also performed his own *Quintette* with the Quatuor Calvet. Dr. Elmer Tidmarsh, an organ student returning for his sixth Fontainebleau summer, wrote in the *Alumni Bulletin* that Casadesus "thrilled everyone and was acclaimed one of the world's great pianists. The piano department is very fortunate in having such a great artist and teacher."[28] Casadesus's emphasis on French repertoire set a new direction for Conservatoire students to follow. By preferring to teach works by his own countrymen, Casadesus encouraged the appreciation, study, and performance of more French music, including newly composed music. The programs of student concerts following Casadesus's initial year bear this out, with more and more performances of French works, culminating in the international broadcast of the Conservatoire's Fauré festival in 1938.

Casadesus was an exceptional professor. Though his choice of repertoire and technique differed from Philipp's, he maintained the high levels of achievement established by his old mentor. Of the piano students who attended the Conservatoire Américain in the 1930s—approximately 412, or just over half of all students—83 received diplomas for Excellence of Execution, many with the coveted *mention bien* or *mention très bien*—high praise indeed.[29] An additional sixty-six were granted diplomas for teaching piano. The most qualified pianists at the end of each summer continued to compete for cash prizes sponsored by the piano-making houses of Pleyel, Erard, Steinway, and Chickering. Selected students also were promoted at recitals at the Salle Pleyel in Paris, and, as radio became an acceptable and practical medium—despite Decreus's allegation that its "mechanical music" would spell an end to conservatories as a whole—concerts by student prizewinners were broadcast in France and in the United States.

The renewed involvement of Casadesus at the Conservatoire was an energizing and crucial event at the school, for it soon became clear that Decreus, Casadesus, and other faculty members would be needed to assist with the administration of the school. Director Maurice Ravel, hoped to be a long-lasting figure at the Conservatoire, was dying. Ravel's last major works had been his piano concertos, completed in 1930 and 1931. Shortly after their premieres he began to experience aphasia and loss of muscle control, marked by bouts of memory loss and speech difficulties. While for the first time Ravel was receiving admiration and acclaim from both critics and audience, he could enjoy it little. Unable to compose, he told a friend that "his mind was replete with ideas, but, when he wished to write them down, they vanished."[30] This frightening loss of mental agility foreshadowed an event just before his death: when asked for his signature, the composer replied, "I have forgotten how to spell Ravel."

At the time of Ravel's appointment as director in Fontainebleau, he was already suffering from the brain tumor that would end his life. The Conservatoire Américain, full of optimism both for Ravel's health and the school's future, knew of his illness but hoped against hope that it was not serious, that a cure could be found, that this great Frenchman could lead the school to never-before-attained brilliance. In the end, the Ravel name aided the Conservatoire more than did the man himself. He died in Paris in 1937, much of his potential unfulfilled. Decreus, previously appointed resident director and assisted considerably by Casadesus, took on the responsibilities of the full directorship, overseeing day-to-day administrative duties, working with the Conseil d'Administration and the Palais staff, and keeping close watch on educational trends and changes so as to keep the curriculum as up-to-date and useful as possible.

As the decade neared its end, individual faculty members and the Conservatoire as a whole faced challenges brought about by societal changes and changes in the music world, including the first stirrings of dissatisfaction with its most widely recognized instructor. Nadia Boulanger began to face resistance from students for the first time as some started to view the revered pedagogue as too personally involved with her students and unfair in her treatment of her pupils. David Diamond, who first attended the Conservatoire Américain in 1937, had a very unhappy experience with the famed pedagogue. Boulanger was in the habit of controlling her students' lives to the smallest detail. She insisted on certain standards of behavior, and there were strictly enforced dress codes for men and women, who were not permitted to wear trousers in her presence.[31] She often took it upon herself to make living arrangements and to oversee even the diets of her pupils.[32] Diamond, a strong personality himself, disliked Boulanger's approach. He was angered by having to wait for lessons and being asked to run errands, and felt that Boulanger had not lived up to his expectations.[33] Boulanger believed that most of her students—especially the American ones—lacked fundamental training. Many accepted this criticism and used it to push themselves to work harder. Diamond was one rare student who dared to disagree with the master. Boulanger accused the young composer of hypersensitivity, but the contretemps raised another, more unpleasant matter: that of Boulanger's anti-Semitism.

According to Léonie Rosenstiel, Boulanger's authorized biographer, Boulanger's exceptionally devout Catholicism included the belief that "each individual Jew was morally responsible for the crucifixion of Jesus."[34] Anti-Semitic intolerance was common in France, and Boulanger's views were no exception. In the interest of not offending students and patrons of the Conservatoire, however, she had to keep a tight rein on the expression of her feelings in this regard. Boulanger accepted many Jewish students at the Conservatoire, but was careful not to take on "too many" at once.[35] Earlier students were not aware of Boulanger's convictions because she was so able to suppress her prejudices in their presence. However, her stance became more apparent when, during this period, she became noticeably less enthusiastic about Copland's music as he explored Jewish themes and the use of Jewish folk materials, and she pointedly refused to play his work *Vitebsk (Study on a Jewish Theme)*. Jewish students continued to attend the Conservatoire, but Boulanger's prejudices had damaged her reputation, and later pupils knew to expect Boulanger's Catholic outlook to flavor her demeanor toward them.

Ambitious students were compelling forces in bringing other changes to the Conservatoire's approaches and curriculum as well. While at the beginning of the 1930s, students were encouraged to follow the practice of their professors and become proficient musicians in multiple areas of study, a new push for specialization brought about a reversal of this policy. Musicians who specialized only in performing were able to devote more time to practice, more time to repertoire, and began to displace the technically less brilliant. Pianists in particular began more and more to devote themselves to single composers or periods. Students of the Casadesuses in Fontainebleau may well have felt the pull of specialization in French music: an enormous new repertoire was being opened up, explored, and promoted by Robert and Gaby, and increasing numbers of their students fell in line behind them. In time, the Conservatoire's widely taken secondary classes, while never abandoned or neglected entirely, became of less importance for many of the performers.

For nonpianists, a summer at the Conservatoire in the late 1930s provided the opportunity to study current French interpretation, widely recognized as differing from German or Russian schools, especially in strings. Cellist Paul Bazelaire, a sought-after soloist, was one especially appreciated professor at the Conservatoire Américain whose students returned year after year.[36] For string players, acquiring the French style meant new approaches to sonority, bow angles, left hand articulation, and phrasing. The real acquisition of French style came after the mechanics had been mastered, at which point a student understood the teacher's point of view and could emulate and interpret as an individual, often after leaving Fontainebleau. Pianists also faced changes to their technique: confronted with new etudes and study-pieces,

they could be called on to alter anything from pedaling to which arm mus-
cles to use in the pursuit of the French sound.[37]

By the end of the decade, critics could stretch a bit and, if so inclined,
make some sort of case for a "Fontainebleau School" of composition. Copland's "American" style, tonal and accessible, was echoed by Thomson's likewise audience-pleasing simplicities. Diamond, too, worked within the tonal
sphere, as did Talma, Beveridge Webster, and numerous other Conservatoire
composers of the twenties and thirties. However, it is difficult to link the
composers with any more musically specific stylistic parallels. The one trend
cited by Copland and others of Boulanger's approach toward composers at
the school was that she never forced any particular student into a style or
method of composition. Instead, through guided work in all areas of musicianship, each came to find a unique voice. Boulanger constantly brought in
new music for her charges to study, new and important composers for them
to meet. Some students, such as Talma, were clearly more influenced by
French music in general and that of Lili Boulanger and Fauré in particular.

Louise Talma was one of Boulanger's most committed students, attending
Fontainebleau for thirteen years as a student before becoming its first American faculty member. Talma had begun attending the Conservatoire Américain in 1926 at the age of twenty and continued studying there well after she
had begun a career at Hunter College. She took piano lessons from Isidor
Philipp during her first years at the Conservatoire, but Boulanger quickly became the most important influence in her musical and personal lives. Her
early compositions show Boulanger's influence very clearly: tonal and neo-
classical, they point to Boulanger's high regard for Stravinsky and her frequent use of his works in her teaching. Talma's works display a solid ground-
ing in counterpoint as well, another area in which Boulanger insisted that
her students be proficient. During her time as a Fontainebleau student,
Talma was developing the style of vocal writing for which she would best be
known. In 1938 she was awarded the Stovall Prize, the top honor for composition students, and a coup for her teacher, who had campaigned for the
treatment of women as the equal to men as composers and who was still officially only a professor of harmony.[38]

The 1939 Conservatoire session opened with the usual fanfare: Mrs. Stovall increased the composition competition Stovall Prize award money to
2,000 francs; Fragnaud, enthusiastic as ever, brought Maurice Martenot to
Fontainebleau to demonstrate his new instrument, the ether-wave ondes
Martenot; concert plans and parties were in the air. Interdepartmental cooperation between composition and piano brought Hindemith and Stravinsky
premieres to Fontainebleau, Stravinsky himself led master classes and, as part

of the Stovall Prize jury, awarded Talma her second accolade as the Conservatoire's best student composer. Tuition was only 7,000 francs that year, or $190, and students were eligible for the French Railroad Reduction Card, offering discounted travel, something many students planned to do at the end of the course.

However, just a few hours' drive from the Jeu de Paume and the Louis XV wing another nation was stirring for war. This would be the last summer for some time that any aspiring American musician would appreciate Fontainebleau's newly paved streets, bicycle through its woods, eat pastry creations in the gardens, meet fellow students at "Rosa's Bull"—sculptor Rosa Bonheur's bronze bull that stood in the center of town, quake with nerves before a harmony class or concert in the tapestry-laden Jeu de Paume, or stand in the shadow of the Horseshoe Staircase. The first era of the Conservatoire Américain came to an end with the final concerts in September. Posters appeared on village walls across France: "One, entitled 'Passive Defense,' warns people that 'enemy bombs may be redoubtable,' and tells them what to do in case of gas attack. The second poster is an *avis à la population* and instructs civilians what to do with automobile headlights and public and private lamps during blackouts."[39] In many areas surrounding Paris, announcements regarding blackout times were made by boys on bicycles equipped with military drums for the purpose of attracting attention. Air-raid sirens were tested. The American Hospital in Neuilly prepared for emergency evacuation, the Louvre closed and sent artworks away to undisclosed safe locations, and in mid-August the government asked for the voluntary evacuation of Paris. The Palais of Fontainebleau closed its doors to visitors and began putting art and artifacts into storage. Students and faculty at the Conservatoire completed the year with frantically hurried exams and final performances, striving to maintain an air of normalcy until the very last days of the session. As the air turned cooler and the students, having packed their trunks with music, Parisian dresses, and counterpoint lessons, sailed home, France went to war.

The first era of the Conservatoire Américain ended that September. As a debate emerged about the future of the school during the war, there was ample time to take stock of its accomplishments and shortcomings: at the age of eighteen, the Conservatoire had reached adulthood, and professors and students alike could analyze the school with an eye toward shaping its maturity. "The Fontainebleau School," wrote Walter Damrosch, " . . . is one of the few beautiful flowers that has grown from the earth drenched by the Great War."[40]

As students rushed home from their summer's idyll in Fontainebleau in advance of the coming war that seemed at once unthinkable and yet inevitable, professors and alumni, optimistic to their cores, and the most dedicated supporters within the town packed up the chateau tightly against the coming storm and looked to the future. The outlook for Damrosch's beautiful flower was more precarious than any brought about by previous crises of finance or conflict with the Palais. In determining the course of action to take, the brief history of the school undoubtedly was considered: was it worth preserving, and at what cost? Was the Conservatoire Américain, that great adventure in international relations and exchange, of value in the rapidly changing world?

While the alumni looked forward, those interested in promoting the historical and continuing value of the Conservatoire looked back: the *Alumni Bulletin* of June 1940 reminded its loyal readers of the success of their fellow students with no fewer than five densely printed pages. Boldface type bragged of the achievements of composers Colin McPhee and Aaron Copland, violinist Romeo Arsenault, singer Maria Montana, violinist Barbara Lull, and pianists Beveridge Webster and Clara Rabinowitch.[41]

Despite the disparities of talent and commitment that the school suffered during its first years, the Conservatoire had established an international reputation as the training ground of the future greats. A vociferous alumni group based in New York saw to propaganda and publicity, making sure that no musician, be it elementary-school music teacher or major conductor, or, for that matter, no prominent and artistically supportive socialite went without knowledge of the school that took place each summer in the Palais. Fontainebleau students used the name of the Conservatoire Américain to promote careers and impress employers. A diploma from the school in teaching or, especially, performance, was a passport to a job in the music world, and a vast network of alumni aided new graduates in making their ways through the maze of managers, concerts, publicity, and teaching contracts.

The American composition students of the Conservatoire Américain were perhaps the best-known products of the school's formative years. However, many trace the similarities and successes of the major composers not to the school itself, but rather to Boulanger, with whom almost all of the composers had some form of contact. In time, though, the teaching processes of Boulanger became inextricably linked with Fontainebleau, and the name of the pedagogue called up this cultural synonym.

No one could predict the effect that the war would have on the school. The first war had led to its creation; the second would lead to its modernization as it passed from youthful exuberance and giddiness to a more mature state. Spending the war in an American exile, the Conservatoire Américain, like many of its contemporaries, came of age in a foreign country, led by a brave few.

Notes

1. *Fontainebleau Alumni Bulletin*, May 1930, 2.
2. Interview with Gaby Casadesus, July 20, 1999, possession of author; interviews with Elsie Watson, various dates July 1999 and July 2000, possession of author.
3. *Fontainebleau Alumni Bulletin*, January 1932, 4.
4. Janet Flanner, *Paris Was Yesterday* (New York: Harcourt Brace Jovanovich, 1972), 67.
5. Photograph, undated (1930s), scrapbook of Hilda Berkey, CA/GA.
6. Gaby Casadesus, *Mes noces musicales* (Paris: Buchet/Chastel, 1989), 40.
7. *Fontainebleau Alumni Bulletin*, January 1933, 1.
8. *Fontainebleau Alumni Bulletin*, January 1932, 2.
9. *Fontainebleau Alumni Bulletin*, January 1939, 2.
10. *Fontainebleau Alumni Bulletin*, January 1939, 2.
11. *Fontainebleau Alumni Bulletin*, January 1934, 1.
12. *Fontainebleau Alumni Bulletin*, January 1939, 2.
13. Letters, Francis Rogers to Maurice Fragnaud, the *Musical Courier*, various dates, CA/F.
14. *Fontainebleau Alumni Bulletin*, May 1930, 1, 6–7.
15. Boulanger's students at Fontainebleau arrived and studied as both registered and unregistered students, with unregistered students frequently having had previous contact with Boulanger. Because of this practice, and because of apparently uneven account-keeping during this period, not all of these names appear on the rolls.
16. Including most of the New York office. Those in administrative positions who had not been students of Boulanger tended to be patrons of the arts with other connections to her, through children, relatives, or friends. Examples include Clarence and Marie Brodeur, Gladys Stubenbord, and others.
17. Fontainebleau brochures, 1930–1939, BMF.
18. Marcel Dupré, "The Part to Be Played by the Student at the American Conservatory–Fontainebleau," *Fontainebleau Alumni Bulletin*, January 1933, 1.
19. Livre des Éleves, CA/F.
20. *Fontainebleau Alumni Bulletin*, May 1933, 2; also, Elizabeth Saylor, "Coming Home," possession of author.
21. Letter, Walter Damrosch to Maurice Fragnaud, January 4, 1932, CA/F.
22. Letter, Charles-Marie Widor to the Minister of Education, March 15, 1933, CA/F.
23. *Musical Courier*, April 22, 1932, Paris.
24. Letter, Francis Rogers to the *Musical Courier*, undated, CA/F.

25. *Fontainebleau Alumni Bulletin*, March 1935, 1.

26. *Fontainebleau Alumni Bulletin*, March 1935, 5.

27. *Fontainebleau Alumni Bulletin*, May 1934, 8.

28. *Fontainebleau Alumni Bulletin*, March 1935, 1.

29. Between 1930 and 1939, the Conservatoire Américain had 737 students. Document tracing enrollment c. 1949, CA/F.

30. Arbie Orenstein, *Ravel: Man and Musician* (New York: Columbia University Press, 1975), 107.

31. Elsie Watson, interview with author, July 1999, possession of author.

32. Interviews with Elsie Watson, July 1999 and July 2000; Jay Gottlieb, July 2000; and Emile Naoumoff, 2000, possession of author.

33. Léonie Rosenstiel, *Nadia Boulanger: A Life in Music* (New York: Norton, 1982), 280–281.

34. Rosenstiel, *Nadia Boulanger*, 198.

35. Rosenstiel, *Nadia Boulanger*, 198. Also demonstrated in correspondence of Boulanger, dating from 1949 to 1978, CA/F.

36. Livre des Éleves, CA/F.

37. Interview with Gaby Casadesus, July 1999, possession of author. Also comments of Philippe Bianconi to students, July 2000, recorded by Jessie Fillerup, possession of author.

38. Livre des Éleves, 1921–1950s, CA/F.

39. Flanner, *Paris Was Yesterday*, 222.

40. Document, "The Fontainebleau Schools," 1984, CA/F.

41. *Fontainebleau Alumni Bulletin*, June 1940.

~

CHAPTER THREE

Interlude 1: Elizabeth Saylor on "Coming Home": An Account of the Session of 1939

Here I was, a year out of graduate school, sailing to Europe in June with my sister Harriet for a summer's study in music at the American Conservatory in Fontainebleau, France. After nine days on the ocean on the Holland-America ship *Veendam*, we landed in England. We finally reached London, and while at lunch in Paddington station we saw a squadron of uniformed, helmeted English soldiers march across the waiting room. We had an instant of the horrible realization of the proximity of hostile nations and perhaps—war. [There were] several soldiers on the train from Paris to Fontainebleau. In Fontainebleau I found my pension and my hostess, Mme Garzan. She was the eldest of four generations living in the large three-story home. Tiny, energetic, dressed always in deep mourning, she was up at six daily to sweep off the sidewalk with her home-made broom of twigs, and to carry a pitcher of hot water up to each bedroom. There at Mme Garzan's I met up with my dear friend Lib Rhodes, also a music major from the University of Wisconsin. My room was on the third floor with running cold water in the wash basin, and a closet concealed in the wall by the wallpaper, which went right on over it.

Meals were in the school restaurant; classes and practice rooms in the palace itself. In the long twilight after dinner we often walked in the gardens behind the palace watching the swans on the pond and admiring the long avenues of trees pruned and shaped so that they looked like the eaves on houses. My organ teacher, Nadia Boulanger, had not arrived, and after one piano lesson my piano teacher, Gaby Casadesus, announced that she would be gone to Paris for ten days! Deeply disappointed I practiced further the things I had been preparing for three months. A weekend trip to Paris included a visit to the Opera after dinner at the Café de la Paix, where I had my first delightful peach Melba and enjoyed dinner for 18 francs (45 cents). At the Opera, where we heard "Damnation of Faust," I particularly enjoyed the promenade between acts, where everyone walked slowly counter-clockwise, getting mild exercise and admiring other people's clothes.

July 1. France warned Germany that she would carry out her alliance obligations to Poland.

Back to school on Monday and my first lesson with Nadia Boulanger. She was perfectly marvelous. Devout Catholic. A very strong, mobile face, beautiful when she spoke or played. Mannish clothes, quite long skirts and flat-heeled men's shoes. Always in half-mourning, all her clothes were in black, gray, or white. Iron gray hair softly waved and done up into a simple knot in back. Rimless glasses on a silver chain. Her mouth turned down oddly at the corners, but she had a lovely rare smile.

Bastille Day, July 14! It was a real celebration for me, for Mme Casadesus arrived for my lesson with her: a whole hour! She assigned two new works: Beethoven's Sonata Opus 110 and Chopin's C minor Nocturne. She was so inspiring. She was extremely pretty, with coal black wavy hair, very white teeth and a heart-shaped face. She wore adorable clothes, mostly pink and navy. She had a beautiful figure and was the mother of two boys, the eldest of whom was eleven. Her interpretation was fiery and emotional, and she had tremendous power in her broad, spatulate fingers. One time she took my hand in her large one and crooned over it, "Poor, poor." Another daily concert finished the school day. None of these continental artists played from memory. A formal dinner in the school restaurant was followed by much champagne and the annual sing on the horseshoe staircase. A great crowd of townsfolk had gathered despite the wet streets and walks drenched by the afternoon downpour. Costumed professionals from Paris danced on a platform erected in front of the staircase. All the students then marched onstage in couples and sang, "There's a Long, Long Trail A-Winding," and what a long trail it was on those cobblestones! Many other songs followed, then the "Star-Spangled Banner" on which the audience rose, and finally our most distinguished soprano sang "The Marseillaise." The singing was followed by a dance. In came a detachment of 10 or so officers of the army, hand-picked by the Fontainebleau school heads to eke out the male population. Very nice fellows and a marvelous party. I was escorted home by the officer who lives at Mme Garzan's in the room next to mine. I like the officers, even if they do wear their spurs dancing.

The very next day was my first piano lesson with M. Casadesus. I was still feeling very relaxed from the champagne, but with a fierce headache. I had some trouble with the Bach, and finally turned to my teacher and said, "Trop de champagne hier soir." At which point he threw back his head and laughed and laughed. The French think it's wonderful that we celebrate the Fourteenth so heartily. Monsieur was tall, blondish and graying. He looked like a prosperous businessman, not handsome, round face and gray eyes and full lips. A very reserved manner matched his restrained classical interpretation, with brilliant contrast between his pearly soft finger work and sonorous, heavy touch. He was grand: more sensitive than his wife in a quieter way. She was fireworks but I felt she would do wonders for my technique, and he for interpretation.

When we went to a movie we saw George Brent and Olivia de Havilland in "Gold Is Where You Find It." It seemed funny to hear them speaking their lines in French. A companion newsreel showed French fortifications in Africa and forty minutes of camels: walking, running, sitting, rising, being branded, drinking and eating thorn bushes—and, well, camels.

One of our next trips was the Sunday we went to Versailles. To the Neptune fountains we went, where the famous Fête de Nuit was to be held. A ballet group was poled across the reflecting pool to the pavilion platform and performed a variety of dances until nightfall, about 10 o'clock, when the beautiful fountain display began around the elaborate Neptune group of statuary. Colored lights played on the fountains, and then came the most spectacular fireworks I have ever seen.

Back at school the following day I saw about a dozen bombers flying south in formation over the palace. Then Lib and I visited the little theatre decorated by Napoleon. The stage floor actually slopes, so that there is real meaning to "upstage" and "downstage." The front rows of blue velvet seats were surpassed in elegance by the first gallery, where the emperor himself sat. Here were the most gorgeous quilted upholstered chairs matching the golden yellow brocade satin walls. Each succeeding balcony was less lavishly decorated, and in the top gallery, behind oval gilt grills, sat the specially invited hoi polloi. This balcony went completely around, so that although the spectators might not *see* the production they could hear it, and above all, view royalty!

July 21. France again warned the German government.

Rich flaky croissants for breakfast were a far cry from the alternative, toast. The French method of toasting was to hack off at least an inch slice of bread and burn it slightly on both sides. The bread is amazing: thin loaves at least a yard long. One saw bakers' boys bicycling along the streets with huge wicker hampers fastened to the handlebars and naked loaves of bread stick-ing straight up out of the baskets. I saw a traveler on the Paris train open his suitcase, pull a loaf of bread out from his clothes and proceed to break off a piece and eat it.

A few days later Lib and I went to the open market. Fun, but the fish smell clung to my clothes for hours. It was a very gay and busy outdoor market: long tables set out, each stall covered from sun and rain. Vegetables right next to laces and notions. And fish. Delicious soft cheeses packed in layers with straw between, a band (mostly drums) playing out in front. Clothing, brooms, buttons, fruit, *fish* (eyes and all), poultry and meat out in the open air and flies, according to the French custom, honey, shoes, pastries, sweets, flowers, everything. And *fish*—salted, fresh, dried. I bought some buttons—glass and pearl.

A most encouraging lesson with M. Casadesus on Friday in which he said, "You are a very good musician," made my practice hours worthwhile. Then came a Sunday trip to Chartres through lovely old French towns where grass and flowers had rooted on housetops between the tiles and were actually growing on the pointed roofs. Organ music filled the church and rolled back and forth as we sat in the nave for the service, looking up toward the altar with the five tall slender windows filled with exquisite glass. It was a unique experience to attend mass in this marvelous 12th century edifice built to the glory of God.

The schedule at the conservatory was a weekly organ lesson with Boulanger and another with M. Panel; a weekly lesson with M. Casadesus and two with Mme. Having had only two years of organ I found my back-ground woefully inadequate, a fact which Boulanger discovered immediately. She had no patience with less than perfection and said to me after a poor les-son, "Tell M. Panel that your teacher wept in your lesson!" In addition to pri-vate lessons and classes I was practicing organ two hours a day and piano four hours. Terribly discouraged, I wavered between studying only with M. Panel and dropping organ altogether. The latter finally won and I began to con-centrate on piano alone.

On a Sunday afternoon two of us bicycled through a lovely woodsy path to the practice field where the army drills every morning. Camouflage, machine-gun targets and piles of old rusty shells made it a horrible place.

A long talk with Mme Casadesus helped me to decide what to do. I told her I enjoyed teaching but *loved* playing for people and wanted to study. She volunteered that with a year's study on technique I'd be equipped and ready to concertize! My head was in the clouds all day. I had written to Isidor Philipp in Paris requesting an interview, and in that afternoon's mail came his answer making an appointment for Monday the 21st of August! Another wonderful lesson with M. Casadesus, who had just been elected to the Legion of Honor. And then he said he *and* his wife were off for a week's concert tour in Holland. While they were gone I had a great weekend in Paris with my sister, who had completed her tour of Scandinavia and was on her way home. At the American Express office I had the most curious experience: lots of Americans were milling around and I couldn't think of a whole English sentence, but instead dozens of French expressions and phrases were running through my head. I went to the Holland-America office and cancelled my passage home.

Back in Fontainebleau I obtained permission for Harriet to attend a class of Mlle. Boulanger's. After Mlle's amazing piano rendition of Bach's organ chorale preludes which are written on three staves for two hands and two feet, a fellow student made the immortal remark, "I don't see how she does it, and with only four hands, too."

Before Harriet left, three of us took the little horse and carriage into the early morning woods, so still and motionless, not a sign of a bird or squirrel. We saw the "Bouquets du Roi," trees pruned to have long, long trunks, and foliage forming a high ceiling above. Truly the trees in clusters looked for all the world like bouquets of long-stemmed flowers: the king's bouquets. We took pictures of the old driver and his darling horse with white crocheted and tasseled ear-covers to discourage flies.

August 15. The French warned the German government for the 3rd time.

At last the 21st arrived and I went to Paris to register at the embassy, only to find that I couldn't do so without passport, three photos and 12,000 francs for an identity card. Then on to Philipp's home, where I sat on a park bench opposite the house until the appointed time of 11:30. M. Philipp was very kind to me. I needn't have worried. He talked to me immediately of the war scare, about which he was very pessimistic and melancholy. He asked me to play for him, so I began with the Beethoven Opus 110 and them played the Prelude to the Bach G Major French Suite. He said, "You are *very* talented," and when I told him that I wanted to continue with the Casadesus until they left on concert tour, he said I could come back any time for lessons! He seemed more than willing to take me on, despite the fact that he has retired from active teaching. I returned to Fontainebleau again walking on air.

A vicious attack of intestinal flu laid me low for a week and demolished both practicing and piano lessons. Finally I went to a French woman doctor who fixed me up with drugs and diet. When I returned to Mme Garzan's I received a letter from home via the clipper saying *come home*. Period. The last straw after all the illness, so I broke down and cried in my room. All my beautiful plans had gone to pot.

In late August von Ribbentrop went to Moscow and on August 23 Russia and Germany signed a non-aggression pact which secretly included partitioning Poland between them and placed the Baltic states within the Russian sphere of influence.

Tension was growing in Fontainebleau with more soldiers in the streets, the embassy in Paris advising tourists to leave and everyone wondering if it was true that Hitler would take Danzig, and France and England combine to aid Poland's resistance. Past the church in town I saw bills posted about the draft and mobilization. Certain ages had already been called—a new group last night. Another bill listed requirements of personal equipment needed by each draftee.

A six-hour blackout was announced for the night, beginning at ten o'clock. At Mme Garzan's I was greeted by a wire from home: "Sail September second. Imperative. Dad." It had been sent at 8:10 this morning. I wished that my parents were not worrying. Strangely enough, though there was a good deal of tension I was not afraid. And the French were not particularly hysterical—or even excited. This was the third mobilization they had had in a year, and as someone said, "The situation has been like a smoldering volcano for ten years, and after all one can't remain in a state of hysteria for a decade."

August 25. The French premier announced that France would support Poland in a German attack, and the same day Great Britain signed a treaty of alliance with Poland. Mussolini declared he could not go to war just then, so Hitler countermanded the orders for the offensive against Poland.

I sent a wire to the Holland-America office asking for a reply to my letter requesting a renewal of my booking or another on the second or fifth of September. By this time I was really frightened and could feel it in the pit of my stomach. It was such a *grim* feeling—not excitement or thrill, but rather sorrow and a fatalistic attitude of stern determination. We heard more and more sad farewells: the owner of the Launoy next door, a World War widow, today sent off her only son. Three more divisions of the army were mobilized today. Of the ten, 1, 3, 4, 5, and 6 had been requisitioned.

I received a wire this evening, thank the Lord, from Holland-America: "Trying to get space. Will notify you soonest possible."

Meanwhile there came the news that the big ocean liners were free to turn around and return in case of war, so long as they were outside the country's three-mile limit. The *Bremen* had just done so. Heaven only knew what became of her passengers and the mail on board—delayed days, possibly weeks.

Then came the news that there might be trouble getting to Rotterdam to catch the boat if the frontiers were closed—*and* with the altered sailing dates no one knew when the boats would leave.

The Americans at the restaurant were a pretty worried-looking bunch of students. The franc had been steady at 37.75 to the dollar all summer, when it suddenly dipped to 40 on August 26. It was impossible to get a telephone call through to Paris, so everyone resorted to wires, which were very inexpensive and fairly quick. Sunday morning Mme Garzan woke me with the news that my neighbor, the officer in the room next door, had been conscripted and left early that morning. And that afternoon was my final exam. Talk about tension: either I worried about the war or else dithered about that final. All my professors were in a semicircle around a large table next to the piano; one looked directly into my face. After playing the Bach, Beethoven, and a Moszkowski etude for them I was questioned in piano pedagogy. I was limp as a rag when I came out of the examining room after twenty-five minutes of a fifteen-minute exam. After tea a group of us went out to the convergence of Rue de France and Rue Royale to see the requisition of horses and trucks. Private saddle horses were being tested for officers' use and were branded with numbers on the hoofs. Cars and delivery trucks were being tested, and then white numbers were stenciled on the driver's door. All the American boys in the Conservatory had been requested to turn in their bicycles to the shops where they had rented them, to trade them for girls' bicycles!

Monday morning I received both a teacher's and a performer's certificate as well as a solfège certificate, the only one granted in the school! My friend Lib returned from the weekend in Paris really frightened. She told many stories of the hysteria in Paris and was determined to leave the next day for Paris and go to Rotterdam on Wednesday to wait for the *Noordam* sailing on Saturday. I envied her passage terribly and could have torn my hair to think I had cancelled mine. But I still thought it wasn't necessary to leave so soon.

August 29. Hitler demanded that the Polish negotiator with full powers present himself on the following day.

Up at seven o'clock Tuesday to catch the train for Paris for my first lesson with Philipp. A wonderful lesson with him. I had brought in several problems in technique and he was kind enough to give me over an hour, although my train had been late so that I arrived twenty minutes after the appointed hour. He called it "an electric lesson" because we covered so much ground in so little time. In the subway I saw two Negro women well dressed in black with long cylinders of khaki-colored metal slung over their shoulders. Gas masks. I joined the long line at Holland-America at 1:30. An hour later along came

Lib! As we stood there talking she overheard a young red-haired woman frantically trying to get rid of a passage on the *Noordam*! Lib shrieked at me and I rushed up to the redhead. God be praised: the doorman let us through the crowd and we got into the office. The young woman was a Vassar student from Denver and had a passage on the *Manhattan*, leaving sooner, and wanted to cancel her *Noordam* sailing. I walked out simply weak with relief, but with a great many last-minute things to do, for the Holland-American agent had advised leaving on the morning train—if it went—the same Rotterdam train Lib was taking. The train was chartered for the passengers of a special ship leaving tomorrow evening from Amsterdam. The problem was to get it through the border, for France had now closed her border. Bought laces and gloves for gifts and barely caught the train back to school: an hour's ride of headache and frantic planning before reaching Fontainebleau for the last time. Three girls at my table at dinner took over for me and had me packed in twenty minutes. I arranged for Mme Garzan's nephew to return my rented bicycle and for my three friends to forward the music I had left at the chateau in my practice room.

August 30. Poland ordered general mobilization.

Up at five o'clock for dawn and sunrise over the chateau. I left a gift for Mme Garzan and stole out of the house at six with my tremendously heavy suitcases. Fortunately the conductor helped me on and off the tram, and I caught the 6:48 to Paris with time to spare. In the crowd at the Gare du Nord I found Lib, who had stayed overnight in Paris and we breakfasted together in the station during an hour and a half wait for the border train. We found a compartment and settled back, tremendously relieved to be actually on the train. The German steamship lines had cancelled all their sailings. No wonder everyone was stampeding the Holland-American office in Paris. Considering the difficulty in getting the train across the border, we had very little trouble: no suitcase searching, and just had to show our passports two or three times. At last, Rotterdam. We found an inexpensive hotel without trouble and gladly fell into bed.

August 31. At the urging of Great Britain, Poland designated a negotiator with Germany, but without full powers.

After registering our tickets at the steamship office we took the bus to Amsterdam. This country was completely mobilized and yet the people seemed happier than the French. Beautiful gray-green army uniforms. Sailors in black uniforms with tiny caps and 9-inch long streamers.

September 1. At dawn German troops entered Polish territory.

At breakfast we learned that Danzig was now part of the Reich. At the American Express office we learned that Warsaw was being bombarded by the Germans, and over the radio heard Hitler's speech of the day translated into English. According to him, Germany was warring on Poland in self-defense to uphold her honor, *liberty* and justice. With mixed feelings I sent a cable home: "Sailing today *Noordam*. Betty." We boarded the *Noordam*, which was scheduled to sail at noon on Saturday, Sept. 2.

Noon, September 2. England and France sent their 24-hour ultimatum to Germany to withdraw her troops from Poland.

Noon came and went and still we lay in port, the crew loading cargo and lettering all afternoon "*NOORDAM—HOLLAND*" in eight-foot letters on the sides of the boat and painting three broad stripes alongside: red, white, and blue. If submarines couldn't see that, we were sunk, literally. It was nerve-wracking waiting for the ship to cast off, as Germany's 24 hours dripped slowly on. At last taking advantage of the tide, the crew pulled up anchor and cast off at seven and we were soon out of the English Channel.

Eleven a.m. Sunday, September 3. England declared war on Germany and mined the channel in fulfillment of the guarantee it had earlier given to Poland. That afternoon during a very solemn boat drill we were told that meat, bread, water, and medicine for *two days* were provided in each lifeboat. In case of fire we were to stay in the cabin until the steward came to relay the captain's order. At five-thirty I saw my first battleship too far away to determine its nationality.

France entered the war at five p.m.

September 4. Hitler forbade all German attacks on French and British passenger steamers even when these were sailing in convoy, possibly with the American public opinion in mind.

Next morning we learned that the *Bremen* was captured the night before, and now came the report of the first torpedoing of an English passenger ship by the Germans. Ninety miles off Glasgow a Cunard ship had been sunk on Sunday, carrying many Americans, the *Athenia*. We were now unable to tell about weather ahead, for no ships would give out radio messages with their location for fear of submarines. An English freighter was torpedoed in the Bay of Biscay.

[At last] we saw the lovely row of lights along Long Island and the Jones Beach tower. I climbed up into my bunk for the last time and watched the lights through the two portholes. Coney Island went by with its Ferris wheel and blue neon lights. Channel buoys floated by frequently with their red lights and warning clangs. Then our vessel stopped for the night. Early that morning came the wonderful sight of dawn and sunrise behind the Manhattan skyline. A thin little crescent moon and the morning star faded away as the dawn became rosier. But best of all was the Statue of Liberty. How many of us on board greeted her with tears in our eyes, now that the long strain was over and we were safe again, for then we knew we were *coming home*.

Note

Extracted from Elizabeth Saylor's essay, "Coming Home," offered to alumni in the *Fontainebleau Alumni Bulletin*, April 1993, possession of author.

PART II

EXILE AND WAR

CHAPTER FOUR

~

At Home in Exile (1940–1945)

Exactly as Elizabeth Saylor relates, after the last students had hurriedly departed from Fontainebleau, France declared war on Germany in September 1939. The lack of military preparedness led to stunning defeats, culminating nine months later with the German army's capture of Paris on June 14, 1940. The French were ready to capitulate. Despite offers from Winston Churchill of an alliance with Britain, Marshal Pétain signed an armistice treaty with Germany. Much of France was occupied, including the Palais de Fontainebleau. In the months immediately preceding and following France's defeat, French and other European artists and composers fled the continent for the United States, among them Bartók, Hindemith, Martinu, Milhaud, Schoenberg, Stravinsky, and, albeit reluctantly, Nadia Boulanger.

Walter Damrosch called an executive meeting of the school's American committee in April 1940 to order to address the worsening condition in Europe and the future of the Conservatoire Américain. The meeting ended with the passing of several resolutions. Perhaps the most emphatic began, "In view of the situation in Europe, and trusting in the ultimate victory of the Allies, France, and England, and as evidence of our concern and sympathy with France, the American Committee will carry on during the intermediate period, cooperating with the Fontainebleau Alumni Association to keep the spirit of Fontainebleau alive."[1]

The spirit of Fontainebleau's American alumni and French professors initially appeared to be only monetarily based, with little planning for the actual continuation of the school's function as an educational institution.

Benefit concerts for both the school and for the war effort were easily organized and executed, and this ability to raise money through performances
was certainly an asset in aiding the beleaguered Gallic populace and the
Allied soldiers stationed in France. Boulanger began a war relief fund that
she herself directed, which received $125 from Fontainebleau alumni and
supporters in its first months of operation.[2] She remained in France until
late 1940, performing benefit concerts and using her car to drive people
out of Paris and away from war zones. Of one of her concerts she wrote,
"I conducted the other day an orchestra of soldiers at the front. You can't
imagine—all these men in uniform, some of them coming down from the
front lines, and an atmosphere of religious attention: Mozart, Bach—and
would you believe it, Debussy's 'Dieu, qu'il la fait bon regarder' heard in absolute silence, enthusiastic[ally]."[3] Boulanger may have been surprised by
the positive reaction to the performances of art music, but the appreciation
was genuine, and she concertized with some regularity for military groups.
However, the unexpected joys of such concerts were eventually outweighed
by the fact that such performances could no longer be considered safe, and
Boulanger accepted a three-year contract from the Longy School of Music
in Boston.[4] There, too, she held benefit concerts for France, often sending
her own fees to relief agencies.

At the same time that Boulanger was conducting in France for war relief,
Robert and Gaby Casadesus were securing a location and making the necessary arrangements for the Conservatoire to operate in exile. Clearly for many
former students and faculty members, playing benefit concerts and writing
checks to the Alumni Association was not enough in the way of preserving
the spirit of Fontainebleau, and those alumni, along with a number of interested new students, made their view known to the Casadesuses. Gaby
Casadesus recalled that she and her husband had been performing (he on his
sixth tour of the country) in the United States and were persuaded to stay
until conditions in France had improved. "The students asked us to stay," she
said. "They were the ones who wanted to continue the classes."[5] As the
Casadesuses were alone in this endeavor, being the only Conservatoire faculty outside of France, the school would operate as a series of piano master
classes only. Should the war continue at length, expansion to something akin
to the school's normal proportions and range might be considered, although
this was initially regarded as a doubtful outcome. The Casadesuses found that
St. George's, a private boys' school situated in Newport, Rhode Island, was
willing to house the Conservatoire during the summer of 1940. St. George's
proved to be most generous in its support of the conservatoire-in-exile. John
Frothingham, a director of St. George's, saw to it that the Conservatoire

Américain was allowed full run of the stately red-brick buildings and expansive grounds bordering the sea. Students and faculty had separate rooms, practice studios, and ample classrooms. The school was also granted use of the chapel, equipped with an organ, which the students were encouraged to use, the library, a lounge, a gymnasium, a concert salon, and gardens.

In addition to the students who had urged the Casadesuses to hold a session of the Conservatoire, alumni of the music school showed great interest in the school's presence in America. Alumni had always been welcome at Fontainebleau, and it was a tradition among them to return to Fontainebleau on a regular basis for refresher courses, to give concerts, or just to visit. With this interest from alumni, the stateside Conservatoire Américain curriculum was expanded from only piano master classes into a more rounded experience. Longtime student and Boulanger protégée Louise Talma signed on to teach solfège and music history, and Marthe Pillois agreed to teach French and diction. The Baldwin piano company supplied instruments at a reduced cost. Despite the war, the Conservatoire opened on July 8, 1940, for a projected two months of intensive study for piano students and alumni. The school continued at St. George's in 1941, where "the usual round of lessons, master classes, picnics, [and] swimming parties" continued far from danger. Students gave and hosted war-relief concerts during that year's six-week term, cut short of the originally planned eight or nine weeks by Robert Casadesus's concert schedule. Repertoire was, as usual, heavily French, with Chopin, Liszt, and Czerny afforded special status as worthy foreigners. Many musical organizations in Allied nations shunned works by German composers during the war, but the Casadesuses, while emphasizing French repertoire as a matter of course, seem to have restricted their students' repertoire choices very little, if at all, and their own concerts continued to include works from the standard German repertoire.

In 1942, when the beaches of Rhode Island were needed for military exercises, the Casadesuses once again relocated the Conservatoire. This time the school settled into Great Barrington, Massachusetts, not far from Tanglewood.[6] Gaby and Robert Casadesus continued their piano master classes there in a Renaissance-style mansion, hosting "les plus grands musiciens du moment" each summer. Casadesus student William Eves wrote:

> The setting was beautiful and quiet, and inspiring for the study of music which in its performance would be imbued with the character and atmosphere of elegance and natural beauty. The mansion itself contained a fine concert hall with stage and atrium with black onyx-type floors and replacements of marble pillars on all sides. There was the "Versailles Room," with gilded fireplace,

where Robert gave his lessons. Across the atrium was the Chinese room, which was Madame's studio. On the outside of the house were two terraces overlooking the expansive lawns with their pool and "jet d'eau." Against the woods at the far end of the pool was a facade of a Greek temple for ornamentation. The gentle splashing of the fountain made a refreshing sound effect, and the pool had another sound effect: from an old bull frog which made an occasional croak in the night; Casadesus referred to him as "Beethov."[7]

However, not all aspects of the summers were as plush as the surroundings. When neither Baldwin nor Steinway could deliver pianos to the new location, the task of finding enough instruments fell to Gaby Casadesus, who canvassed New England's colleges, music schools, performers, and music lovers, borrowing pianos for the students. Students, including pianist Charles Rosen, who attended in 1942, lived in crowded quarters in the mansion, several to each room. A handful assisted the Casadesuses or worked for their studies by taking care of secretarial responsibilities, housekeeping, and waiting tables on the terrace, which served as the restaurant.[8]

Despite the relative hardships of running the school at Great Barrington, the Fontainebleau-like atmosphere of postdinner concerts prevailed. Eves wrote that after meals:

> The group of pianists, guests, and the Casadesus began to drift back into the big house, at the cue of the lead by Monsieur and Madame and their friends, two of whom were Mr. and Mrs. Zino Francescatti, he the violinist. Now gathered and settled comfortably into the concert hall, the tuning of the violin . . . became the last call to hush, and then the music of the great piano and violin sonatas commenced. Music of Beethoven, Franck, Fauré, Ravel, and Debussy was augmented by Bach sonatas for unaccompanied violin, and special treats were the *Poème* by Chausson and the *Introduction and Allegro* by Saint-Saëns, with orchestral parts having been transcribed for piano.[9]

In addition to their serious concerts, students also presented an annual "show," in which they performed skits, dances, and imitations of their professors. Jean Casadesus, the eldest child of Robert and Gaby, contributed his skill at playing jazz and boogie-woogie, and Robert was known to join in on renditions of "Tea for Two" and "Misty," to the delight of the audience. At the end of each session all present gave a concert for war-relief funds or for the local hospital.

By 1943 the Conservatoire in exile had some forty piano students, an impressive number given the financial situation of the day, the uncertainty of each summer's location, and the full-time faculty of two. Dividing the students by level, Robert Casadesus generally taught the more advanced pianists in the style of a master class and Gaby provided more detailed lessons for the intermediate artists. This pair of dedicated teachers was sufficiently busy that a nurse had to be hired to watch after the newest Casadesus child, Thérèse, who had been born in 1942. In addition to their teaching, the Casadesuses frequently played for French Relief concerts, both as soloists and in two-piano appearances. Gaby Casadesus paired with Albert Einstein in a performance for British Relief in 1942, and Robert often played his own works with other noted French musicians for similar benefits.

Notably lacking in the continuation of the Conservatoire was Nadia Boulanger. Although she had missed the first year of the conservatoire-in-exile's operations by staying in France, she was invited to teach during the second year of the school's residence in Newport. Citing what she felt was the intention of the Casadesuses to use the Conservatoire as a school primarily for pianists, she declined to attend an organizational meeting of the school earlier that spring, and made plain that she would not participate in the school's American existence. Because it was clear that by asking her to join them the Casadesuses were emphatically not planning the kind of piano-only school she ostensibly protested, Boulanger appears to have been concealing her real reason for not wanting to participate, and her correspondence with her former students confirms this. Letters written by her New York Conservatoire office confidantes suggest that she felt a kind of resentment at her lack of a leadership role in the school's day-to-day affairs and at the role of the Casadesus family in managing the school's operations.[10] Much of this sentiment can be traced to the differences between Boulanger's status within the musical world at large and her position at the Conservatoire.

Having grown accustomed to celebrity status in the United States, Boulanger was not celebrated as much in her home country, where instead of being a sensation, she was viewed rather as any other member of the musical establishment. Composers and pianists from the Americas and from Eastern Europe often idolized their teacher, and she contributed a significant number of students to the enrollment rosters of the Conservatoire. However, she was treated as the equal of her colleagues in Fontainebleau rather than as superior to the rest of the faculty, receiving no higher pay or position than any other full-time professor. Certainly her stagnant position as professor of harmony—rather than composition—and the implications that that role had as a subordinate position within the composition department must have been a disappointment to Boulanger, whose abilities and fame had led her to performances as the guest conductor of major American orchestras and as a guest lecturer. Instead of working with the Casadesuses and the alumni association to continue the classes of the Conservatoire during the war,

Boulanger chose to spend her first American summer visiting former students who were sisters at a convent in Sinsinawa, Wisconsin, making plans to teach at several schools within the United States. Although she did make arrangements to teach at the Longy School of Music in Boston where her pupil Melville Smith was the director, and the Peabody Conservatory of Music in Baltimore, where Reginald Stewart, yet another former student, was in charge, Boulanger's approach was problematic. She summarily dismissed her Peabody students as ignorant, and demanded complete access to Longy's financial and artistic planning sessions, as well as a salary raise beyond what had been agreed on. Both of her former students found themselves in awkward situations, resulting in what Rosenstiel describes as "one of Nadia's greatest fears": losing control.[11] Finally, citing fatigue from her prior teaching schedule, Boulanger spent the remainder of the war in California. Although she continued to teach privately and made trips to Wisconsin to work with the Dominicans at Edgewood College, she did not entertain the idea of a rapprochement with the Casadesuses or consider teaching at the Conservatoire-in-exile. Her influence in the Conservatoire's sphere was thus diminished over the period of the war.

Most Conservatoire professors remained in France after the occupation, some for the entire duration of the war. During the German occupation, musical events were subject to censorship. Many musicians, including Conservatoire cello teacher Paul Bazelaire, were prohibited from public concertizing for refusing to submit to such draconian conditions. Others, such as singer Gilberte Lecompte, toured in neutral Switzerland and were hired by the Entertainments National Service Association (ENSA)—the British equivalent of the USO—for performances in England. Pianist Isidor Philipp fled Paris by automobile on the very morning the German army descended on it, braving "the terrors of the highways," as the *Fontainebleau Alumni Bulletin* described it. Others musicians were mobilized prior to the German occupation, and Jacqueline Bickford, an interpreter for the combined Conservatoire Américain and École des Beaux Arts, was interned for the duration of the war.

In Fontainebleau itself, as in Newport and Great Barrington, something quite extraordinary was happening. The American-educated Lucie Délécluse, first a nurse to the Conservatoire and later the secretary to the director's office, recorded the events in her diary, later published in the *Fontainebleau Alumni Bulletin*:

> The German General Headquarters established its office in Fontainebleau and for several months we were "Ville Fermée"; nobody could come into

Fontainebleau from the outside, and we could not go about in the vicinity without a special "Ausweis" [permit]; a curfew was imposed. The town was reeking with staff officers. Von Brautchitz, von Keitel, von Milch, and many others were stationed in or about the town, changing residences every few days.

Such clicking of heels, saluting and goosestepping. The last seemed such a ludicrous performance to the French that they could hardly refrain from laughing outright, faces twitching to hide the amusement going on inside. Of course, the Palace was occupied, but all the furniture, tapestries, carpets and works of art had been evacuated in 1939 to central France where they still are. The Conservatory wing was turned into offices; quite a few demonstrations went on in the Palace and on the grounds. Hitler came to confer with his commanders, but so secretly that only the big heads knew of it, and he left before the beginning of a celebration which was to take place in the Palace. Seems he did not feel so very secure, even among his adoring countrymen.[12]

Delécluse was issued a rare permit that allowed her to enter the Palais in order to speak with the Frenchmen still on guard there and record the daily goings-on inside the school's home. German troops installed antiaircraft and machine guns on the Palais roofs and Horseshoe Staircase, a sacrilege to Fontainebleau's citizens. While the Frenchmen convinced the occupying officers that the chateau would receive protection as an historical monument only if unarmed, and the big guns were moved to more discreet locations, nothing could remove the enormous Nazi flags in the courtyard and on the roof. Guards of the French museum inside the chateau were able to clandestinely place a very small French flag on the roof as well, clearly showing Fontainebleau's defiant spirit and preventing the chateau from becoming a bombing victim.

At the onset of Fontainebleau's occupation, more than twelve thousand troops were garrisoned in the town, the usual population of which was fifteen thousand. The five hundred soldiers who remained after the initial invasion devastated the village, vandalizing buildings, looting homes, and displacing and occasionally arresting citizens. Among those arrested was the mayor of Fontainebleau's sister town of Avon.[13] He died in a prison camp in Hamburg. Other victims from the immediate area included five monks, one of whom was Admiral Thierry d'Argenlieu, a retired Free French naval commander; thirty-seven members of Fontainebleau's resistance group; and several young men and women. Most were executed without benefit of trial, and their fates were unknown until months after the end of the war.

Twenty-three trainloads of furniture, art, and other valuables—even clothes and shoes—left Fontainebleau on convoys bound for Germany, never to be recovered. Delécluse, concerned that property of the Conservatoire

Américain also was being stolen, conspired with one of the French Palais guards: together they removed many Conservatoire belongings, including documents, linens, mattresses, and silver. Delécluse and the Palais manager hid all of this behind a false wall built by French staff workers overnight between the Conservatoire's Rosa Bonheur Room and the offices of the Beaux-Arts office. Although the entire building was searched thoroughly before visits by dignitaries, the hiding space—and the school's property—was never discovered.

The music of the Conservatoire Américain's music library had an even more dramatic rescue. Delécluse received an urgent summons from the Palais manager, and upon arriving at the Palais she discovered that

> The Germans were throwing out the music from our library. I rushed to the rescue. They had needed the biggest bookcase in the library and had dumped all the music on the stage stair-case of the theatre. At the same time a performance by some German theatre was being staged. So we had to get to work in a hurry. Mr. Bray [the conservator of the Palais] got some of his garden attendants with wheel-barrows, and we had all the music trucked away to the Rosa Bonheur room.[14]

The school's pianos, too, had to be similarly hauled away to the relative safety of their makers' Paris vaults on short notice.

In the United States, the Fontainebleau Alumni Association made strong efforts to aid the town. Seeing the name of the association in relation to a relief effort, alumni began to send money, food, clothes, blankets, diapers, and other staples for Fontainebleau citizens. Packages were regularly dispatched to Paris and Fontainebleau, where townspeople collected and distributed the contents. Many former students served actively in the war: fighting, translating, performing for troops in military bands or with touring groups, composing for radio broadcasts, and nursing. An address made by Henri Bonnet, the French ambassador to the United States, sums up the French appreciation for the association's actions, while also conveying a bit of the bitterness felt by many French toward their liberators:

> It has often been said that Art belonged to no country in particular, and this seems to be true in many respects. A symphony of Beethoven, a painting by Rembrandt, a sculpture of Rodin, convey a feeling of beauty to everyone sensitive to Art. Whatever the native language may be, the fact remains nevertheless that countries with a long inheritance of culture, and a great wealth of Art production throughout a number of centuries accumulate on their territories masterpieces of every sort, and that these surroundings as well as the tradition which is responsible for their production, create an atmosphere most

favorable to the development of young talent. Thus for over a century, young French artists have been sent to Rome to the "Villa Medicis" where in that beautiful building overlooking the Eternal City, they have had an opportunity of getting acquainted with the beauty of the past.

Nothing appears to me more beautiful than such an influence, and I am proud to think that the French Government went a step further in that direction when it created in the old Palace of Fontainebleau the first school ever opened by one nation for the exclusive benefit of another.

From 1921 to 1939, within the walls of that historical mansion so favorable to the stimulation of emotional and creative activities, young American artists have had the opportunity to live in the shrine of French artistic production.

Although this has been interrupted by war and the difficult conditions of the postwar period, it is to be hoped that the schools of Fontainebleau may look forward to their re-opening within the shortest possible time.

The spirit of goodwill which has presided over their creation and promoted their success is still there, in both sides of the ocean, and is kept alive in this country by the devotion and activities of the former students of the Schools. The resumption of the publication of the *Bulletin* of the Alumni Association, which was interrupted during the war, is a very good omen. I wish to express my appreciation of the understanding and sympathy which the Alumni Association of the Fontainebleau Schools have always extended to France and I congratulate them for having resumed the publication of their Bulletin, with the hope that it is the harbinger of a speedy renewal of even closer ties between their country and the—France of today.[15]

The "France of today," of which Bonnet spoke, was one in great need, as the Conservatoire's faculty and students soon discovered.

A division of Patton's 3rd Army arrived in Fontainebleau on August 23, 1945, destroying bridges and crossroads behind them. "What infinite joy it was," wrote Lucie Delécluse, "you *cannot possibly* imagine. I don't know if in our emotion we conveyed to your boys how overjoyed we were." In Paris, Conservatoire alumna Jessica Luginbuhl said, "Oh how we greeted you here in Paris—your troops. I cried myself hoarse! [. . .] Now we are living in the midst of soldiers—all the houses around here are occupied by Americans so [sic] good it is to hear them down the streets. It reminds me of dear old Fontainebleau and the Palace . . . ."[16] The American army entering Fontainebleau found it relatively intact after the destruction seen in other parts of the country. Homes were still standing, although relieved of their contents. The synagogue, not surprisingly, had been destroyed by dynamiting, but it was the only completely ruined structure in the town. Soldiers, jeeps, and tanks prowled the cobbled and dirt streets of the town. Officers were moved into the Conservatoire's Louis XV wing of the Palais, dances were held in the school's hotels, and a doughnut shop was opened. Most food, however, was still severely rationed, with scarcities in meat, milk, sugar, fruit, and nuts. More readily available were wine, bread, and the vegetables grown in side-yard plots by townspeople. Shoes, stockings, linens, cotton, and wool were not to be had except by special ration coupons, although newlyweds were entitled to a pair of sheets and towels.

The Conservatoire's own corps had suffered casualties during its exile: Camille Decreus, the director, had died in 1939. No one was appointed in his place owing to the uncertainty of the wartime situation. Maurice Fragnaud, one of the school's founders and chairman of the French Conseil d'Administration, had also died. Another third of the aging council died before 1945. Remaining American military personnel and the Military Academy of St. Cyr, the French West Point, occupied the Palais. The United States government urged citizens not to travel in Europe.

Despite these warnings from the United States and the privations that they knew they would face, many European exiles who had passed the war in America were now determined to go home, including Robert and Gaby Casadesus. They returned to Fontainebleau in 1946 with their three children, eager to restore the Conservatoire to all its glory, in its proper home in the Palais. The Casadesuses were followed a year later by Boulanger. A new era of the Conservatoire Américain was about to begin.

Notes

1. *Fontainebleau Alumni Bulletin*, June 1940, 1.
2. *Fontainebleau Alumni Bulletin*, June 1940, 3.
3. *Fontainebleau Alumni Bulletin*, June 1940, 3.
4. Léonie Rosenstiel, *Nadia Boulanger: A Life in Music* (New York: Norton, 1982), 314.
5. Gaby Casadesus, interview with author, July 20, 1999, possession of author.
6. In fact, the mansion in which the Conservatoire Américain was housed was ceded to Koussevitsky when the Conservatoire Américain returned to France in 1946, and became part of Tanglewood. Honegger and Martinu gave composition lessons there.
7. William Eves, unpublished essay, possession of author.
8. Eves, unpublished essay. Also: Thérèse Casadesus Rawson, conversation with author, July 2000.
9. Eves, unpublished essay.
10. Letters, Marie Brodeur to Lucie Delécluse, March 29, 1968; May 16, 1971; November 11, 1974, discussing the rift between Boulanger and the Casadesuses,

CA/NY, CA/GA. Brodeur blamed the Casadesus family for behaving as if the Conservatoire "was a family affair" and denying Boulanger her deserved place as the focal point of the school.

11. Rosenstiel, *Nadia Boulanger*, 324.

12. *Fontainebleau Alumni Bulletin*, November 1945, 1, 3–5.

13. Fontainebleau is linked with the town of Avon, with which it shares a railway station and some municipal facilities.

14. *Fontainebleau Alumni Bulletin*, November 1945, 1, 3–5.

15. *Fontainebleau Alumni Bulletin*, November 1945, 1, 3–5.

16. *Fontainebleau Alumni Bulletin*, November 1945, 6.

CHAPTER FIVE

~

Reconstruction (1946–1948)

Throughout the war, the American Committee and the Conseil d'Administration met regularly in order to plan for the future of their school. When Gaby and Robert Casadesus brought nineteen piano students to the Palais de Fontainebleau in 1946, the Conseil had already appointed Robert director of music in a meeting held almost a year earlier, in September 1945. Marcel Dupré was granted the position of director general, although his busy performance schedule and teaching obligations at the Paris Conservatoire limited his involvement; he delegated most administrative power to Casadesus and later Boulanger and made only a few appearances at master classes each summer. A noted French architect, Jean-Paul Alaux, would take over Fragnaud's position as President of the Écoles d'Art Américaines.[1]

These positions, unanimously decided by the Conseil, the American Committee, and Walter Damrosch, came as no surprise to the Casadesuses. While continuing to operate the school in the United States, they had been in constant touch with the various administrative organizations—as much contact as possible considering the problems with overseas mail to and from the Conseil in France. There was no doubt in the minds of those who met in 1944 and 1945 that Robert would be offered and would accept the position: he and Gaby had shown outstanding dedication to the Conservatoire, carrying on its traditions and upholding its standards through the difficult emergency relocation and establishment in America. The Casadesuses had saved the world-famous Conservatoire Américain from almost certain end. Revitalizing a school that had lain defunct for the entire duration of the war may well have proven impossible. Keeping the school alive in exile had ensured that it would not disappear without a fight.

However, many of her supporters and students had led Nadia Boulanger to believe that the directorship of at least the Conservatoire, if not the entire Écoles d'Art Américaines, would be offered to her.[2] In fact, it was not; according to the records of the Conseil, she was not even considered. She would remain a professor of harmony and, taking on a position that had long been hers in fact if not formally, composition.[3] Despite the warm welcome given to her by the Conservatoire administration and faculty, Boulanger felt that she had been snubbed.

Plans for the reopening of the Conservatoire Américain were enthusiastically made: professors were approached, funds were raised. Recruitment was especially difficult, because the United States government strongly warned its citizens not to travel abroad. However, the fact that the Casadesuses were willing to return with their young children encouraged prospective piano students. In the months preceding the reopening, Gaby Casadesus spent much of her time writing to anxious students and their parents in order to reassure them regarding their personal safety in Fontainebleau. In the end there were nineteen music students, just two more than the seventeen set forth by the Conseil as a minimum for the school to open.[4] In addition to the Casadesus role model, the American Committee had the foresight to continue promotion of the Conservatoire during the war. The *Alumni Bulletin* was published at regular intervals, and the *France-Amerique*, New York's leading French-language newspaper, offered the *Bulletin*'s editors space for Fontainebleau-related articles every two weeks. This clever public relations tactic enabled the American Committee to maintain ties to the French community in the United States as well as in France, since the paper was circulated there as well. No one would forget the Conservatoire Américain because it was out of sight and hence out of mind; its admirers would have constant notice of it.[5]

The Conseil had a number of problems hiring faculty and staff because of the low salaries that it could offer. Fortunately, enough prewar professors and new teachers wanting to teach at the school signed on as part of a skeleton faculty. Paul Bazelaire was engaged for the summer, as were voice and violin instructors, and an assistant piano teacher was hired.[6]

Other logistical problems were likewise readily attacked and rapidly solved. The restaurant, damaged by the occupation, was repaired, as were sites within the Palais. The Casadesuses requested that students bring as much music as they could transport, since contents and condition of the Conservatoire's library were unknown. Alumni and friends of the Conservatoire pledged funds for the restoration of the organs, which, after being abandoned for six years, were in extremely poor condition. Piano maker Maison Pleyel offered the school fourteen pianos for the summer, even at the risk of the school not opening. Alaux, a true believer in the Écoles d'Art Américaines, negotiated with the Palais, which saw in the postwar confusion the chance to permanently remove those bothersome Americans as lodgers in its wings. The officials of the chateau wanted to use the rooms that had been loaned to the Conservatoire for a museum instead of a dormitory. Reminding the chateau staff and officials of the generosity of Rockefeller, the rapport between the French and Americans, and the recent assistance of the United States in the war, Alaux secured a new agreement with the Palais de Fontainebleau, allowing for classroom and practice space in addition to limited living quarters. Arrangements were also made for students to be housed in two residential hotels, the Pension Launoy and at the Villa on the Rue Royale. The Casadesuses took up residence in the palace, adding to their cachet of leadership and sophistication. The younger Casadesus children were delighted with the free run of their summer home, and Jean's tours of the chateau became a favorite event for students. By living in the Palais, Robert and Gaby Casadesus continued binding the location to the institution, and instilled for those first brave postwar students a sense of grandeur and scale, despite the damage that had been done to the buildings. Secure in his success, Alaux planned the official reopening for the Fourth of July, hoping to celebrate the twenty-fifth year of the Conservatoire Américain in style.

Nadia Boulanger was one of the few professors for whom the 1946 resurrection of the Conservatoire was somewhat of a nonevent. With only one student, she taught at her apartment in Paris, going to Fontainebleau only for occasional group classes.[7] In addition, she was requested to hold classes for the Casadesuses' piano students. Her place in the administration under Robert and, in effect, Gaby, could not have but wounded Boulanger's considerable pride. Her earlier belief that the Casadesuses were interested in turning the school into a piano-only academy, coupled with the decision not to name her director, followed finally by this perceived slight—that so many students attended for the Casadesuses but only one for her—appears to have created a drive in Boulanger to become if not the actual head of the school, then a de facto one. This ambition began to inform all of her decisions over the next two years at the Conservatoire and affect the future of the school. Seeing the emphasis put on the piano department over other areas, Boulanger again believed that their intentions were to close out the other instruments and departments of the Conservatoire. While she worked intensely with as many students as possible during each session, revealing her opinions of the Conservatoire's leadership and direction only to close confidantes, she nonetheless routinely convinced many of her students that the Casadesus family expressed a feeling of entitlement regarding the Conservatoire and were the heirs-without-contest to the creation of Robert's uncle Francis. Learning her lesson—that her withdrawal from Conservatoire affairs during the war had possibly cost her the directorship—Boulanger began to make sure that the administration knew of her interest in advancing her position within the school, and cultivated supporters on the Conseil and Board.

Of the students who braved the deprivations and problems of traveling to France, quite a few were military veterans, assisted in paying the $225 tuition by the Veterans Bureau. A new group formed just after the war, the Société des Amis des Écoles d'Art Américaines, also provided subventions for the school and scholarships for students. Jean Casadesus escorted arriving students through "the melee of Cherbourg,"[8] and onto the Paris train, and Alaux and Robert Casadesus met the first students of the postwar era at the Gare St. Lazare and brought them to Fontainebleau, delighted that they had arrived safely. The faculty was not alone in welcoming the students: The municipality of Fontainebleau, despite its often-fractious chateau workers, was eager to help the Conservatoire Américain regain its feet in its hometown. Many had benefited from the care packages sent by the Fontainebleau Alumni Association during the war, which included blankets, eggs, soap, needles, coffee and tea, and vitamins.

In its first postexile year, the Conservatoire Américain was naturally known for its excellent pianists. Six concerts were given, of which four were broadcast on the radio. Student Edith Turpin recalled, "Music, music everywhere—from the harmony students holding forth downstairs, with the strains of the 'Caseys' [Robert and Gaby Casadesus] on the second floor, topped off by the cacophony of all ten pianos on the top floor going like mad!"[9]

Although the session had fewer students than in its prewar days, the studies were no less intense: the weeks were filled with lessons, sight-reading, master classes, faculty recitals, and vocal-ensemble class, in which Boulanger, on her trips to Fontainebleau, began a Conservatoire tradition of studying Bach's cantatas, a course of study she had initiated with her private students in Paris a decade earlier. The Pleyel pianos were installed on the third floor of the chateau, a floor above the Casadesuses' residence, and practice began at seven-thirty every morning. Repertoire, as might be expected, was mostly French: Debussy and Ravel were performed in abundance. Guest artists, as before, appeared frequently at the school. The highlight of 1946 was the visit of Soulima Stravinsky, who played through some of his father's works with Boulanger in one of her rare classes at the Palais.

In the year of the school's reopening, fêtes and parties resumed as if the school had never closed. Students were treated to parties given by the American Army troops in Fontainebleau and by Lucie Delécluse, Alaux, and the Casadesus family. Gaby Casadesus's birthday party was planned and hosted by the students, and faculty and students alike enjoyed the Bastille Day carnival— Robert Casadesus was "seen on the Dodgems . . . happily bumping every car in sight."[10] The town itself was "hospitable and charming" for the students, who frequented the movie houses, restaurants, and cafés.[11]

The Conservatoire's reopening set back the school's finances considerably: by the end of the summer, it was running a deficit of $5,000. A budget for the following year was set, and the Fontainebleau government suggested a grant from its own coffers for the 1947 session. The Tourist Board offered to help with costs and with the problem of finding adequate housing for the male students, since there was a shortage of rooms in the year of reopening. With considerable work and despite financial struggles, the summer of 1948 was laid out, publicized, and warmly anticipated.[12]

Indeed, the session of 1948 did open on time and with a noted increase in student enrollment, up to forty-eight, thanks in part to diligent promotions in the United States and to the efforts of the town of Fontainebleau. In April that year, the Conseil had been able to purchase a hotel, the Hôtel d'Albe, at 11-13 Rue Royale, close to the Palais. The hotel, complete with a lovely garden, contained many of the modern conveniences American students found lacking in the chateau and in the homes of townspeople who hosted them: full-sized bathtubs with running hot and cold water, even showers. During the part of the year when Conservatoire Américain students did not live in the hotel, it would be rented to the Uniforce military headquarters for use by their staff.

The increasing enrollment and growing material acquisitions of the Conservatoire Américain, under the steady and progressive directorship of Robert Casadesus, promised a smooth and successful future for the school. It was not to last. More turmoil lay ahead for the school's direction and administration. During the summer of 1948, Thérèse Casadesus, the youngest child and only daughter of Robert and Gaby, contracted polio from a Fontainebleau student. Her older brother, Guy, also was stricken but managed to escape the worst outcomes of the disease. Thérèse, in critical condition, was evacuated from Fontainebleau to the American Hospital in the Paris suburb of Neuilly, accompanied by her devastated parents. For several days it was unknown whether she would live, and following her recovery from the initial onslaught, Robert and Gaby traveled to Switzerland, the United States, the Netherlands, and Great Britain in search of treatments and therapies for their daughter. Robert Casadesus resigned his position as director of the Conservatoire and the family returned to Princeton for half of each year, spending the other six months at their home in Paris on the rue Vaneau. Gaby Casadesus found the memories of Thérèse's illness in Fontainebleau horrifying to the degree that she would not return to the town for many years.[13]

With the sudden and tragic departure of Robert Casadesus, the Conservatoire Américain was once again in need of a director. Here Boulanger saw a chance to move up within the school. Citing her reputation and her long involvement with the Conservatoire, Boulanger applied to the Conseil d'Administration for the directorship and with the cooperation of her allies there and on the American Board she was appointed to the position she had long coveted.[14] Still holding the view that the direction of Robert Casadesus would have turned the school into a piano-only program, Boulanger's new plans for the Conservatoire did not include the Casadesuses in any meaningful way. Robert returned in 1949 for two days of master classes and heard a selection of pianists chosen for the classes by Boulanger. Although the fame of the "First Family of the Piano," as Robert, Gaby, and their eldest son Jean were becoming known, continued to rise, Boulanger did not accord them the welcome given to many other great artists involved with the Conservatoire, even those only peripherally attached to it.

Regardless of her feelings for the Casadesus family, Boulanger was eager to begin a new era at the Conservatoire Américain, and she embraced her responsibilities and duties wholeheartedly and with energy few could match. As France, Fontainebleau, and the Conservatoire itself began to recover more fully from the effects of the war, Boulanger began to build the school into a personal cathedral intended for the worship of absolute musicianship.

Notes

1. Notes of the Conseil d'Administration, September 1945, CA/F.
2. Léonie Rosenstiel, *Nadia Boulanger: A Life in Music* (New York: Norton, 1982), 336; and Elsie Watson, interview with author, July 1999, possession of author.
3. Interview with Gaby Casadesus, July 20, 1999, possession of author.
4. While the accounts of Gaby Casadesus and the *Alumni Bulletin* of June 1947 agree on this number, the Conseil d'Administration meeting notes of October 1947 give the figures of 112 Beaux Arts students and 57 Conservatoire students. I believe this to be an error in the typewritten report.

5. *Fontainebleau Alumni Bulletin*, November 1945, 3.

6. Livre de Detail, financial records kept from the 1930s to the 1950s, CA/F.

7. Interview with Gaby Casadesus.

8. Edith Turpin, "Another Start," *Fontainebleau Alumni Bulletin*, June 1947, 3.

9. Turpin, "Another Start," 4.

10. Turpin, "Another Start," 4.

11. Turpin, "Another Start," 4.

12. Report of the President, October 1947, CA/F; Report of the Reopening of the Schools for the Session of 1947, October 1947, CA/F; letter, author unknown, attesting to the accomplishments of Alaux, 1953, CA/F.

13. Casadesus, *Mes noces musicales* (Paris: Buchet/Chastel, 1989), 156. Also conversation with Thérèse Casadesus Rawson, July 1999, July 2000.

14. Undated document, early 1949, announcing her new position, CA/F.

CHAPTER SIX

~

Interlude 2: Gaby Casadesus on Her Return to Fontainebleau in 1946

All the students we used to have, they said, "Why don't you teach?" Well, during the war we were [in the United States] for maybe three months and so we received from the French government the order—to my husband—to stay to do the masterclass in the summer. So we stayed . . . The students came because we were French and we were continuing what we did before. My husband was head of the piano department in 1936, and we were at least four pianists and assistants [in the department]. In America we had just piano and French.

The school [in New England] managed to let us stay, because they said, "You cannot go back to France now." They said, "You must stay for three months," and we received the apartment, the car. The first and second years at Newport—a prep school—we were by the sea. We were always together, it was like a family. The school began as three months, then two.

We kept [the school in America] for six years, and after five years it was possible to come back but all the American people said, "You cannot go back—it is too soon, you should stay." And so we stayed until '46 and were able to bring back only nineteen pupils [when we did return] because they were afraid of not having enough food. Many of their parents were hesitant to send their children to France while rationing continued. The year 1946 was a truly important time in our lives. Among everything else, it was the year of our return to France after six years' absence, but it was also the year of Jean's professional debut.

[By the time we returned,] the chateau was battered. The food was difficult to find. I brought a lot of beef.

Nadia did not come back right away—I think in '47. We just had piano. The architects came in '47. We had to find ways to get back into the part of the Palace we used to be, which was the Louis XV. We had to occupy the chateau because otherwise it would have been on its way to becoming a museum, like it is now.

It was difficult because there was not so much to eat for the Americans. But they [the people of Fontainebleau] were surprised to see them coming back so soon. And glad because it was the life coming back to France. It was marvelous. When my husband was going to have a concert in Switzerland we took all the children [students] to it—they were willing to follow us. They went to the concert. There were only nineteen pupils the first year, because it was difficult and the American government said, "Don't go too soon, there is not enough to eat in France. Don't go." But we knew it was possible. We took things with us—shampoo, toothpaste—to keep the Americans with what they were used to having. I told my daughter, "You are going to eat good French bread." I did the baking by hand.

The reopening of Fontainebleau was 4 July, you know, Independence Day for the Americans. Robert was named Director. At the beginning of August, we gave a party for the students. I remember the date—it was the 9th, my birthday. The students literally covered me with flowers! Robert and I played the works of Spanish composer Manuel Infante, who was with us for the reopening of the school.

We brought back the school, really. It was very important to us to be there, to teach there.

Note

All materials are taken from the author's interview with Gaby Casadesus, Recloses, France, July 20, 1999 (assisted by Thérèse Casadesus Rawson); and Gaby Casadesus, *Mes noces musicales* (Paris: Buchet/Chastel, 1989).

PART III

"LA BELLE DAME SANS MERCI"

CHAPTER SEVEN

~

A New Era (1949–1957)

"Nadia Boulanger, for the first year of her Directorate, organized a most brilliant series of concerts for the students, twenty-one in all," reported the *Fontainebleau Alumni Bulletin* in November 1949.[1] "The classes were regularly attended, with a good grade of students in each class. Mr. Casadesus came for two days at the end of August and heard the best pianists in three Master Classes." An open letter from the Alumni Association to the *Bulletin* echoed this sentiment and its support for Boulanger: "In the Music School, Mlle. Nadia Boulanger, who was confronted with the difficult task of succeeding Mr. Casadesus, gave proof of her extraordinary activity in organizing a series of twenty-one fine concerts which attracted many notable visitors."[2]

The summer of 1949 was abuzz with activity on the part of the new director. Boulanger spent a great deal of time continuing the restructuring of the Conservatoire as begun by Casadesus: new faculty members were hired, and financial assistance was doggedly sought from alumni and from the traditional supporters of the school. The process of creating a new faculty and increasing student enrollment was not easy. The drop from forty-eight students the previous year to only twenty-eight following the departure of the Casadesuses was a cause for concern; Boulanger immediately proposed a clarinet class to help make up the difference and approached Ginette Neveu about taking over the violin class. The famous violinist's decision was never known: she died just days later in a Paris–New York plane crash, and Boulanger was forced to quickly find yet another head for the violin department, selecting Jean Pasquier and his siblings to lead the string students.[3]

Other classes suffered the pains of reorganization as well. The organ class worked under poor conditions owing to the state of the instruments, which were in disrepair. Boulanger made arrangements with a local church to have students practice there, but those organs were not in any better shape, and before the summer was out the Conseil had voted to start repairs at once on the organ in the Jeu de Paume. The notes from the meeting read, "The cost will be very heavy, but we shall be able to meet a large enrollment next year."[4] Four electric harmoniums were to be reconditioned before the start of the next season, in addition to the repairs in the Jeu de Paume.

Voice students were sent to Paris for lessons with a succession of teachers as one after the other fell ill or were unable to complete the summer's course. In the end they finished their course under Boulanger, who also oversaw piano students and the vocal ensemble, in addition to her duties as professor of composition and harmony. Three concerts by students were given: one evening each for vocal ensemble, voice, and piano.

In addition to hiring, scheduling, and material concerns, there were financial difficulties. The school had just purchased the Hôtel d'Albe, and the restaurant had required considerable plumbing, carpentry, and painting repairs. Members of the French committee, including President Jean-Paul Alaux, gave the Conservatoire personal loans totaling some 700,000 francs, but still the school operated in the red.[5] A deal to lease the Albe to the Uniforce headquarters during the winter became hopelessly tangled in red tape, and the expected payments did not materialize. And to add to these complications, a group of demanding students added to the financial crisis.

"A group of veterans [students studying on the GI bill] came to ask for a refund of board and lodging on the plea that the School was charging more than they were worth and that they could work it out more economically themselves. [. . .] We made the error of refunding three students at the beginning," wrote Alaux in his notes of the session.[6] It was, indeed, an error. No sooner had the three students been given their refunds than the school office was deluged with a wave of demands for similar treatment. Students began to "insinuate a lack of honesty in the administration of the Schools," Alaux reported, horrified: "One . . . had such an insolent attitude that [we] decided to expel him." The affair didn't stop there: a petition was circulated among the students. Thirty-three students signed a notice complaining of the Conservatoire's unfavorable fees and policies, arguing that they wanted to stretch their dollars as far as possible in order to stay on in Paris for the winter. The petition was sent to the American embassy, which, to the relief of the Conservatoire, ignored it. The embassy had dealt with similar student protests, usually led by student veterans, at the École des Beaux-Arts, and was unwilling to get involved.

Some of the financial strain was relieved over the summer by the receipt of a gift from the Myron Taylor Foundation. They owned the Villa Anabel on the Riviera, a house that had once served as a home for musicians, but the foundation had decided to close down its programs. The foundation offered the villa to Alaux to use or sell, however he saw fit. Alaux found the villa beautiful, and although the market for such a luxury was not optimal, he suggested finding a buyer right away so that the proceeds could be used to fund scholarships and organ repairs.[7]

During Boulanger's first season as director, the Conservatoire's whirlwind social schedule continued unabated. A monarchist, Boulanger regularly socialized with nobility, and brought Queen Elisabeth of Belgium—the patron of the international competitions for piano and violin, held in her name—to the last student concert of the year.[8] After the students had sung for Mass in the Palais's Chapelle de la Trinité, Alaux and Boulanger presented the queen to the students in the Salon des Laques. Bastille Day found the students serenading the citizens of Fontainebleau from the Horseshoe Staircase with national anthems and folk songs, and a troupe of Scottish dancers from Uniforce appeared at several evenings' entertainments. A "diner de têtes" in July was followed by a costume ball in August, Baron and Baronne Hottinger and the Comte de Noailles hosted student receptions, and the Préfet of Seine et Marne gave a garden party in Melun for students and faculty.[9]

In 1949 Fontainebleau itself was still recovering from the hardships of war. Alumna Elsie Watson recalls that, "the French kids were always smaller [for their age], and less developed than American . . . kids, probably because of the lean years of the war."[10] Indeed, while European travel was increasing again, travel guides of all types warned Americans about the conditions they would face on the Continent. One book helped visitors to France prepare themselves by offering advice on "How to Live without a Bath," which begins with an illustration captioned, "This is a bidet."[11] This same tome of enlightenment for France-bound twenty-somethings also details the difficulties of using the telephone ("making a phone call means trouble"), of exchanging money in a time of rampant black-marketeering in currency, and then describes shocks an American was likely to have if a doctor's visit were required ("some doctors are using penicillin while others are using cups [. . .] go to the American Hospital in Neuilly").[12] However, the reputation of the school was enough to overcome the reservations of students who otherwise might have waited for better days on the Continent, and the brochures written by the school included reassuring information on Fontainebleau's up-to-date medical clinic and accommodations.[13] Eight-year-old piano prodigy Idil Biret arrived in Fontainebleau for the first time that summer, as did Charles Lindbergh's daughters Anne, who studied in the Beaux Arts division, and Reeve, a flutist. By the time the next summer came around, enrollment at the Conservatoire Américain had grown to 125—its prewar standards.

However, financial problems still plagued the institution, and President Alaux continually was required to plead for frugality on the part of Boulanger. In the early days of 1950 he wrote to her, recounting the poor financial state of the school and asking that, as director of the Conservatoire, she take more responsibility for its business affairs. Boulanger was asked to justify her expenses more clearly; her expenditures were leading to a crisis for the school's continued existence. Boulanger was undeterred in planning for a gala 1951 season commemorating the school's thirtieth anniversary. "Next year," she wrote in September 1950, "for in spite of everything there will be a next year (we do not accept defeat except under the evidence of overwhelming circumstances), we shall have [master classes, concerts, and increased enrollment]."[14] Boulanger's optimism and force of determination in continuing the school is clear, and, indeed, the following year proved the best attended since the departure of the Casadesuses.

In 1951 the school opened with 126 Music and Beaux-Arts students, and it carried a deficit of 2,200,000 francs, which rose the next year to 3,100,000. The new director replied to Alaux's concerns with plans to secure better currency exchange rates and increased fund-raising, both in France and America. Alaux, alarmed by the proposed costs of salaries and at renovations to the school's instruments and facilities, negotiated for two years to obtain subsidies from the Ministry of Foreign Affairs and from the Department of Seine et Marne for a total of 600,000 francs. It would not go far. In August 1953, Boulanger designated a salary of 200,000 francs for her 1952 directorship duties, an additional 220,000 for her teaching stipend, and gave herself a raise the following year, taking 400,000 for the directorship alone and 200,000 for teaching. Boulanger allocated 120,000 francs for her assistant Annette Dieudonné, though the two were to have the same number of students. Instrumental teachers received an average of 100,000 francs, though piano professor Alice Gaultier-Leon, a protégée of Albeniz, held out for 250,000 francs for teaching seventeen students and with some wrangling was finally awarded that amount.[15] The Ravel and Durand Composition Prizes were 200,000 francs each in 1953, twice the average instrumental instructor's pay. Tuition hovered between $435 and $450 during the first half of the decade, insufficient to cover expenses. In September 1953 Alaux resigned his position as president, citing his failing eyesight. Of his tenure, he wrote,

> The situation was eminently difficult. If we did not reopen the Schools [in 1946], we were threatened to have to leave the Palace at the approaching expiration of our lease. [. . .] Our difficulties have been many—taxes, social securities, repairs to the restaurant, repairs to the grand organ, increase in salaries, the lease of pianos and the bus-trips, have year after year weighed heavily on our budgets.[16]

Though departing, Alaux stressed conservative spending for the future: Nadia Boulanger, he wrote in a memo to Quinto Maganini, "intends to spend now her amount of the [currency] exchange excess in plans for the 1954 season."[17] He emphasized that the subsidies and grants from the government and other donors must be used "solely for educational purposes."[18] This advice, given twenty years earlier by Maurice Fragnaud, went unheeded. Instead, Boulanger relied on charity concerts by celebrity performers, donations, and the work of the alumni office in New York to take care of funding, as well as urging increases in tuition and registration fees, doubling the tuition between 1951 and 1956. Large, already organized groups of students were accepted during this period for the hefty fees they generated, regardless of the levels of musicianship they achieved, and despite the widely recognized fact that such students brought down the overall quality of the session. Several examples of this are evident in the correspondence of Boulanger and the New York secretary, Myra Davis, who wrote to her in 1953 with several proposals from potential students: A Mrs. Hazel Dorey wanted free piano lessons in exchange for bringing [a] group of students. Some she does not know and they are of varying levels of proficiency. Should Mrs. Dorey get free lessons? How many does she have to bring to get free lessons? Shouldn't the Conservatoire Américain admit them individually rather than as a group? "Knowing how opposed you are to 'tourists' rather than 'students,'" remarked Davis, "I should tell you that Mrs. Dorey and her husband have formerly conducted tours in Europe for Thomas Cook, and Mrs. Dorey has in mind contacting our students about a planned tour following the Fontainebleau session. Do you think this would be well received?"[19]

Mrs. Dorey was not the only one with such an idea. Pianists William Battaile and John Westmoreland had similar ideas. Westmoreland led a choral group from Elon College in North Carolina. The heads of their French department and the Music department (also an accompanist) would be their chaperones. What kind of deal could be worked out?

In the case of the last request, Boulanger implied to Westmoreland that one of every five students would get a full scholarship, resulting in three or four scholarships for the group of seventeen. Westmoreland agreed to have the Conservatoire Américain vet each student individually but was concerned about what would happen if one was turned down. Bargaining with Boulanger, Westmoreland also suggested that their chaperone act as interpreter for the school while in Fontainebleau in order to defray costs.[20]

Groups such as these were not uncommon in the 1950s as the Conservatoire strove to secure its finances and future. The school faced serious stateside competition for the first time from the Tanglewood Festival, which had just opened a year-round office in New York and was active in recruiting young performers from the top American conservatories and universities. Confronted with the poaching of Fontainebleau students, Boulanger and the Alumni Association arranged for truly stellar concerts and master class opportunities: Students in the mid-1950s were treated to classes and concerts by Yehudi Menuhin, Clifford Curzon, Pierre Bernac, and Francis Poulenc. Pianist Seymour Bernstein was awarded a work dedicated to him by Milhaud, as a result of taking first prize in 1953, and students in 1954, such as Idil Biret and Salabert Composition Prize winner Luise Vosgerchian, found that their competition pieces had been composed especially for the Conservatoire by Auric, Copland, Dutilleux, Françaix, Milhaud, and others. All students participated in the staging of Jean Françaix's opera *Paris á Nous Deux*, which was presented in the Fontainebleau Municipal Theater in honor of Menuhin, who conducted the performances. Students winning the Prix d'Excellence, Premier Prix, and the named prizes (including the Durand Prize, the Ravel Prize, the Jean de Polignac Memorial Prize, the Friends of Dinu Lipatti Memorial Prize, and the Lili Boulanger Memorial Prize) were presented at concerts at the American embassy and at Radio-Diffusion Française. Students poured in to bask in the glow of Boulanger, members of Les Six, instrumentalists and singers like Doda Conrad, Maurice Gendron, and Menuhin, and to take their chances at winning fame and starting a career. The Conservatoire Américain de Fontainebleau seemed to have entered a new golden age, despite its financial difficulties.[21]

After Alaux's resignation, Boulanger was in a position to choose her own president of the Conseil, someone who would follow her lead in determining the future of the music school. The roles of director general and president of the Conseil were amalgamated into a single position, and Boulanger had just the man for it. She chose François Valéry, the son of her close friend and famous poet Paul Valéry. Valéry's family connections aided the Conservatoire and his involvement grew as he spent time at the school and with its faculty and students. Completely fluent in English and an excellent diplomat, the levelheaded and imperturbable Valéry would see the school through decades of change in the directorship, class emphasis, and relations between the French and American committees.

The 1950s were a time of change in repertoire and in approaches to interpretation. The burgeoning recording industry grew during the postwar years, creating a need for more recording artists. Concurrently, consumer expectations for recordings rose, and musicians were forced to refine techniques and interpretations for permanent sound media as well as for live performances. The blasé, one-take recording sessions of the past were scorned in favor of multiple-take sessions and, when available, sophisticated editing of takes to produce a polished, albeit composite, product. Consumers who became accustomed to perfection gleaned from recording techniques applied their expectations to recitals as well, and students had to be ready to withstand the scrutiny of the most discerning ears. Tastes in the concert hall also changed: historically appropriate interpretations began to gain ground as performers looked into musicological research and applied it to performance practice. The early music movement, long a fringe element in the performance world despite its early adherents, among them Francis, Henri, and Regina Casadesus, began to acquire more devotees as audiences and performers alike became more aware of stylistic suitability in terms of tempo, rubato, vibrato, portamento, tone color, and instrumentation itself.[22]

Students at the Conservatoire Américain were aware of the new approaches to playing, and their professors were careful to include instruction in the current practices. Economy of gesture and a heavy emphasis on analysis led students to cleaner and more carefully considered interpretations. Students recalled the long hours of practice for their lessons and analysis of everything from chant and Josquin to Mozart and Poulenc, and they recalled the vocal ensemble's performances of Tallis and other Renaissance composers.[23] Even Pierre Fournier and Paul Bazelaire contributed to the early-music repertoire by performing Marais at their concert in 1954. Of musical tastes, Boulanger asked students, "What more is style than conventions accepted?"[24] Yet she herself was immensely conscious of style and tastes and pushed the Conservatoire Américain instrumentalists to be on the cutting edge of performance, although the repertoire and compositional styles favored by Boulanger often truncated the student composers' exploration of the serialist and more avant-garde techniques that she disliked. Boulez, for example, was never discussed or heard, and student artists could be sure of *not* performing on concerts in the Jeu de Paume or anywhere else if their works were not deemed suitable by Mademoiselle, regardless of whether the work in question had become part of the standard repertoire or was deemed a crucial element in a student's development by a professor.

For the most part, though, repertoire at the Conservatoire Américain during the 1950s certainly did not shy from the edge of contemporary works. Debussy and Ravel being well accepted as part of the standard canon, students in Fontainebleau turned to more recent French composers, including Messiaen, members of Les Six, Robert Casadesus, and those who composed for the student competitions, and they looked to music being written by non-French composers for additional repertoire. The standard historical repertoire served as text for analysis. Students attending the 1954 session included in their classes the study of Josquin's *Missa La Sol Fa Re Mi*, Bach's *Musical Offering*, and the *Art of Fugue*, Beethoven's String Quartet op. 130, Hindemith's *Ludus Tonalis*, Stravinsky's *Concerto for Two Pianos*, Bartók's *Divertimento*, and other quartets of Mozart and Beethoven.[25]

Overall, Boulanger's acceptance or rejection of works for either performance, study, or as student compositions, seems primarily based on their artistic genealogy: Messiaen was a clear descendant of Debussy, had studied with Dukas at the Paris Conservatoire, and was considered by Boulanger to be an Impressionist carrying along the tradition of the earlier part of the century. A devout Catholic whose religious mysticism must have struck a chord with the equally devout Boulanger, Messiaen was acceptable. Poulenc, too, was in good standing as a compositional role model for Conservatoire students. He was also a composer of the neoclassicist vein whose works found favor at Fontainebleau, his songs often being assigned to voice students. Boulez, on the other hand, was one of the major composers of the day completely ignored by Boulanger, his relevance in contemporary music notwithstanding. Considered "a perfect Wagnerite,"[26] his iconoclastic approach to composition and conducting made him unsuitable for the aesthetic nurtured at Fontainebleau, where students learned to appreciate the traditional output of the Paris Conservatoire rather than that of its latter-day renegades.

Despite the welcome much of the new repertoire received in the analysis classes, student compositions that applied contemporary compositional trends were dismissed, and the use of approved approaches from earlier periods and stricter rules for the creation of music were rigidly enforced. Composition students often spent the entire summer working on fugue and counterpoint in the most traditional style, learning from Bach and Beethoven. Although Boulanger, when questioned, admitted that, "Electronic music is an experiment and one must encourage research," she vehemently argued against works by the most experimental and innovative of contemporary composers. "The majority of musicians cannot hear anything," she declared.

"It is for this reason, this great lack, that crazy, pointless, worthless music is being written today."[27] In the end, Boulanger's own preferences led her to limit the scope of works studied and created by her composition students.

Of course, not all was work during the Conservatoire's reconstruction period: parties and fêtes continued as they had before. In 1954 two students became the proud owners of a goose they named Françoie (*oie* being French for "goose") when they won him at a Bastille Day raffle in the Fontainebleau market. Françoie was housed in the women's lodgings at the Hôtel d'Albe, where he had unfettered run of all the bathtubs until the end of the summer, when he was donated as dinner to the concierge.[28] The early 1950s seem best remembered by the students who wrote for the *Alumni Bulletin* as one whirlwind social event after another, from the welcome party to Boulanger's postconcert cocktail parties to the costume balls held at the end of each season, Versailles, Black-and-White, and Medieval being just a few of their themes. Group trips to Barbizon, Giverny, Sens, and the Loire Valley provided respite from practicing and from solfège classes. The Beaux Arts division and musicians collaborated for the Françaix opera in 1954. Bastille Day celebrations and the end-of-summer ball became joint endeavors as well, with the artists providing costuming and set design for the musical productions and theme nights.

The living standards of the students at this time were enviable. Students in Paris could live on eighty dollars a month and in the *banlieues*, or outlying suburbs, the cost of living was even lower.[29] Students regularly visited the capital, picking up French editions of music and luxury items found much more expensively at home. Accommodation in Fontainebleau was apparently sumptuous as well: Elsie Watson was thrilled to stay in room 6 at the Albe: "It's elegant!" she wrote, describing the room in her diary.

> Marble fireplace and mirror, two blue velour wing chairs, two desks and desk chairs, two beds, a huge wardrobe with double mirror and a smaller wardrobe where we keep our luggage. The window reaches from floor to ceiling, has curtains and blue and silver brocaded damask drapes. Right next to us—adjoining— is an immense bathroom with double basins, a toilet, bathtub and some sort of a wardrobe and still plenty of space left to move around.[30]

Despite the outward appearances of the Conservatoire, its luxurious student quarters and impressive guest roster, financial difficulties continued to batter the school even after tuition was nearly doubled between 1950 and 1959, when it cost $885 to attend for the summer. The students were not unaware of the problems the school faced, and in 1956 students worked together to collect money to assist the school. They presented the fund to Boulanger at the final dinner of the session. Touched, Boulanger earmarked the money to be used "to the best advantage of future students in a manner which will prove most useful to them."[31] At the same time, the New York office and Alumni Association continued the scholarship benefit concerts begun before the war. Alumni performed gratis at these events and at the annual Alumni Association dinner in order to raise funds for instrument-specific scholarships.

However grim the bank balance must have looked, it did not stop the Conseil, under Boulanger's direction, from spending more and more. In 1957, the Conservatoire acquired the Barassy Hotel at 15 Rue St. Honoré for the lodging of male students. Not long after the purchase, the Alumni Association began asking its members to contribute for the furnishings the building desperately needed. "[T]hese men will not care to sleep on nicely polished floors," ran the copy, "and even new bathrooms lose their charm if one must wait after the bath until the air has dried him."[32] The association was not subtle: "Any sum, no matter how small, will be joyously received." Contributions were, naturally, tax deductible.

In September 1957 Boulanger celebrated her seventieth birthday, amid much fanfare from students, friends, and admirers. Jean Françaix's gift to Boulanger, a cantata entitled *Komm meine heilige Nadia*, gave observers a sense of the teacher's great following and of the admiration that her students and colleagues felt for her. Required to retire at that age from teaching at the Paris Conservatoire, Boulanger became even more control-oriented in regard to the Conservatoire Américain. Her directives and desires would change it from a school designed for the fostering of great talent and international artistic collaboration and friendship into a place where her philosophies could be paramount, a place where she could enjoy the adoration of both students and alumni, and a place where she would be able to direct every nuance of life, from students' practice schedules to their manners, within the school's confines. Able to devote herself full time to directing the Conservatoire, what for any other musician might have been twilight years of rest and pleasure were for Boulanger a time for continuing to create in Fontainebleau the ultimate expression of her musical philosophy.

Notes

1. Document of the Conservatoire Américain, November 4, 1949, CA/F.
2. Letter of the Alumni Association, November 1949, CA/F.
3. Document of the Conservatoire Américain, November 4, 1949, CA/F.
4. Conseil d'Administration meeting notes, November 1949, CA/F.

5. At this time the French franc was valued at 331 old francs to the U.S. dollar (Werner Antweiler, pacific.commerce.ubc.ca/xr).

6. Document of the Conservatoire Américain, November 4, 1949, CA/F.

7. Document of the Conservatoire Américain, November 4, 1949, CA/F.

8. Letter, Jean-Paul Alaux to Alumni Association, *Fontainebleau Alumni Bulletin*, November 1949.

9. Document of the Conservatoire Américain, November 4, 1949, CA/F.

10. Elsie Watson, letter to author, undated November 2000, possession of author.

11. Helene MacLean, *There's No Place Like Paris* (New York: Doubleday and Co., 1951), 106.

12. MacLean, *There's No Place Like Paris*, 165.

13. Documents of the Conservatoire Américain, various dates, CA/F.

14. Letter, Nadia Boulanger to Charles DuBose, September 2, 1950, CA/F.

15. Conservatoire Américain Budget, 1953, CA/F. Also: Letter, addressee unknown, undated, 1953, disclosing salaries, CA/F.

16. Jean-Paul Alaux, letter of resignation, CA/F.

17. Memo, Jean-Paul Alaux to Quinto Maganini, undated, CA/F.

18. Memo, Jean-Paul Alaux to Quinto Maganini, undated, CA/F.

19. Letter, Myra Davis to Nadia Boulanger, Lucie Delécluse, and Jean-Paul Alaux, undated January 1952, CA/F.

20. Letter, Myra Davis to Nadia Boulanger, Lucie Delécluse, and Jean-Paul Alaux, undated January 1952, CA/F.

21. *Fontainebleau Alumni Bulletins*, 1954–1959.

22. Robert Philip, *Early Recordings and Musical Style: Changing Tastes in Instrumental Performance, 1900–1950* (Cambridge, U.K.: Cambridge University Press, 1992).

23. Elsie Watson, diaries, 1959. Also: *Fontainebleau Alumni Bulletin*, November 1959, 2.

24. Jay Gottlieb, letter to author, undated August 2000, possession of author.

25. Fontainebleau Schools of Music and Fine Arts Brochure, 1954, CA/F.

26. Nicolas Slonimsky, *The Concise Baker's Biographical Dictionary of Musicians* (New York: Schirmer Books, 1994), 119.

27. Jay Gottlieb, letter to author, undated August 2000, possession of author.

28. *Fontainebleau Alumni Bulletin*, November 1954, 5.

29. MacLean, *There's No Place Like Paris*, 14.

30. Watson, diaries, June 21, 1950.

31. *Fontainebleau Alumni Bulletin*, November 1956, 4.

32. *Fontainebleau Alumni Bulletin*, April 1957, 1.

CHAPTER EIGHT

~

La Belle Dame sans Merci
(1958–1979)

This afternoon, a strange little black-bearded fellow from Paris played the Beethoven op 110. Mlle Boulanger considered him an intruder and pouted throughout his performance. [Later] Ann Fiore and I went to our favorite place for tea and soon Jim Harrison rushed in to say that Miss Johnson was bringing Mlle Boulanger and Curzon for tea. We took the hint, found ourselves another table; some left and the proprietress asked some others to come another time. Such a commotion! As if it were the queen![1]

After nearly a dozen years as director of the Conservatoire Américain, Nadia Boulanger was, at the time of her retirement from the Paris Conservatoire, finally able to devote the bulk of her time and energy to the school. Having had to wait longer than she wished to become director, Boulanger's assumption of authority grew to proportions that soon caused consternation and no small amount of resentment among the administration, faculty, and even the students, as Elsie Watson's diary entry above indicates. Boulanger no longer seemed content with teaching her own classes and overseeing the financial and logistical concerns of the school. Instead, she became increasingly anxious about the decisions made by professors and other administrators. Concerned that music and materials prepared for performance or used in other classes somehow would not be appropriate for audiences or students, she dictated to the professors the repertoire she desired the students to learn each summer, regardless of individual professors' objectives and of the ambitions or abilities of the students. She told guest artists—not least of whom was Soulima Stravinsky, who came to play works of his father's—what to perform at their Fontainebleau recitals. In addition, she established an extracurricular system of oversight in which she set dress codes and enforced a code of moral behavior applicable to all students from prodigies to returning alumni.[2] She served as the principal liaison between the school and the city of Fontainebleau, and was a one-woman promotional board. Undeterred by her advancing age, hearing difficulties, and declining health, Boulanger relied on contacts in the musical and jet-set worlds for support for all of her projects, not only those related to the Conservatoire. As Boulanger passed her seventieth birthday, more and more students came to Fontainebleau, hoping to study with the master before it was too late. In essence, Fontainebleau became Boulanger, and Boulanger *was* Fontainebleau.

Boulanger's teaching methods were stern, her approaches precise, and her students both adored and feared her. Though she believed that her American charges were often underprepared, lacked proper background for her classes, were undisciplined, and constantly struggled to keep up, Boulanger admitted large numbers of students to her classes in the later years of her life. She did this for two reasons, the first of which was to maintain the Conservatoire's long-standing status as a symbol of French musical influence.[3] She also accepted record numbers in part to boost sagging enrollment figures, which were blamed over time on the Vietnam War, inflation in the United States, and Tanglewood's aggressive marketing and promotion tactics, such as maintaining an office open year-round.[4] Students who went to Fontainebleau to study found this policy to be a double-edged sword. While they might be receiving training and immersion that they would not have gotten had admission requirements been more stringent, they also faced the intellectual and musical challenges and emotional turmoil that came with such study.

Students found that it was not complicated to enter Fontainebleau and to study with Boulanger: the difficulties lay inside the classroom, where standards were high and patience often ran thin. As time went on, Boulanger often taught specifically to one or two select students— frequently her young, hand-chosen prodigies. Other students did not fare as well. One older woman was chastised to the point of tears in an overcrowded harmony class, and another student escaped from a particularly long lesson by exiting through a classroom window into the Palais's Jardin Anglais. Pianist Elsie Watson wrote in her diary on one occasion that she had survived Boulanger's harmony class "unscathed," but more often reported that classes could be tense. "No big fireworks but everyone was expecting them at any moment," she noted.[5]

Boulanger's own training and professional experience were evident in her treatment of the Fontainebleau students. She had long given up her own career as a composer when she became a professor at the École Normale in 1920. A student of Fauré and Vidal, Boulanger had an illustrious, award-studded career at the Paris Conservatoire before setting up as a private teacher herself. After several failed attempts to win the Prix de Rome, Boulanger sat for the contest again in 1908. The competition jury eventually gave her a Second Prize, but her approach to the composition of one test-piece was seen as a flaunting of the rules, and the resulting uproar among the contestants and governing body won her no admirers. Camille Saint-Saëns went so far as to chastise her in a letter of May 1908, charging her with wanting to "create a sensation."[6] While he praised her capabilities, the older composer wrote that, "shooting past the target is not the same as hitting it, and that a studied effort to make an impression is very often less effective than naturalness and simplicity."[7] Boulanger competed again the following year, and, not surprisingly, found no new success.

Boulanger's run-in with Saint-Saëns was not the last battle she would have in her campaign of attacking established musicians and their conventions, and her experience with him did not seem to temper her approaches. When denied a teaching position at the Paris Conservatoire in 1910, she placed the blame on Debussy, who responded to her accusations with a letter defending himself, while flattering her in terms that make clear his view that she was brash, assumptive, and not a little arrogant. Boulanger's personality was not the only thing criticized: Amadée Boutarel, critic of Le Ménéstrel, found her works insipid and banal, and suggested that while the young woman was a finely trained musician, her composition could use some improvement.[8]

But Boulanger was a competent composer and aspired to the forefront of the French musical world. Her plans were dealt a practical and psychological blow with the sudden decision of her equally musical and more compositionally talented sister Lili to devote herself to composition full time. Lili had always been fragile in health and appearance and was the cosseted baby of the family, which lent to her the preternatural halo of the youthful and gifted, predestined for the short but prolific life, much as Keats had been viewed in poetic circles. With Lili's choice of a career in composition, Nadia had to face the fact that her own gifts would be completely overshadowed by those of her sister, whom Le Ménéstrel, in contrast with its opinion of Nadia, had described as a composer of "great brilliance."[9] There was a single face-saving solution: Nadia became Lili's sole tutor, giving up her own composition for the sake of Lili's future. Turning instead to conducting and performance, Nadia spared herself most of the comparisons that might have been made had she remained devoted to composition. Lili Boulanger achieved what her less talented, more irascible sister had been unable to do, and became the first woman to win the Grand Prix de Rome, stunning the judges with her cantata *Faust et Hélène* in 1913.

Nadia Boulanger's shift from composition to performance did little to polish her sometimes abrasive and unyielding approach to situations. As a performer, she traveled extensively with her friend and mentor, pianist Raoul Pugno. Female conductors still were rare, and wherever she took the podium, Boulanger attracted praise and criticism for musical and political reasons alike. Female soloists, while more widely accepted than those wielding batons, were far too often also viewed as novelties, and Boulanger's unapologetically strong appearance—no opera-singer frills or lady-violinist froth was found in her wardrobe—lent to her an image of a determined and serious musician, something some more traditionally minded male musicians had trouble accepting. Boulanger's exceptional musicianship gained her countless admirers among French music aficionados, but she made enemies as efficiently as she curried favors. In Russia, an ailing Pugno asked Sergei Rachmaninoff to take his place in a concert with Boulanger. When the celebrated Russian pianist and composer refused, Boulanger forever added him to her list of foes. As her students quickly learned, his name could not be mentioned nor could his music be played in her presence under any circumstances. Boulanger's fame and stature grew, taking her to other countries and performance venues, and this less than tactful outlook accompanied her. While audiences often were impressed with the rarity of so professional and competent a female conductor and performer, orchestra members were not always enthusiastic, especially when Boulanger complained about the inferiority of American and British musical training.[10]

In 1918, Lili Boulanger died, aged twenty-four. Nadia entered the full and then half-mourning that would characterize her dress and frame of mind for the rest of her life. Interest in Lili's works grew, and Nadia clung even more firmly to her goal of refraining from composition in favor of conducting and teaching. Added to those two areas was a new mission to memorialize her sister, and she worked to promote the small body of works left by Lili, overseeing dozens of concerts and recording projects.

There is no doubt that her own training in one of the world's most stringent music schools influenced Boulanger's approach to her students, both those she taught privately and those under her tutelage at the Conservatoire Américain. Boulanger's approach to her Fontainebleau students demonstrated her belief that while all people could benefit from the study of music, only the very best should be encouraged to make it their life's work. Students with talent were hand-picked for special attention; just as frequently, secondary-school music teachers and other students already embarked on professional careers were counseled to change their courses of action or to consider music only as an avocation.

Composers began with private lessons from Boulanger, but most students were first exposed to her in the classroom, where she focused on ear-training and harmonic analysis. Students took classes both with Boulanger and with her long-time assistant, Annette Dieudonné. Both included solfège manuals of the Paris Conservatoire and Hindemith's *Elementary Training for Musicians*, Bach chorales, exercises prepared by both teachers, and a plethora of scores representing the span of music history from the Renaissance to the contemporary as their standard texts. Boulanger carefully placed students into five levels of solfège classes according to their abilities, and she knew well the rigors of the assigned work. The daily dictations and exercises were designed to both push the limits of their abilities and to show them their weaknesses and failings as musicians-in-training. "Very difficult," she told one young composer of the work he must undertake, not without humor, but in all seriousness, "very boring."[11] Despite the prestige associated with having taken and survived a Boulanger class, attrition was a problem in these classes, with a third to one-half of all students dropping out of them before the end of the summer.[12] However, Boulanger kept a close watch on attendance, especially that of her own personal composition and piano students, and even those studying in other areas were rarely truant if they wished to acquire and retain her good graces.

Private composition lessons often were more difficult than the group classes. Students were admitted into Boulanger's apartments in the center of the Louis XV wing; in her later years she was escorted by a nurse. There, surrounded by mementos of her life, students would seat themselves at the piano with their newly composed scores, ready to submit to Boulanger's critique. "Here I was," recounts composer and pianist Joe Kerr, who later became part of the Conservatoire's administrative staff, "just a kid from Texas, and I wanted to write music, and I'd written this little piece . . . anyway, I'm sitting there and she's got photos of all these people she knows all over the place, signed, 'Love, Igor.' I mean, it's all kind of overwhelming."[13] Many students were asked to forget all that they knew and to start over at the beginning with rudimentary exercises and studies. Some balked; others swallowed their pride and complied. Lessons, scheduled for set blocks of time, could run late by the hour; waiting students knew better than to leave, despite having to sit in the hall for unpredictable lengths of time. Inside, composers were being asked to do anything from writing species counter-point to playing a harmonic progression through all of the keys at the piano. Expectations were high, and students' attempts frequently met with disap-pointment on the part of Boulanger.

Boulanger's piano and organ students found similar demands waiting for them. Of her requirements, Boulanger related, referring to her own practice as a child,

> Each week I had to play a prelude and fugue by heart. But you know, you mustn't exaggerate, a prelude and fugue a week, that's not much! In my course I require as much of my pupils. I make them write out the separate parts from memory after which they should be able to reconstruct the whole piece. After a training of this kind, they have well-furnished minds.[14]

For many summers, Boulanger chose a theme for the session's focus: a composer, genre, or period, by means of which harmony and form would be studied. In 1965, for example, piano students were all assigned one or more Beethoven sonatas, and Boulanger's classroom lectures and master classes fo-cused almost exclusively on this repertoire for the duration of the summer. During other summers she dealt with Renaissance masses, Bach's preludes and fugues, Mozart's sonatas, and Stravinsky's orchestral works. This holistic approach was one that made eminent sense to the faculty and students, and it has influenced the ways in which harmony and repertoire classes are ap-proached in American conservatories today.

Composition and piano were the dominant fields of study at the Con-servatoire under Boulanger's direction, and consequently works equally worthy of study by pianists and composers alike—such as Beethoven's piano sonatas—often formed the backbone of a given summer's program, with in-strumental and vocal music on the periphery. This emphasis was not as wel-coming or as practical for instrumentalists and singers as it could have been, and in fact, as Boulanger's ability to direct the school developed and as the board's trust in her leadership grew, she proposed ending instrumental and vocal classes altogether. During the 1960s, she managed to scale instru-mental classes back to the point where students were required to travel to Paris for their lessons rather than having the professors come to Fontainebleau. Boulanger also requested that the American office make it a policy to deny scholarships to instrumentalists in order to encourage a de-cline in their enrollment, asking that the majority of funds go instead to pi-anists and composers. While some members of the board agreed with this plan, there was dissent. Such a radical proposal raised several flags for long-time Fontainebleau watchers. Boulanger's scheme for limiting enrollment was a strangely familiar echo of what she had so hotly accused the Casadesuses of attempting in the 1940s and against which she had railed to the point of distancing herself from the school's American incarnation. Luckily for the many talented singers, violinists, cellists, and other instrumentalists who attended the Conservatoire from the 1960s through the late 1970s, the majority faction of the board prevailed, and classes with Yehudi Menuhin, Maurice Gendron, and the Pasquiers continued apace.

Comparison with competing schools was also a factor in many of Boulanger's decisions as the Director of the school. Many stateside summer programs, including Tanglewood and Aspen, were focused on instrumental performance with an emphasis on orchestral training; and other summer schools, including Yale's Norfolk Festival and the Marlboro Festival, were dedicated to chamber music. In order to retain its standing in the summer-music-school continuum, the Conservatoire needed to provide a wide range of performance opportunities and musical exposures. In addition, much of the school's prestige came from its association with top instrumental performers: Henryk Szering, Yehudi Menuhin, Paul Bazelaire, Maurice Gendron, the Pasquier Trio, and Doda Conrad had brought scores of talented string players and singers to the school.

Finally, finances were an ever-present issue and the school faced pressing questions each year as its administrators planned for the next summer: Would composers and pianists alone generate enough revenue for the school to stay open? What constituted a viable number of students to assure success each summer? How large would scholarships be, and how would they be overseen and dispersed? In the end, continued instrumental study, limited fund-raising by the Alumni Association, and support from Boulanger's society patrons ensured the continuation of the school in its traditional form despite perennially operating at a deficit.[15]

Boulanger's strong personality filled the chateau, and students constantly were aware of her presence. Her most faithful protégés were encouraged to report as informers back to Boulanger any indiscretions made by other students: women wearing trousers, men dating Fontainebleau's resident women, students who practiced less than they might. From the beginning of her tenure as a professor, Boulanger had taken it upon herself to monitor her students' behavior. She had been involved intimately in their lives, from making living arrangements for them to counseling them on their love lives. She taught table manners and social skills at her parties.[16] The youngest students became surrogate children to Boulanger, whose belief that a woman's primary role was that of mother led her to consider adopting a child. The conflict between this belief and her own overwhelming ambition as a female composer and pedagogue led to inconsistencies in her teaching of female students. The most talented, such as Louise Talma, who became a faculty member at Hunter College and the Conservatoire Américain after spending her youth studying with Boulanger each summer in Fontainebleau, were encouraged in their professional lives. Yet Boulanger seemed hesitant to push them as she did her male students, and encouraged many to seek out non-musical careers. Women of less apparent talent—whether for composition or performance—were likely to receive advice from Mademoiselle urging them to marry and raise a family while maintaining an amateur interest in music. Not a few women were told to give up music altogether for obvious lack of skills, but were also supposed to find consolation in their ability to produce children and create a happy home.

Boulanger's attempted domination of the student body often conflicted with her ability to run the Conservatoire even-handedly and in an organized manner. She resisted putting out publicity materials for the summer sessions in advance, relying instead on word-of-mouth advertising. This kind of promotion, Boulanger felt, would encourage former students and faculty to send their own students and colleagues, and would lower the number of applications from the less talented who might be tempted to reply to a general advertisement.[17] However, this kind of publicity often resulted in a professor-student patronage system that led to accusations of unfair distribution of scholarship funds.[18]

Hiring visiting artists and clinicians was also left to last-minute planning, and Boulanger was not always aware of what was desirable to American students coming to France. Although the American office tried to guide Boulanger in her choice of performers and clinicians, they rarely succeeded in changing her mind or promoting one artist over another, once she had decided that one better met her requirements for a Fontainebleau appearance, regardless of his or her status among the students. In order to raise enrollment, Boulanger began promoting Robert Casadesus's master classes and Jean Casadesus's private teaching. The American office expressed disappointment with this plan, urging her to engage artists more recognizable to the American students. Marie Brodeur wrote in 1966, "I'm sorry to say that he [Robert Casadesus] is the master class man for 1967. It will mean another small piano enrollment."[19] She went on to report to the American council in 1973 that Boulanger

> spoke [to me] of the bad drop in enrollments, and blamed it on the political situation. I said no, it seemed traceable to the change in leadership of the piano

master class. Upon which, she asked me point-blank what the Casadesus name was worth as a drawing card. I said, "Nothing. Aside from their immediate personal pupils . . . they have no following." I told her frankly that to revive the piano master class, she needed other leadership.[20]

Boulanger, however, had made her peace with the Casadesus family, and was now reluctant to let them go. Their students continued to be some of the best pianists at the Conservatoire each summer, but enrollment numbers remained lower than the school desired.

Specific master class arrangements also were a matter of some contention. Robert Casadesus, Clifford Curzon, and other artists were invited to Fontainebleau for two to three days of cocktail parties, classes, and recitals, and a great amount of excitement surrounded these visits. Naturally one would suppose that the master classes were reserved for Conservatoire students, but the reality was quite different. Students judged to be the best of each piano teacher's studio were heard by Boulanger and Jean Casadesus in closed auditions; Boulanger then selected those who would play for the guest clinician. Once these appropriate representatives of the Conservatoire had been allocated times to play, Boulanger then made phone calls and extended personal invitations to nonstudents to take part in the classes. This policy was alluded to in the school's brochures, which read—a little condescendingly—in part:

> Participation [in] master classes. Young talented artists having already started on their career or participated in great competitions may be chosen to play at the Master Classes, though not members of the School. This participation proves of great value to the regular students too.[21]

Students were naturally dismayed to find that they and their colleagues were denied participation in the classes in favor of outsiders. Especially difficult for students were the occasions when even the most highly esteemed students were not invited to play. Watson's diary records that,

> The first of Mr. Curzon's three master classes began today [July 19, 1965] with many more Beethoven sonatas. Mlle Boulanger has invited many of her pianist friends to "make" the master class and only Charles, one of our tablemates, has the opportunity to play. Naturally, many of the students are disappointed, and feel that they have been misled by the literature that reached them before they arrived.[22]

From her insistence on selecting each student's repertoire to overseeing their manners and making herself available in only limited ways, it is clear that Boulanger encouraged what later administrators of the school would call the "cult of Boulanger." As former Mannes president Charles Kaufman recounts, "Everything sort of swirled around her, to one degree or another. She and her approach to things were the focus of the whole institution. Everything else was sort of the spokes of the wheel, so to speak."[23] Louise Talma and other early acolytes of Boulanger sent students to her long after it was generally agreed that the pedagogue was well past her prime and wont to ramble and lecture unproductively at her scheduled classes. Elsie Watson noted in her diaries in 1965 that "Many of her master classes are not well prepared and we sit while she hums and sings to herself and enjoys the music."[24] The situation did not improve over time. Watson found that the following year, "There was a master class given in the Jeu de Paume by Mlle Boulanger—supposedly on French music, but, as usual, she hummed, sang, rambled on for two hours and a half while I wished I were at the piano."[25]

Watson was not alone in her observations, nor was she the first to remark on them: Virgil Thomson first became critical of Boulanger's methods as early as the 1930s, when Thomson wrote to Copland of their teacher that "Nadia is not the same as when we were there. The flattery and guidance was precious to us and inspiring and the counterpoint lessons were competent enough and that's all there was." Thomson goes on to relate Boulanger's later approach: "The counterpoint was still fair [. . .] but the main thing was all changed. The guidance wasn't worth a damn. On the contrary, quite troublesome. Once the habit of composition was established, she used every art of sympathy and generosity to make it grow in her own pet channels." He was equally revolted by the aura of infallibility that surrounded the pedagogue, writing that "she lives in a temple of adulation and knee-bending that is disgusting."[26] Copland conceded that Boulanger's "pet ideas" and the "maternal means" of communicating them were forced on students but commented that students should "throw them overboard" after thorough internalization and reflection.[27] Indeed, many students applied a method of selection of ideas and tools usual among those who have undertaken sessions of master class–style study, as opposed to that of years of tutelage under one teacher: use what works, don't use what doesn't, remember it all so that it can be presented to one's own students, who also may well likewise pick and choose. However, as Boulanger aged, there became less and less from which to choose.

Gradually it became clear that, for students to be completely indoctrinated into Boulanger's world and thus receive her full attention, they would have to begin working with her at a very young age. There was an increase in the number of prodigies at Fontainebleau in the 1960s and 1970s as

Boulanger began to take on younger and younger students, hoping to mold and train them during their most formative years. In its earliest days, students younger than eighteen were rarely, if ever, permitted in the Conservatoire, but by the end of Boulanger's life and tenure as director, Emile Naoumoff had been studying with her for several years beginning when he was just nine years old. Idil Biret and Juliana Osinchuk were but two more children taken under the wing of Mademoiselle for training. Some older child talents— pianist Jay Gottlieb, for example, was brought by Louise Talma to Fontainebleau as a teenager, and Jean-Pierre Marty, also in his teens when he began his work with Boulanger—were showered with attention. Generally, though, Boulanger gave her undivided attention to one chosen child hoping to foster a complete musical and even social upbringing for the prodigy of the moment. Photographs from in the 1950s and later often show the director surrounded by such children, many of whom continued their studies with her in Paris after the Conservatoire closed each September. As she aged, Boulanger began accepting increasingly younger students, perhaps searching for her last protégé or for someone she could train as her successor as a ped- agogue. However, this is only conjecture, as, in the end, her own egotism in this regard nearly caused the Conservatoire to be closed for good.

There can be no question as to Nadia Boulanger's influence on the Con- servatoire Américain and on the musicians whom it educated during her tenure as director there. The Boulanger heyday began with her installment as director and continued into the mid-1970s, with polished artists and am- ateur music lovers alike flocking to Fontainebleau in order to bask in the eru- dition of the celebrated pedagogue. Boulanger pushed and prodded students to excel, coaxed them to create, and ruthlessly struck down the hopes of those she felt unworthy. She was the midwife of generations of works from American composers and performers, whose skills and insights into the work- ings of music were passed along to their own students. Her techniques, honed in the years as a professor at the Paris Conservatoire and the Conservatoire Américain, still shape countless ear-training and musicianship classes throughout the United States.

For the Conservatoire Américain, Boulanger was a force that was both vi- tal and damaging. Her energy, dedication to teaching—for whatever reasons, be they egotistical, devotional, or charitable—and her professional and per- sonal contacts proved essential in bringing students and guest artists to Fontainebleau each summer, subsidizing pianists and composers, and raising the name of the school to legendary status. Her domineering personality, self- centered approach to administration, and lack of foresight caused the Con- servatoire Américain to run at a financial loss, alienated former students and potential supporters, and caused the school great difficulties after her death. Boulanger was a one-woman graduate school, as Thomson had said: admissions committee, professor, dormitory proctor, financial administrator, and juror all in one. Students willing to undertake the rigors of a course with Boulanger, and who were capable of withstanding the firestorms as well as the praise, found that their careers were bettered for the experiences under Mademoiselle's hand, and they reveled in being Fontainebleau alumni. Others, especially the instrumentalists who existed in a sphere outside of Boulanger's immediate concern, found her inspiring but not directly influential. Finally, the schoolteachers and older students who attended Fontainebleau on a regular basis held a third viewpoint: that Boulanger was wrapped up in her own world, an often indifferent administrator and a sometimes callous teacher. Regardless of individual reactions to the director, the atmosphere at the Palais de Fontainebleau was, under Boulanger's vitality and that of the professors she employed, one of intense study and musical accomplishment that considerably influenced Conservatoire students, their careers, and those of their students.

From Boulanger's takeover of the Conservatoire Américain until her death in 1978, scores of first-rate performers and educators flowed from the Palais, having experienced that intense study. Composers Louise Talma, Bathia Churgin, Krzysztof Meyer, Yung Shen, Charles Wuorinen, and Kenton Coe; pianists Malcolm Frager, Seymour Bernstein, Idil Biret, Robert Levin, Jay Gottlieb, Luise Vosgerchian, and Emile Naoumoff; cellists Kermit Moore and Pierre Djokic; and vocalists Norman Farrow, June Anderson, and John Ferrante all passed through the halls of the chateau and out into performing and teaching careers. Narcis Bonet, Jean-Pierre Marty, David Montagu, and Yuko Satoh were all alumni of the Conservatoire Américain between 1959 and 1970.

The 1960s and 1970s were both exciting and unstable times for the school. Boulanger continued to attract celebrated clinicians and a moderately large student population. The climate of "Flower Power" and the attitudes engendered about the war in Southeast Asia only subtly altered the conservatory's atmosphere. Mini-skirted women appeared to play in Robert Casadesus's master class,[28] but it appears that music held sway over politics as part of daily conversation, although no one could have missed seeing Fontainebleau graffiti, "U.S. stay with us," spray-painted in front of the post office near the Palais, pleading for the United States to continue its assistance with French foreign affairs.[29] Attendance apparently was unaffected, and the fact that female music students outnumbered male music students in the final years of the 1960s and early 1970s could be attributable either to the American draft or to the fact that this often was usual at the school.[30] However, there was evidently some concern and emotion among the students during this period about the war, and as a response to this, the collaborative fête of 1970 was based on Euripides's *Iphigenia*. Of the work, on which musicians and Beaux-Arts students worked together in order to create an evening-long installation, painter Bicky Homer wrote, "We used the story of Iphigenia and her sacrifice in contrast to the formidable attitudes of a warrior."[31] In addition to their artwork and musical contributions, students undertook exercises in drama and physical improvisation in order to better express themselves during the exhibition, which featured nude dancers and models and charcoal-dust finger-painting by students and observers alike, as part of the reaction to the movement and "music of death" provided by composition students.

Classes were conducted apace of their previous direction, although Boulanger herself led fewer and fewer of them, relying heavily on Annette Dieudonné. Repertoire ran less to the avant-garde and the newly composed than before, and starting in 1960, students were taken to Solesmes each summer for a seminar on Gregorian chant with the famed scholar-monks there. An afternoon of intense study at the abbey helped to prepare them for their summer-long project on chant and mass settings, which culminated in the performance of a mass by Orlando de Lasso for the Feast of St. Louis, the patron saint of Fontainebleau, at the end of the session. The trips to Solesmes led to greater interest in early music among students and faculty that year, and a madrigal group began to meet regularly for sight-reading. Instrumentalists dropped in and accompanied other Renaissance vocal music, and, not straying too far historically, Boulanger's classes focused on the *Well-Tempered Clavier*. Most repertoire during the 1960s remained solidly French to the degree that even French Renaissance composers were given preference over Italians and others in the early music sight-reading sessions, with French music festivals occurring every few years. However, one notable concession was made to American tastes and burgeoning interest in jazz among the students: two saxophone professors were hired for the first time in 1961.[32]

With the proliferation of prodigies and young virtuosos at Fontainebleau, there was a surprising increase in interest and performance of ensemble music, considering the demands made on the musicians' time as soloists and Boulanger's distaste for instrumental courses. The school was host to several ensembles-in-residence each year, including wind quintets, string quartets, a vocal ensemble, and a handful of trios. Performances increased in frequency with the advent of the ensembles-in-residence, and it was not uncommon for nightly concerts to take place for consecutive weeks without an evening off. Formal concerts still were held in the Jeu de Paume and other chateau venues, and students presented works in a more relaxed setting at the student restaurant after meals as well. The student "stars" of the summer used this type of recital equally as much as did the less confident or less advanced did: pianist Idil Biret and the ensembles-in-residence often used the restaurant to try out works before programming them on a larger, more public concert or in a master-class setting.

Young students increased in number during this period, but the Conservatoire also began a concerted effort in the United States to attract older performers. Students at the Palais had begun to complain about the proliferation of children in their classes, and made their views known to Marie Brodeur of the American office. Brodeur reported on this phenomenon to Boulanger, who replied that she had personally tested each incoming student and found the younger ones to be better students.[33] Brodeur was unsure as to Boulanger's testing methods, evaluative scale, or whether the director entirely grasped the problem causing the complaints. However, as a longtime Fontainebleau administrator from the American side, Brodeur was savvy enough to understand the need to placate the more mature students. The American office's publicity material repeatedly referred to study at Fontainebleau as "nine weeks of graduate level study," and made sure that no prospective student was intimidated by the language barrier; all classes would be with "French professors speaking English."[34] In 1963 Elsie Watson was relieved to find a substantial contingent of students her own age to offset the under-twenty set.[35]

Despite these enticements, even the most prepared students could not assume their success at the Conservatoire. Conductors and composers had no better luck than instrumental performers in any given year. Students in these two disciplines were most likely to be given remedial work to do, without hope of completing it in time to undertake original projects before the close of the session. One observer reported that in 1962, "most of the composers were not permitted to compose and only three of the conductors got to conduct."[36] Scholarship students were faced with perhaps the worst situation: as part of the Conservatoire Américain's work-study program, they were required to take on tutoring, copying, and arranging assignments which were to be completed before their own assignments and practicing could begin. There is little wonder that some complained of learning more about running a music school than about music over the course of the summer.[37]

One attraction for students on the brink of professional success was the vast alumni network that had been growing since the school's inception. Louise Talma, once a wunderkind composition student at the Conservatoire, repeatedly took students with her to Fontainebleau each summer, where she introduced them to Boulanger and other artists who would be able to assist in the establishment of their concert careers. With the school boasting Queen Elisabeth Competition winners, noted composers, and a number of prodigies appearing in major concert halls, the possibilities were endless for career advancement. Concerts, parties, and dinners proved the perfect grounds for effecting introductions, and students judged ready for the greater world found themselves invited to numerous soirées during the summer.

However, the number of alumni involved in the admissions process led to problems with cronyism and nepotism. The halls of the Palais became filled, not with students from all over the United States, representing many different conservatories and music schools, but increasingly with students from the home institutions of professors. Talma was notorious for admitting her own students and funneling large scholarships their way. Marie Brodeur became infuriated with the manipulation of scholarship money and insisted that Talma not serve in any capacity for granting financial aid to Fontainebleau students. "She *must not be scholarship chairman*," Brodeur wrote in 1968.[38] Regardless of the control exercised by the New York office, Boulanger had the final say in accepting or refusing students, and since Talma was one of her most trusted, inner-circle confidantes and assistants, Hunter College was always well represented at the Conservatoire.

As new generations of performers rose through the Conservatoire so did the faculty. Professors who had become Fontainebleau institutions by teaching at the school for many years, some since its opening, began to retire or die. Lucie Delécluse retired in 1963, Maurice Gendron took over the cello classes and master classes on the death of Paul Bazelaire in 1958, and Jean Casadesus, eldest son of Robert and Gaby, had begun teaching at the school as a primary piano instructor in the early 1960s. Jean, born in 1927, had begun his musical studies, naturally enough, with his parents, later moving on to the Paris Conservatoire. During his parents' stay in the United States, he had studied at Princeton University and in 1946 won the Philadelphia Orchestra's concerto competition. He made his American debut with the orchestra, playing the Ravel Concerto in G. By the time he started teaching at Fontainebleau, this eldest child of Robert and Gaby was already being recognized as an outstanding and stylish soloist, and he collaborated with his parents as well as with other instrumental soloists on concerts and recordings. Jean was a charismatic and enthusiastic teacher. Boulanger seized on his charm and magnetism and sent both talented and less talented students to him: the more talented would learn quickly, while those with limited career potential would have reason to practice, attend their lessons, and return to Fontainebleau to study with the young artist. In short, Jean Casadesus became a piano-department money-maker in the way his parents no longer were.

The younger faculty, coupled with the ubiquitous lure of Boulanger, may have contributed to the school's large numbers of students who returned to the school for several years in a row during this time. While some returned for the same course and professor, as many piano students did, others studied in several areas. Robert Levin began attending the Conservatoire in 1960 for piano and harmony, added composition to his curriculum in 1961, and concentrated solely on composition in 1962 and 1963. Jay Gottlieb alternated studying piano, harmony, and composition for several years. For especially talented students, such a plan of multiple undertakings was not unusual, and, in fact, reflected the aims of Francis Casadesus, who had fostered the idea of the complete musician in his building of the Conservatoire's initial curriculum. For other students, it led to disaster. More than one student hoping to follow the course of complete musicianship—the study of harmony and composition in addition to his or her own instrument—met with Boulanger's resistance. Instrumental instructors occasionally warned students not to pursue study with Boulanger if they were registered primarily with other teachers. Her pride and ego were wont to interfere with such students' progress. She did not envision them as potential long-term, private students for herself. "All day long I've been turning over in my mind whether I should 1) enroll in harmony for lessons with Mlle Boulanger or 2) ask her to teach me piano," wrote Elsie Watson in 1972, after many years of study at the school with other pianists, including Jean Casadesus. "[. . .] I decided to ask Mlle Dieudonné what she thought of the idea. . . . She indicated [. . .] there wasn't the slightest chance of [Boulanger] acquiescing to my request."[39] In truth, Watson confesses, she was "rather relieved" to be told this, knowing that the experience she was seeking would be a difficult one to endure.

Boulanger's reputation was still intact in the United States, and, as Watson's writings show, among students who had first encountered Boulanger in earlier days. However, new students at the Conservatoire began to lose their awe of her as her tactics became harsher. Harpist Lillian Phillips attended the Conservatoire in 1963 and wrote an account of her dealings with Mademoiselle:

I had hoped to take Harmony classes. Only the Boulanger private students were permitted to attend. [. . .] Boulanger's master classes: are they to exploit her one or two most talented and make complete fools of the others[?] I saw too many people made fools of and ridiculed by her—adults and even college professors. Maybe this is European teaching, but I went to all of those classes of hers and they were a waste of time. [. . .] Yes, I learned a tremendous amount: How not to teach.[40]

Boulanger's teaching was not the only aspect of her iron grip on the school with which students, disappointed in the master teacher, found fault. Music teachers in public schools often attended Fontainebleau for advanced training and because a certificate of attendance from the Conservatoire Américain would allow them to bypass stateside refresher-course requirements. This was a common enough request that had rarely, if ever, been refused in the past. But Boulanger believed that these students were not acceptable participants in her empire, despite their often paying full tuition and thus contributing significantly to the school's coffers. On more than one occasion she was rude to students requesting these certificates, explaining in blunt terms their shortcomings and inabilities that made it impossible for her to endorse their study at the Conservatoire Américain. One music teacher wrote that, after being denied the standard paperwork by Boulanger, she approached the faculty for help. What she was told was reminiscent of a highly stratified, feudal society in which the honoring of one's betters and self-deprecation were steel guide wires for behavior:

> Later one of the instructors explained how best to heal my offence. I should not tell her (Mlle. Boulanger) that I was studying what I wanted in the school. Rather I should apologize for not choosing to become one of her students as I felt unworthy of her honored instruction.[41]

The student summed up what was the consistent issue with Boulanger's administration and teaching approach:

> While Mlle. Boulanger may be very famous and very inspiring to certain students, she endangers the very existence of the school through her lack of ability to manage it. In truth, I would say her fame has not improved her character but created a god-like sense of being capable of no error.[42]

When Virgil Thomson had made this same statement in the 1930s, it was downplayed by Boulanger admirers, and it was essentially unthinkable that anyone should agree with his assessment of the famous musician. However, with students complaining at the end of each session, the Conseil d'Administration and the American Committees began to take note. Not only was Boulanger's severe treatment and judgment of students questioned, but her faculty appointments and logistical planning capabilities were also criticized. Students flooded the New York office with accounts of Dieudonné falling asleep in classes, losing her place in the exercises and repeating lessons; of the school's inability to provide enough pianos or to secure enough practice rooms appropriate for large instruments; and of the lack of adequate instruments for harpists. The French class was given by an actress with scant English skills; Boulanger and Dieudonné did not inform students before arrival of the music they would require; they failed to make provisions with the Fontainebleau music store for ordering it; classes were irregularly scheduled; certain students were blocked without notice from attending classes for which they were qualified and had registered.[43] Composition, analysis, and harmony students questioned the repertoire covered in the classes and noted the absence of serial and other techniques disliked by Boulanger.

"Nadia has always been brutal since I have known her," wrote Marie Brodeur in response to some of the grievances, noting that even Boulanger's closest companions suffered from her professional cruelty.

> She used to frighten people so that they could not answer, or would not answer the most simple question, for fear of ridicule or sarcasm. . . . [but] many weathered her classes, and many still do. [. . .] The thing I do not understand is the way she sticks her head in the sand and ignores Boulez, etc., instead of having them out for lectures or concerts. She should not ignore them. She feels that if nothing is said, they will go away and everyone will forget the tone row. [. . .] Nadia has a way of walking over some people. She condemned Louise [Talma]'s opera, all but a few measures. After the performance in Frankfort, Nadia refused to mention it. Also, when Grant Johannessen played her new piano work with the Buffalo Symphony, Louise sent a recording to Nadia. She never even acknowledged it . . . just ignored it.[44]

Consternation over these problems reached the Conseil d'Administration through various channels, and François Valéry made the suggestion that somehow Boulanger be persuaded to hand over the directorship while continuing to teach. This was an impossible solution for Boulanger supporters, and the proposal was never made directly to Boulanger herself. Students continued to come and study with her, but the veneer of her reputation was beginning to show signs of wear at the hands of those who had less-than-optimal experiences and were honest enough to acknowledge it both to themselves and to the rest of the musical community.

To most observers and casual acquaintances of the school, the Conservatoire shone with the brilliance of celebrated artists and teachers during a time when many minds were caught up in the ugliness of the outside world. An annual alumni radio broadcast was instituted after many years of delinquency in order to promote the school's finest products. Students of the

1960s and early 1970s ranged from those already concertizing, as were Idil Biret and Jay Gottlieb, to those about to become stars. Samuel Sanders, Andre-Michel Schub, Jeremy Menuhin, and June Anderson all began concert careers after attending the Conservatoire. Performers and composers were not the only American musicians made in France: musicologists of both the historical and analytical sort came out of the Palais as well: Bathia Churgin, Susan Forscher Weiss, and Severine Neff studied at the school, taking courses in instrumental performance as well as composition, harmony, and theory.

On their concert programs and through their own teaching, these Conservatoire Américain students transmitted to their own students the repertoire, techniques, and points of view of their French professors and mentors. Pianist Douglas Buys remained faithful to the texts used by Dieudonné at the Conservatoire and used the Paris Conservatory solfège method book in his own ear-training classes at the North Carolina School of the Arts, just as Bruce Eicher adopted the French fixed-do system for his classes at the Peabody Conservatory. Don Campbell's study at the Conservatoire led to working with music acquisition among very young children and Jay Gottlieb became a specialist in twentieth-century and French piano music.

Repertoire at the Conservatoire remained solidly Francophile, with the occasional nod to a master unlucky enough to have been born elsewhere. Rameau, Franck, Ravel, Couperin, Fauré, and Debussy all had annual airings. Messiaen and Françaix represented more recent generations for French composers, although their works did not always find student acceptance, despite the annual presence of Françaix staging operas, teaching piano, or holding master classes. Singers were given Poulenc, Duparc, and Grétry to study, and foreigners Stravinsky and Chopin were admitted into the realm of honorary Frenchmen.

Composers, like their performer classmates, were encouraged to study French music and consider its language. While Conservatoire students rarely emerged from the curriculum sounding like French composers, they often assimilated some aspects of the style that had enveloped them for the summer. Exploration of instrumentation and color, tonal versus atonal techniques, and the challenges of writing for small, mixed ensembles were all issues dealt with by the composition students, especially as time went on and Boulanger realized that not all of the composition students would be satisfied with a summer of basics, starting with simple counterpoint exercises.

As in previous years, students found time for a social life in both Fontainebleau and Paris. Although student demonstrations occurred in Paris during the Vietnam War era, the musicians of the Conservatoire Américain

seem to have felt few repercussions of the unrest among their French counterparts, aside from the graffiti and conversation mentioned earlier. There are
but a few hints as to the political nature or attitudes of the students at
Fontainebleau: for their formal group photos they appear conservatively
dressed, with some longer hair and shorter skirts mixed in, and written de-
scriptions mention the occasional "hippie" in the Beaux-Arts division, but
within the music school it appears that there were no flamboyantly dressed
flower children, no confrontational demonstrators. In the eyes of the faculty,
in the 1920s and 1930s, jazz was a distracting and regressive form of music-
making best avoided by the students. Surely there was no lack of appreciation for popular music during this period at the school, but it passes by, un-
noticed for the record by students and professors alike. Major concerts given
by Soviet artist Sviatoslav Richter were sold out, and politics ended at the
door to the Salle des Colonnes.

Most students, no longer living in the Palais, made their homes in the
school-owned hotels near the chateau. Most coveted was a room in the Hôtel
d'Albe, where a typical room "just couldn't be any more French than it is."

> It's rococo in style with very high ceilings and gold ornamentation and murals
> on the walls. There's a seven-foot mirror flanked by crystal chandeliers which
> illuminate a beautiful, marble-topped dresser. In the center hangs a big chan-
> delier reflected in [the] mirror-doored wardrobe.[45]

The Albe was also the site of a garden bordered by a terrace and balcony,
often used for parties, and a pavilion that housed a piano and table tennis.
Aristocratic supporters of the Conservatoire Américain invited students to
their country homes and chateaux, and tours bused them to Versailles,
Chartres, and the south of France. Students spent Sundays, when the Palais
and therefore the practice rooms were closed, assisting in the town's effort to
clean up the forest. "Les Amis de la Forêt" trooped out into the woods each
week with gloves and bags to haul away debris left by campers and picnick-
ers, and were rewarded for their efforts with guidebooks to the forest, scarves,
and other tokens.[46] The traditional costume balls and Fête St. Louis celebrations were highlights of the social schedule, as were the Bastille Day events.

Bastille Day in Fontainebleau often began not with French observances
but with an early-morning concert on the Horseshoe Staircase by Conservatoire Américain students. They sang "The Marseillaise" and "The Star-
Spangled Banner," followed by French and American folk-song arrangements. Composition students often were inspired to create their own
arrangements of the two national anthems, sung with varying degrees of suc-

cess. In some years a reception followed at the Palais or Town Hall, complete with champagne and hors d'oeuvres. Classes took up the remainder of the French holiday, but the evening found students watching the fireworks in Paris or at the Bastille Day carnival, a traveling assortment of games, rides, and food vendors set up in the former stable area of the chateau.

In 1967 Nadia Boulanger celebrated her eightieth birthday amid much fanfare at the court of Prince Rainier and Princess Grace of Monaco. Guests included Marc Chagall; Igor Markevitch and his son Oleg, a Boulanger protégé; Elliott Carter; Philippe Entremont; Mieczyslaw Horoszowski; Yehudi Menuhin; and some thirty Conservatoire Américain alumni. Boulanger was described as excited and pleased to be feted, with accolades being presented one after another throughout the year. However, Boulanger, despite her activity, was beginning to decline. While she persisted in refusing to scale back her teaching or to relinquish command over the Conservatoire Américain's affairs in any way, the French and American councils quietly began looking to the future without her.

Notes

1. Elsie Watson, diaries, July 19, 1960, possession of author.

2. Documents of the Conservatoire Américain, undated 1960s, CA/F. Also: Letter, Nadia Boulanger to Soulima Stravinsky, undated 1975, CA/F.

3. Notes of Conseil d'Administration, May 1977, CA/F.

4. Memo, Nadia Boulanger to Clarence Brodeur, undated 1954, CA/F. Also: Letter: Nadia Boulanger letter to unknown recipient, undated April 1972, CA/F.

5. Watson, diaries, July 2, 1965.

6. Jérôme Spycket, *Nadia Boulanger*, trans. M. M. Shriver (New York: Pendragon Press, 1987), 22–23.

7. Spycket, *Nadia Boulanger*, 22–23.

8. Léonie Rosenstiel, *Nadia Boulanger: A Life in Music* (New York: Norton, 1982), 104–105.

9. Rosenstiel, *Nadia Boulanger*, 105–106.

10. Rosenstiel, *Nadia Boulanger*, 295.

11. Joe Kerr, spoken monologue, "How I Killed Nadia Boulanger." Performed July 28, 1999, at the Hôtel d'Albe, Fontainebleau.

12. Kerr, "How I Killed Nadia Boulanger."

13. Kerr, "How I Killed Nadia Boulanger."

14. Bruno Montsaingeon, *Mademoiselle: Conversations with Nadia Boulanger* (Boston: Northeastern University Press, 1985).

15. Letters, Marie Brodeur to Martha Crawford, July 12, 1970 and March 14, 1969, CA/NY.

16. Jay Gottlieb, interview with author, July 2000, possession of author.

17. Documents of the Conservatoire Américain, various dates, CA/F.

18. Letter, Marie Brodeur to Martha Crawford, November 22, 1968, CA/NY.

19. Marie Brodeur, letter to Martha Crawford, November 6, 1966, CA/NY.

20. Clarence and Marie Brodeur, "Report on the Conditions at Fontainebleau," 1973, CA/NY.

21. Conservatoire Américain brochure, 1961–1962, 15, CA/GA.

22. Watson, diaries, July 19, 1965.

23. Charles Kaufman, interview with author, March 24, 1999, possession of author.

24. Watson, diaries, August 16, 1965.

25. Watson, diaries, July 27, 1966.

26. Anthony Tommasini, *Virgil Thomson: Composer on the Aisle* (New York: Norton, 1997), 99–100.

27. Aaron Copland and Vivian Perlis, *Copland 1900 through 1945* (New York: St. Martin's, 1984), 195.

28. *Fontainebleau Alumni Bulletin*, November 1963, 4.

29. *Fontainebleau Alumni Bulletin*, November 1966, 3.

30. Conservatoire Américain student registries and *Fontainebleau Alumni Bulletins*, November 1967, November 1968, November 1970, CA/F.

31. *Fontainebleau Alumni Bulletin*, November 1971, 1, 3.

32. *Fontainebleau Alumni Bulletin*, April 1961, 6.

33. Letter, Marie Brodeur to Martha Crawford, October 10, 1968, CA/NY.

34. *Fontainebleau Alumni Bulletin*, April 1961, 9.

35. Watson, diaries, 1963.

36. Letter, Ethelston Chapman to Louise Talma, undated 1960s, CA/GA.

37. Letter, Marie Brodeur to Gladys Detweiler, November 22, 1968, CA/GA.

38. Letter, Marie Brodeur to Martha Crawford, October 15, 1968, CA/NY.

39. Watson, diaries, July 5, 1972.

40. Letter, Lillian Phillips to Georgia Vraz, September 22, 1963, CA/GA.

41. Letter, Marie Ellen de Bolt to Georgia Vraz, October 6, 1963, CA/GA.

42. Letter, Marie Ellen de Bolt to Georgia Vraz, October 6, 1963, CA/GA.

43. Letter, Lillian Phillips to Georgia Vraz, September 22, 1963, CA/GA.

44. Letter, Marie Brodeur to Peggy and Quinto Maganini, September 6, 1966, CA/GA.

45. Barbara Gable, "Dear Diary," *Fontainebleau Alumni Bulletin*, November 1963, 3.

46. Watson, diaries, August 14, 1966, possession of author.

~

CHAPTER NINE

Interlude 3: Emile Naoumoff on Growing Up at Fontainebleau (1970s)

Many child prodigies began studying at the Conservatoire Américain de Fontainebleau during the 1950s, growing up surrounded by major artists and teachers while at the same time playing hide-and-seek in the Palais corridors. Pianist and composer Emile Naoumoff began studying at the Conservatoire Américain when he was eight years old.[1]

I arrived in Paris in the winter of 1970 and I met Nadia Boulanger in an ad hoc meeting that was scheduled over the fall during our stay. We were from Bulgaria. We were behind the iron curtain, so it wasn't like something you could do from back there. My father obtained the authorization to travel abroad in a western country, which was very difficult. . . . So [using the pretext of his father's participation in a medical congress], we took the train and traveled on the Orient Express for many days and nights. While in Bulgaria, where I started music when I was five, my piano teacher mentioned the name of Nadia Boulanger by adding: "she is probably dead by now." Because of the communication of the time, in context, things were not so obvious.

Nadia Boulanger received only on Wednesdays in Paris. Wednesday was the sacred day for her analysis class. It was like *the* group class; the rest she taught privately. And it was an institution, these Wednesdays, because she taught this for the past, probably fifty years. [After] the Wednesday class, she would allow people to come and meet her, guests, friends, students, musicians; and it was a salon, open to art culture in France, all kinds of people who gathered in her apartment. So, one of those Wednesdays I went there, and I performed for her. In one of her books she remembers this—but I remember it even more vividly since I interrupted my playing to tell her that I would like to play for her a minuet I had composed. I played for her and at this point she stopped me after my minuet and she asked to talk to my parents, who were in the room, among other—unknown to me at the time—friends, who were composers like Jean Françaix and Stravinsky's son. [She] asked my parents for me to be able to study with her for ten years. She would not ask for any fee, and she would even find scholarships for me. She asked my parents for them to find ways to find income so that they could stay around, so I was not alone. [I was] eight years [old], and she was eighty-four.

Ten years [almost] happened. It was nine and a half, actually. And it was planned like this for every week: two or three private three-hour lessons with discovery, lesson practice, examinations. It was private sessions as well as exercises, counterpoint, fugue, harmony, sight-reading, keyboard. Basically the idea was to make a complete musician. Because I was thirsty and hungry with my God's gift, as she would say, I had more responsibility to work harder. And for somebody her age to want to do something [for] ten years is almost visionary or irresponsible. For my parents it meant, of course, never seeing Bulgaria again, because it was impossible to travel. So when I was there I was a child and she was a very old lady.

The first summer of mine in Fontainebleau was July of '71, the fiftieth anniversary of the school. And so my first lesson was in fact in Fontainebleau, after this meeting [in Paris]. I began discovering music in Fontainebleau. [That year] I saw Copland come and play his pieces in the Salle des Colonnes and I saw Souzay come to give master classes and Stravinsky's son came to give master classes and I played for him too. And so many people of such different backgrounds came to pay homage to the school, of course, to [Boulanger] mostly, at that point.

I had three or four private solfège lessons of two hours a week . . . as well as Nadia's three-hour lessons each week. Plus the group student classes at Fontainebleau as well as in Paris . . . the analysis class, keyboard harmony . . . within two or three years I was able to write complex thoughts in music, which were in my brain but I couldn't exteriorize . . .

I was receiving all this knowledge of the nineteenth century, of a complete musicianship attitude—part pianist, part keyboardist, part accompanist of singers, transposing, sight-reading, as well as playing the accompaniment of the Bach cantatas we sang there each summer in Fontainebleau . . . and therefore played a continuo in the three parts without any, hopefully, mistakes in the voice leading. In the sight-reading, even, on the keyboard. At the same time, [I had to] practice technique on the piano. In other words, [she wanted us to] be challenged to be the best you can at several disciplines, organ included. It could have easily driven me crazy, if I hadn't been as hungry and thirsty for music as I had been, so I think she must have been amused—she used to call me the gift of her old age.

She could, I guess, transmit a certain essence of what she was, century-long, from her teachers, like Fauré, to her early students like Copland or her incredible sister. I arrived about sixty or seventy years after all these people in her life and so she, [at the] sunset of her life passed me this torch and Fontainebleau presented literally the headiest moments of my life because every summer I was even more so close to music-making without boundaries, so to speak.

For me Fontainebleau was expected like the moment of pure joy because from the crack of dawn until the evening late at night, I would be in a musical bath and she let me be as such very free in my endeavors in music, composition-wise, and interpretation-wise to some extent. She didn't dictate, you know: feel like this, how don't you dare hear it like me. She insisted, [though I was] a child, on a monstrous discipline in exercises, be it counterpoint, fugue, scales, or whatever it is. So on one side I understood that I'm allowed no consideration and on the other side I was allowed all the freedom that the nonconcessions were allowing. Very early [Boulanger and Dieudonné made me] understand in my consciousness that I was able to receive discipline in order—and at the same time, in my creativity, to develop my freedom.

Fontainebleau was even more so interesting [than study in Paris during the year], because in two months, or a month and a half, of the intense sessions of days that were long like weeks. [Because] of interaction with an incredible amount of various musicians, the Americans as well (that's where I learned my American language, phonetically—because she was teaching with her French accent—it was hilarious) but nevertheless, this interaction between the students, this proximity, the lunches and dinners with the students, improvised concerts, the sight-readings, the transcriptions of pieces that weren't called as such, just in order to sing them, play them, love them, discover them, build them, rebuild them; and [we were] basically playing with Legos, with cantatas by Bach.

[The Conservatoire Américain de Fontainebleau] allowed all of these various aspects of Nadia's musicianship to be geographically in one place, and what a place. And at the same time it gave the impression that she was going to teach the indigenous knowledge. This was the way she was criticized by those who didn't like her, Messiaen and others—that she was so involved with the American students and it was jealousy in many ways because of her incredible influence on American musicians. And that *was* Fontainebleau.

My relationship with Boulanger was far from being the teacher-student—it was more like a way of life that I was taught. I was taught all these things about hearing music, and Fontainebleau, when I calculated at one point—nine summers, ten summers as a student—represented almost two years of the most intense moments.

I went from childhood to adolescence—of course being a child prodigy and, in the '70s, I was not the typical adolescent of today. I was mastering reversible counterpoint, I couldn't tie my shoe, I was perfectly unadapted for everyday life. I was the perfect example of a child prodigy, with its awkwardness . . . so Fontainebleau represented a place where I was comfortable because all the realities of life didn't exist. The restaurant and the hotel, and the concerts and the visiting professors and the accompaniment and the Bach cantata build-up and Nadia's classes and private lessons and the ping-pong games at the Hôtel d'Albe and the Frisbee games, my first words in English, all my American friends, my first girlfriend—everything had to happen—all this happened, basically, in Fontainebleau. Like you are told in summertime, do the things that are necessary in the development of a human personality. I happened to do them in Fontainebleau. I met my wife in Fontainebleau, but that was after Nadia's death.

The advantage of Fontainebleau for me that was the most important wasn't even her, as much as the fact of being around all these incredible Americans, young people. One morning in August when I went to breakfast full of fugues and counterpoints in my hands, at the restaurant's breakfast one of them said, "The King died today," reading the Herald tribune, for Elvis Presley and I remember saying, "Whooo?"—the same way there was this *Love Story* movie, and in one section of the movie they walk after she performed a Bach harpsichord part in a Brandenburg concerto in a private house and he goes, "You're good at it, I think you should study music." And she goes, "Who says I won't? I'm going to study with Nadia Boulanger." And he goes, "Whooo?"

American students were for me the only link to America other than John Wayne and dubbed French westerns on TV, which is the only thing I knew of America. It's true you see them drink milk and not Coca-Cola. [I thought] it was very American to drink Coca-Cola but instead they all drank boxes of milk. And the King died and everybody was crying, and I was just like, "Whooo?" so I did realize that I was sort of out of phase with things, obviously. They must have had a lot of fun with me at the time. Some of them remember me as being one of those odd kids, but in any case it's true that Fontainebleau represented more for me than for somebody who would go there as a young adult for summers, which is already an incredible endeavor when you think about the castle, and Boulanger and all that.

[Fontainebleau] created for me an enormous amount of friendships. In '84, I visited New York for the first time in my life, and went into Juilliard, where Cathy, [now] my wife, was studying at the time. I entered Juilliard, and it was like—I could hear five or six people going, "Hi Emile," in the cafeteria—people who were finishing studies after Fontainebleau who were there. I go someplace else unexpectedly, somebody says oh, I was in Fontainebleau in '73, remember me? '76? Remember me '73, '74? That's why the Alumni [Association] sends the famous bulletin—more or less to try to keep up with this enormous, powerful army of alumni.

On the makeup of the classes at the Conservatoire Américain and being a child among older students:

[In having a child in a class of mostly adults, it is necessary to] balance the part of the frustration on the part of the adults, who feel this—it's too easy for this kid, it's too easy—he's arrogant. Nadia's treatment, humanly—not musically—but humanly, of me was that of an adult. It had drawbacks. But it had advantages. In that the students saw no complacency of hers toward me other than the fact that the fact of the two human beings next to each other must have been, as an interaction, something fascinating to watch. In the majority of [classroom] situations where I was involved, things went very well. I didn't teach [the older students] anything; I wasn't condescending to them, because I had perfect pitch, for instance, though they couldn't sight-read a Bach cantata with all the clefs. No, in fact, Nadia made it a point at the beginning of my studies with her, not to teach me, the child prodigy, but the young musician, as she used to say. Therefore, as a child prodigy I didn't have the exposure; I wasn't exhibited as such, in concert halls or such. She refused my name to be—at least when she was the one in charge of the program—next to my age.

[She did] lots of things like that, to make a certain sense that "Emile is one of us." Of course, her religious belief was so strong, and that created a morale of humility. For her, those who could do more—those who received more, in her eyes, from God—should be even more humble than others. Which is a double-edged sword because it can hurt those who are very advanced as well as it can unnerve those who are not.

She divided [the students] in her mind into two: the awakened ones, and the sleeping ones. That didn't mean that she didn't teach the sleeping ones, in fact, one of the best teaching lessons I got from her, a pedagogical lesson, was assisting at some other people's lessons, where I could see them be slow as lumps to understand something. This is where she opened her mouth and said she unpeeled me like an orange, she didn't teach me—but I guess with some you have to build the elements in order to create the fruit, not just unpeel the already ripe fruit. I remember after asking her one day, why did you spend so much time with the students who couldn't figure out whatever cadence she was trying to have him to play for such a long time, and she said, mon petit, it's important, you always have to listen to the other.

On Fontainebleau's "civilizing" events for students:

Fontainebleau dinners though added more formality because she would be the one in fact to create the opportunities for the students to have scholarships besides her teaching the students, she had this sort of protocol. [There were] dinners with Khachaturian, or dinner with Stravinsky's son, or with so many people like Markevitch, or so on. It had this kind of strange fun, but unimaginable today when you meet in-vogue personalities of this level.

Concerts were given in Fontainebleau every Tuesday and Friday evening, [and] you would have the postconcert reception in Nadia's apartment. You were in fact selected by names, not by choice, [so] all of the students ended up going once to one of those cocktails. [You would be there] with the artists who just performed, in person, which is amazing [that] me, a student, a no-body, would meet and talk with Bernstein or Copland and all these people. Of course, I'd be scared to death to speak and I'd try to show a lot of presence and all these people—they would be so debonair. Nevertheless Nadia would like to have students come to this postconcert drink at her place. And drink this monstrous punch that she would make which was a horrible drink. After these cocktails we would go to the restaurant, to a special room, where she would have the dinner. Another [group] of her students would then be only the ones to get this dinner table; [there would be] the guests, the performer, and a few students and of course some of her friends, the countesses and husbands or wives, writers, and God only knows who they were—most of us didn't know who they were anyway. Except that they were very intelligent and outspoken, speaking about everything and nothing and so French and that kind of apparent superficiality compared to knowing people who would just say what they had to say. When you're being bombarded by attitudes like this, you end up relatively at ease with adults, as I was.

Nadia would show which fork to use with which meal and all these little things. It was kind of odd that a lady like her, at the Himalayas of [musical] stuff, would care about such basics like your fork, this, that. But mostly for young American students usually came by holding their forks straight and putting their knives in between the fork tines to cut their meat. Nadia didn't mock that, she just tried to help them feel comfortable. For instance, if I would cross my foot and a student—a girl—was sitting next to me, she would interrupt her class to teach me a lesson about how to put my leg.

Later, when I went to Marlboro, Rudolf Serkin's festival, what did I see but the rest of Marlboro, [where] their tradition is to throw their dirty napkins at each other. They have a dirty napkins fight. I was like, "Oh are they going to have the napkins fight?" Mr. Serkin will send it to Mr. Lipkin, Mr. Lipkin will send it to me, I'll send it back to whoever, and I was amused by this, looking at this thinking "Gee, that's fun." And [at Fontainebleau] we were like, and what will I say to the countess such-and-such and will I make a fool of myself if I don't remember the quotation that Nadia used during the lesson. So, every place has its own, and builds its own need for, traditions.

On the legacy of study:

My parents brought me all the way from Bulgaria, because [Boulanger] represented this kind of person who would know what to do with a child that had this potential. Of course, by being around her so long, and in a situation where I was a child, so devoted to her, completely free to receive all her [knowledge] . . . unlike some students who arrived to adolescent or young adults, already formed, somehow, somewhere, and they had to fill up gaps retroactively, in their understanding of their knowledge of music. With me it was all built more linearly.

When I [observed] Nadia being so patient with some relatively mediocre student, compared to some other students, she taught me a lesson of life. She didn't teach me a lesson of music only. I felt, since I saw Nadia give so much, what she gave me was not for me to keep. I cannot pretend to be all of Nadia's meaning. I was the meaning of her last ten years. It's already enormous, but that's what it is. I have to be humble.

Note

1. All materials in this chapter are drawn from the author's interview with Emile Naoumoff, October 14, 2000, possession of author.

PART IV

"APRÈS ELLE LE DELUGE"

The Palais de Fontainebleau, circa 1921. (CA/F)

The Louis XV wing of the Palais, where students and faculty lived, circa 1921. (CA/F)

The Henri IV wing, home to the Conservatoire in the 1980s and 1990s, circa 1921. (CA/F)

The class of 1921. In the front row, Camille Saint-Saëns is eighth from right; Mabel Tuttle is ninth from right; Maurice Fragnaud is tenth from right; Francis Casadesus is eighth from left; Gaby Casadesus, seventh from right; and Robert Casadesus, last row, left. (CA/F)

The violin class of 1921. (CA/F)

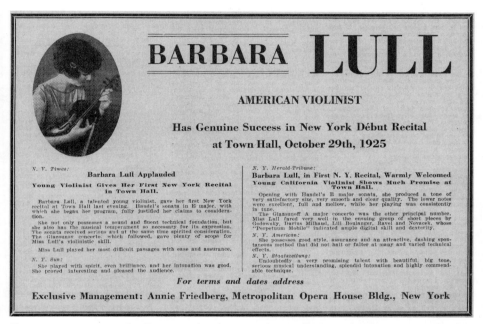

Concert announcement for Conservatoire alumna Barbara Lull, circa 1925. (Possession of author)

MARIA MONTANA

Soprano

Sang at Town Hall January 18th

and the critics wrote . . .

" . . . a voice of good size—clear and even . . . top tones were sung with power and firmness. Her interpretations were musicianly and showed understanding of the atmosphere and emotional significance of her songs to an unusual degree which was exhibited in Schubert's "Nacht und Träume" and especially in a poetic and sympathetic performance of Brahms's "Der Tod, das ist die kuehle Nacht" . . . expressive ability marked Brahms's "Botschaft," exhibited also in the Boito aria and the Respighi songs."

Francis D. Perkins, N. Y. Herald-Tribune, Jan. 19, 1939.

" . . . revealed earnestness, experience and taste."

N. Y. World-Telegram, Jan. 19, 1939.

"A voice of generous range."   —N. Y. Times, Jan. 19, 1939

Season 1939-40 Now Booking

Concert Management: MILTON BENDINER

Steinway Hall   New York

Concert announcement for Conservatoire alumna Maria Montana, née Ruth Kellogg Waite, circa 1939. (Possession of author)

Beaux-Arts students pole music students across the Etang des Carpes in a fish boat as part of the 1925 Bastille Day celebrations. (CA/GA; scrapbook of alumna Hilda Berkey)

Diploma for Excellence d'Execution in cello, signed by Maurice Ravel, circa 1934–1936. (CA/F)

The Casadesuses' combined piano class in 1938. (CA/F)

Nadia Boulanger's pedagogy class in 1938. (CA/F)

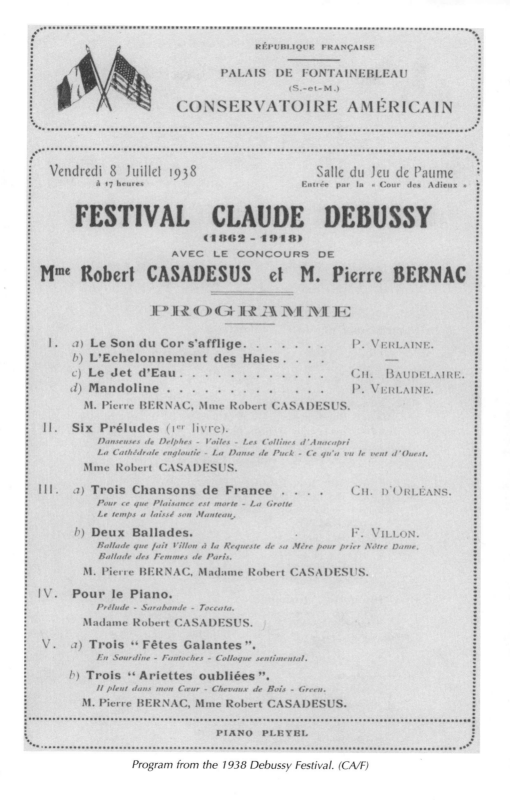

Program from the 1938 Debussy Festival. (CA/F)

PALAIS DE FONTAINEBLEAU
(S.-et-M.)

CONSERVATOIRE AMÉRICAIN

Mardi 5 Juillet 1938
à 15 heures

Salle du Jeu de Paume
Entrée par la « Cour des Adieux »

FESTIVAL MAURICE RAVEL
(1875 - 1938)
AVEC LE CONCOURS DE

Madeleine GREY **Emile BAUME**
André ASSELIN **Paul BAZELAIRE**

I. **Sonate pour Violon et Violoncelle.**
   Allegro - Très vif - Lent - Vif avec entrain.
   M. André ASSELIN, M. Paul BAZELAIRE.

II. *a)* **Histoires Naturelles** (Jules RENARD).
       Le Paon - Le Grillon - La Pintade
   b) **L'Enfant et les Sortilèges** - Air de l'Enfant (COLETTE).
   c) **L'Heure Espagnole** - Air de Conception (Franc NOHAIN).
   d) **Ronde** (Paroles de Maurice RAVEL).
       Madeleine GREY.
           Au Piano : Gilberte LECOMPTE.

III. *a)* **Pavane pour une Infante défunte.**
    b) **Gaspard de la Nuit.**
        Ondine - Le Gibet - Scarbo
    M. Emile BAUME.

IV. **Trois Mélodies Hébraïques.**
       a) *Kaddisch* (Prière pour les Morts, en Hébreu).
       b) *Meyerke* (En Hébreu).
       c) *L'Enigme Eternelle* (En Yiddisch).

    Don Quichotte à Dulcinée.
       d) *Chanson épique.*
       e) *Chanson à boire.*

    Madeleine GREY.
           Au Piano : Gilberte LECOMPTE.

V. *a)* **Oiseaux tristes.**
   b) **Alborado del Gracioso.**
       M. Emile BAUME.

PIANO PLEYEL

Program from the 1938 Ravel Festival. (CA/F)

Class photo from 1938. (CA/F)

Class photo from 1958. (Possession of author)

Class photo from 1982. By this time the Conservatoire had moved into the "Kitchen" Quarter, or Henri VI Quarter of the Palais. (Possession of author)

The salamander, symbol of Francis I and seen throughout the Palais de Fontainebleau, was adopted by the Conservatoire Américain as its mascot.

CHAPTER TEN

⁓

"Après Elle le Deluge" (1980–1987)

The Conservatoire Américain marked its fiftieth anniversary in 1971. A half-century had passed since Francis Casadesus and Walter Damrosch had begun their venture, the creation of a renowned institution of musical learning.

Planning for celebratory events began in the United States, where the American office pursued prominent alumni for their support and sought their presence in Fontainebleau during summer 1971. A golden, shining façade was created by the presence of Aaron Copland; Yehudi and Jeremy Menuhin; Queen Fredericka and Princess Irene of Greece; Beveridge Webster; Soulima Stravinsky; and Janet Price; but away from the parties, commemorative concerts, and celebrity master classes, the French and American councils were facing the problem of Boulanger's decline, and with it, the possible end of the Conservatoire.

Some tensions had always existed between the French Conseil d'Administration and the American Fontainebleau Alumni Association. Written off as cultural differences, the ubiquitous problems of controlling the student admission process, hiring professors, and distributing funds diminished in the wake of more serious issues of preparing the school for Boulanger's eventual death and finding her successor. However, as it was with many of the common matters raised between the school's two governing bodies, much talk occurred but little action was taken. Jean Casadesus, sensing an opportunity in the making, began to agitate for the Conseil to appoint him as assistant director.[1] He was refused, and the American office branded him as overambitious and grasping. Unhappy with the way Jean had tried to promote his

119

classes at Fontainebleau without its blessing, the New York office wrote of his proposed appointment that, "We feel certain that Nadia is not even aware of this. The officers of the Alumni refuse to do anything to hurt Nadia. She is still the Director, no matter what Robert, Gaby, and Jean think."[2]

However, Jean was not wrong in his belief that the Conservatoire needed an heir-designee to the throne. Nadia Boulanger's health was declining at an alarming pace: her eyesight failed to the point of blindness, despite cataract operations; and her hearing was poor enough to require hearing aids for both ears. Her sense of pitch was considerably affected; and her arthritis had crippled her to such extent that she was reduced to teaching from a wheelchair, asking students to play their exercises on the piano for her. She could no longer do it herself.

Of concern, too, were the numerous summer music programs that were gaining popularity in the United States. American students were no longer expected to study in Europe in order to be considered finished musicians but could remain at home and, for comparable or lower costs, study with important performers and instructors. The Tanglewood and Aspen festival schools, along with the festival held at Marlboro and Yale's summer study program, had begun to gain prestige prior to Boulanger's ultimate decline and had grown enormously popular and successful. The Conservatoire was going to have to compete increasingly with university-affiliated and orchestra-affiliated summer programs—sometimes both, as in the case of Tanglewood. While these stateside schools carried with them the support of their affiliates and could rely on large endowments or consortiums of dedicated concert artists for funding, Fontainebleau stood alone.

That the Conservatoire Américain should have had such problems staying afloat was unbelievable to those who read the lists of alumni names and saw the rosters of the faculty hired each year. However, the school's French administrative duties continued to be carried out by volunteers or by students and alumni working for scholarships and small honoraria. The American office of the Fontainebleau Association was entirely an amateur endeavor, and little was done to rally alumni around their summertime alma mater other than plaintive begging that ran in the corners of the *Alumni Bulletin*. The operation was marked by an ineffectiveness that was perplexing to its more sophisticated supporters. Alumni seemed to be somewhat indifferent to the fate of the school, perhaps assuming that it received all it needed from the French government or American governmental and private arts foundations. In planning for the Conservatoire's golden anniversary, a monumental direct-mail effort was put forth by the volunteer officers, but to little avail. "I see Copland will give a program," wrote Marie Brodeur, head of the New York office, of the upcoming celebrations. "He does pay dues. I wish he would give some real money, for a change. I am discouraged, where to look for money."[3]

With numerous attractive opportunities to study in the United States available, students accepted by the Conservatoire often declined to attend, citing inability to finance a summer abroad when similar training could be had for less at home.[4] This left the school in a poor position financially, because faculty salaries and other arrangements were budgeted before a final tally of enrollments was made.

Social changes also affected the handling of matters. Students accustomed to the attitudes and mores of the 1960s frequently circumvented Boulanger's strict codes of behavior, and officers of the councils and board were well aware that any successor to Boulanger would have to be more forward-thinking in terms of students' perspectives. Women might actually be allowed to wear slacks in the presence of a director, and the "hippie" students, as criticized by Clarence Brodeur, nonetheless paid much-needed tuition, and would have to be cultivated as alumni supporters of the school.[5] Faculty would have to be flexible as well. Jean Casadesus proved popular with students, although a deep dislike of the Casadesus family remained among Boulanger's clique. Marie Brodeur was strongly enough opposed to the Casadesus family that she repeatedly made mention of what she retrospectively judged to be a devastating choice for the school:

> I'm still kicking myself; when Fragnaud cabled me (when Philipp quit on [the Conservatoire Américain]) and said the choice was to Casadesus or Cortot. Casadesus was getting quite a reputation around America then and Cortot was fading out, so I cabled back, Casadesus. I sometimes wonder if it wasn't a big mistake.[6]

The Casadesuses—who were teaching, coaching, and mentoring students as usual, as well as trying to plan for the school's future—weren't really the problem, but few administrators were willing to admit where the real issues lay. The more immediate problem was getting Boulanger to accept the fact that she would not be able to retain her hold on the school forever. The view from the French Conseil d'Administration was that while Jean Casadesus might very well make a worthy director, some kind of compromise acceptable to the Americans would have to be made. But in the interim, time seemed to be on Boulanger's side, and then the issue of a successor was further complicated by a tragedy in the Fontainebleau community when Jean Casadesus was killed in an automobile accident on January 20, 1972, while on tour in Canada. The Casadesus family was shattered, and Jean's students likewise mourned. The 1972 session of the Conservatoire Américain opened on July 4 with a mass for Jean, attended by the entire student body. True to form, the discipline of the students was not altered significantly: there was still practicing to be done for the upcoming concerts and lessons. Elsie Watson wrote:

> Of course the day began with practicing and then at 11:30, there was a mass for Jean Casadesus. Lila Gene and I went—lots of music, a recording of the slow movement of a Mozart concerto—Jean's own recording—Ed Phillips played the organ and M. Derenne sang. It was very sad.[7]

Despite the loss of its most popular piano professor, the summer progressed much like any other at Fontainebleau, but with a few important distinctions in the behavior of visiting artists. The steady decline of Boulanger, an aging faculty, and what was perceived as the Conservatoire's reluctance to change with the times, brought about, for the first time, some very vocal criticism by traditional supporters of the Conservatoire's students and methods. Sir Clifford Curzon, Nikita Magaloff, Soulima Stravinsky, and Jeanne-Marie Darré gave master classes that seem often to have been harsh. Elsie Watson wryly remarked on Magaloff's teaching:

> Mr. Magaloff is very negative and highly critical. He uses such terms as "ruin," "spoil," "distort," "you don't understand," "monotonous" to describe the students' efforts. He himself makes a beautiful sound on the piano and knows all the literature so well it is a pity he is so insensitive to the students' feelings. For two days he has been belaboring the fact that we (the students he's heard) *hit* the keys. We are all disposed to try to think of ways not to.[8]

The *Alumni Bulletin*, normally an organ of positive reinforcement of Fontainebleau traditions and events, included an article referring to the classes: "Whether this superlative coaching was always understood is another matter, for the ego is tender, and the master-class situation is sometimes agonizing for the performer."[9]

Typically, Boulanger chose students to play in the master classes: her younger protégés almost always played in every class, with the remaining time allocated for older students, a long-term tactic appreciated less and less by the nonprodigal students, who, not infrequently, had passed up other opportunities to attend the Conservatoire. Other students came to Fontainebleau only to be asked to leave again: instrumentalists frequently had been obligated to travel away from Fontainebleau for their instruction, but usually not farther than Paris, an hour away by train. Violin students of Yehudi Menuhin who arrived at the Palais to study with the virtuoso were informed that all violinists were required to travel to Menuhin's home in Gstaad, Switzerland, for their lessons. Because of the distance and expense involved, they journeyed en masse to Gstaad, where they stayed in Menuhin's home for a week of coaching. The violin students were in fact studying with Menuhin, but they were not actually *at* Fontainebleau. They resented not experiencing classes, events, and student life at the Palais, causing several to complain about the arrangement. Their musical training, which they anticipated being in the style of the Conservatoire's earlier days, fell short of expectations. Fewer and fewer students were allowed to take part in master classes and concerts as Boulanger filled them with guests or allowed select students to monopolize student performance op-portunities. Angry letters disturbed the American office, and enrollment fell steadily. By 1974, Conservatoire President François Valéry was forced to admit that the New York office was bankrupt and that the school was in danger of closing permanently.

In France, Boulanger and her assistants worked to increase class size and recruit sponsors and spokesmen for the Conservatoire. Concert repertoire was managed by Boulanger with the goal of increased audience attendance and therefore profits. Fontainebleau's citizenry could be counted on to at-tend recitals of French music sprinkled with bits of Bach and Mozart, and that is exactly what they got. Professors taught the same works year after year, hoping to create their own brand of performer through the use of the administration-approved French repertoire, but instead this often led the students to create bland and indistinguishable performances. Students occa-sionally were required to pay for their own tickets to the biggest events, a consideration that did not sit well with many, especially with those who had attended in previous years and had become accustomed to open admittance to all Conservatoire-sponsored concerts.[10] The monies went to scholarship and general funds; every dollar and franc was desperately needed.

The repertoire selected for concerts during this time appears remarkably staid in light of contemporary composition and of the works being produced by Fontainebleau's student composers. Works by Messiaen were presented at only two concerts, and while Poulenc and Dutilleux were accepted, along with perennial Fontainebleau figure Jean Françaix, no other avant-garde French composers were heard. The Conservatoire may have encouraged its students to prepare and present French works, but those of Jolivet, Boulez, Murail, and other composers whose works were widely accessible, though not purely tonal, were rarely performed. The occasional "foreigner" slipped in: Dallapiccola, for example, enjoyed a brief vogue among students. However, the substance of student and faculty concerts alike was drawn from the late nineteenth and early-twentieth centuries: Fauré, Debussy, Ravel, and Couperin appeared repeatedly on programs given in the Jeu de Paume and Salle des Colonnes.[11] One could count on hearing Ravel's "Tzigane" and at least six piano works by Debussy played more than three times each summer.

The composition of the student body changed significantly in the 1970s as well. The founding by-laws, established in the 1920s, prevented more than a small number of non-American students from attending the Conservatoire. At a March 1972 Conseil meeting, falling enrollments and strong competition from stateside summer programs and academies prompted a discussion among members about the admission of large numbers of non-American students. In addition, the minimum number of students the Conservatoire Américain required to open, starting in 1973, was established at 100 to 110. Tuition was raised in order to offset the decline of the franc, and concerns were voiced that American students would balk at the price tag of $800, up from $750 the year before. At the same time, Boulanger asked for professorial and administrative salary raises. To offset these costs, she argued, the Conservatoire would have to accept students from Europe and Asia.

In order to do this, François Valéry commented, the by-laws would have to be altered somewhat. After all, the school had begun as a summer conservatory for Americans, and should the majority of students be non-Americans, the Conservatoire would be in violation of its original charter and purpose. Despite this argument, Boulanger was firm. She was willing to risk having a smaller number of Americans in exchange for improved classes—meaning more students, better students, and wealthier students. Clinicians should, with Boulanger's heavy-handed guidance, be able to select students of any background to perform for them. Valéry conceded that the admission of students to master classes was up to the clinician, but that overall the ratio of American to non-American students must remain high.[12] Enrollment rosters show that the number of students from Asia and the Continent rose slowly but steadily after this meeting, including many young French musicians. The school began to achieve a more diversified and cosmopolitan atmosphere, something much appreciated by the students, but the easing of the restrictions on student nationalities also paved the way for non-French musicians to serve as faculty members. Once again the issue of the Conservatoire's purpose would have to be raised and defined.

Despite the fact that inclusion of non-French citizens contravened the desires of the Conservatoire's founders, other Europeans and Americans had served as faculty from the school's beginning, often bringing with them musical styles and interpretations reflecting their own backgrounds. Earlier administrations had been reluctant to alter this tenet formally, although, in the

1920s, Francis Casadesus had required a Russian singer to take out French citizenship in order to become a member of the faculty. As the era of Boulanger waned, it became clear that strong American intervention would be needed to keep students returning to Fontainebleau. Thus Casadesus's nationalistic intentions were thrust aside by practicality.

As Boulanger declined into a state of physical and mental collapse, several of her students were finally but informally recognized as her successors. Two of Boulanger's students stood out as natural leaders following her tenure: Louise Talma was Boulanger's godchild, a formidable and well-regarded composer and teacher in the United States. Robert Levin, an American pianist, conductor, and composer, was a perfect choice to fit the role as well. Unfortunately for the school and both of these musicians was the fact that they shared one ineradicable flaw: they were not French, and, apart from the loosening of strictures regarding student nationality, the director still had to be French. With American officers lobbying for a change in the Conservatoire's statutes, the French Conseil stood its ground on this matter and would not allow changes to the dictate that had so long governed the conservatory: French musicians, led by a Frenchman, teaching American musicians. More limiting was the fact that a formal search for an heir to Boulanger was postponed again and again as she persisted in attempting to control the school herself.

Boulanger was not the only person resisting the inevitable. At an Alumni Association meeting on April 12, 1976, a statement was made to the effect that "Mademoiselle Boulanger feels better every day." Members of the American office lauded the director's stamina and drive, but none truly was cognizant of her condition. The French Conseil knew that the Americans were deluding themselves by believing such fairy tales, and François Valéry wrote time and again to the Alumni Association providing a more realistic view of the situation. He also put forth his aims and intentions in his correspondence: he wanted to keep the Conservatoire Américain as a place that preserved Boulanger's traditions, but he did not want to see it limited to any particular instruments or professors. The Conservatoire obviously needed to keep its relationship with the United States strong, although with recent changes, would admitting even greater numbers students from countries other than America become more acceptable?[13]

Valéry also stressed the need for increased funding, suggesting a partnership with Yale or another university or conservatory. He hoped to use the names of Copland, Boulanger, and others to raise the money necessary to create a one- to two-million-dollar endowment. Boulanger herself was no longer capable of such fund-raising work, and this all-important task would necessarily fall to others. Writing to the Brodeurs in February of 1977, Valéry described his most recent meeting with Boulanger, on a ceremonial occasion:

> I found Nadia exceedingly tired. She could not stand and hardly replied to the President's address, though she talked with me afterwards with her usual presence of mind, quoting Saint Paul, etc. But I feel sure that, if she is to come to Fontainebleau, she will only be able to see one or two students every day. Annette [Dieudonné] is very pessimistic, and sees her declining from week to week. I am extremely worried. What are we to do? If our students come expecting to study with Nadia and find she is not there or cannot give lessons, what will be their reaction. On the other hand, we cannot cancel our session. Last but not least, it is impossible to discuss the situation with Nadia. Annette told me that only her work keeps her alive. "It would kill her if she thought she would not go to Fontainebleau." It's all very sad and disquieting.[14]

Clarence Brodeur replied to Valéry in harsh tones, characterizing the president's idea of fund-raising "a fantasy," and insisting that Boulanger was capable of recognizing the status of her own health and dealing with the problem of finding a successor. Brodeur went on to demand Valéry's silence on the whole matter, asserting that the Conservatoire would be sued by students if they arrived in Fontainebleau prepared to study with Boulanger and found her unavailable for any reason.[15]

In May, Valéry wrote again to the American board, pleading for assistance. Boulanger was getting much worse, and a solution was needed immediately. Valéry had been in contact with a number of American music professors, among them Conservatoire alumnus Robert Levin, then teaching at the State University of New York at Purchase. Levin, James Harrison, and Louis Martin, two other students of Boulanger's, were asked by Valéry to step in and assist the school. Levin began teaching classes at Fontainebleau in 1979, and Harrison served as president of the board of trustees in New York. The trio began to make concrete plans for the school's future. "My job," Harrison commented, "was to get the best out of all possible situations."[16]

While the administrators of the Conservatoire struggled against time and one another, the students continued as before. Each June, young American musicians arrived at the Fontainebleau-Avon train station and made their ways to the Hôtel d'Albe and the Palais. Little changed during this time, and in fact, students began to chafe at what appeared to them as old-school approaches and methods.

By the mid-1970s, Boulanger no longer taught in any realistic sense, and her classes were taken over by Dieudonné, Talma, and Levin. Dieudonné and Talma tried to present the "Nadia style" to the fresh, new Fontainebleau students, but met with limited success. Talma's own style and personality over-came her deference to Boulanger-type tactics, and Dieudonné's teaching was growing stale, a formula made old by year after year of rote instruction.[17]

In 1978 Boulanger taught her last classes at Fontainebleau. She addressed the student body as a whole, held a few group classes, and met with private students during the first few weeks of the session. Not long after the session had begun, it was announced that Mademoiselle would not be teaching for the rest of the summer; indeed, she spent much of the rest of the session in the local hospital, relocating to her Paris apartment at the end of August. Students felt sympathy for the famed pedagogue, but Boulanger no longer commanded the same attention, respect, and fear that she had before.

Beginning in June 1979, the Conservatoire at last had begun making con-cessions to the decline of its leader. Robert Levin essentially took over the program, designing a new format for chamber music and analysis. Repertoire assigned to chamber music ensembles was the same as that studied in the analysis class, an idea so obviously practical that it was embraced by the stu-dents wholeheartedly. A quartet-in-residence was hired to coach the students and to perform in the Jeu de Paume concerts, and private lessons were pro-vided for guitar and wind players. While Boulanger was physically present at Fontainebleau during a portion of the 1979 session, her health was such that she did not receive students or teach, and her mental condition was equally poor: she had difficulty recognizing familiar faces and often was confused. Staunch supporters could no longer delude themselves into believing in the myths that had so long prevailed concerning her unflagging ability to rise up from dissent, depression, or ill health to continue her work; everyone present knew that it was simply a matter of time before she died. Yet no formal pro-ceedings were undertaken to replace her before her death: discussions were conducted in hushed and reverent tones, as if such planning might somehow offend the unaware director. No audit was conducted to assess the financial situation of the school during this period, and it appears that none of Boulanger's former or current protégés or long-time acolytes entered into meaningful conversation with their mentor to address her intentions or de-sires for the school's future.

When Boulanger died on October 22, 1979, the Conservatoire Améri-cain was left without a director, a dictator, or a determined future. In meet-ings of the French and American councils, a committee was formed to su-pervise the Conservatoire's transition from the Boulanger era into a new age. Much like the committee that had established the school in 1921, this group included composers, performers, and a member of the Casadesus fam-ily: François Valéry, composers Henri Dutilleux, Pierre Boulez, and Olivier

Messiaen; former Boulanger protégé Igor Markevitch; violin professor Zino Francescatti; flutist Jean-Pierre Rampal; and Gaby Casadesus were all present. Matters were grave: curriculum and finances needed stability, and the Palais administration deemed it necessary to remove the school from its home in the Louis XV wing to the Henri IV wing in the rear of the chateau. At a meeting of the Conseil in November 1979, Narcis Bonet was appointed director of the conservatory.[18]

The committee's choice of Bonet was startling to some. After all, commented Emile Naoumoff, "when Nadia died, we felt like Louise Talma could have been the sort of immediate continuator, since Louise was her godchild and she dressed like her, she imitated her voice like her; she was the senior woman, female American composer, she was . . . sort of Boulanger without all of the severity."[19] However, Talma was seventy-three when Boulanger died, and the school needed a director with energy and immense managerial experience, something Talma lacked. At the time, Bonet was the assistant director at the École Normale de Musique in Paris and thus well accustomed to the logistics, politics, and countless other facets of running such an institution. A French citizen born in Barcelona, Bonet had studied composition with Boulanger and Igor Markevitch at the Paris Conservatory. At the time of his appointment as director of the Conservatoire, he was well known for his École Normale position and had won several prizes for his music. Proud of his Catalan heritage, Bonet's works were firmly centered in the neoclassicism of Stravinsky, as Talma's had been, while employing Catalan folk music and cultural influences. The head of several Catalan associations and clearly adept at managing personnel, financial resources, and developmental requirements, he seemed to the committee a natural choice to lead the Conservatoire Américain.

The immediate crisis was keeping the school open. Without the gravitas of Boulanger's name and influence to hold them, wealthy donors and patrons disappeared. "It was clear that the halcyon days of a hundred students, Bernac and Curzon were over," says Harrison of the period. "We couldn't pretend that it would be the same kind of place [without Boulanger]."[20] The planned move to the Henri IV quarters of the Palais—which, according to the chateau's chief architect, was absolutely necessary for safety reasons—was projected to cost more than one million francs, and the Ministry of Culture was unable to guarantee the school the necessary subsidies for the relocation. Valéry proposed naming the school "École Nadia Boulanger" in hopes of increasing income and recognition, but the councils did not take up the idea. An affiliation with the State University of New York was discussed, but for the 1980 session, the Conservatoire remained independent.[21]

The 1980 session was overshadowed by Boulanger's death. Dozens of memorial services were held in Paris and Fontainebleau, and maudlin eulogies spilled from the pages of the *Fontainebleau Alumni Bulletin* and from the letters of students. With members of the board and faculty stepping into their roles fully for the first time, constantly worrying about finances and continuing Boulanger's traditions, and participating in the frequent concerts marking her passing, much of the day-to-day work fell to those who had been with the school the longest, regardless of their formal rank. Of this situation and the 1980 session itself, Emile Naoumoff commented that, "the summer after Nadia died, I basically carried it all on my shoulders because a., I spoke English, b., I was a member of the 'furniture,' and c., I was enthusiastic."[22] Naoumoff's remark about being part of the "furniture" of Fontainebleau was made with both pride and bitterness. He had been at the Conservatoire for so long that he was taken for granted: he would teach, he would administer, he would hold the school to its past as Boulanger's territory. Yet, he said, "There was nothing to propose other than that [which] was post-Nadia. How many years can you do every program, 'In memoriam Nadia Boulanger?' I'm the first to have asked to stop that, but in a way it sold the program." His complaints rang true: in their efforts to continue Boulanger's empire, the Conseil d'Administration and faculty were stymied by a lack of vision and by an absence of the force necessary to create a new purpose for being.

At the same time, though, the name of Boulanger still did "sell the program." Students continued to pour through the doors of the Palais and the Hôtel d'Albe. The faculty coped as best they could. Bonet himself taught solfège, conducting, and theory, and Naoumoff taught analysis, ear-training, solfège, and chamber music. Levin, too, gave courses in chamber music and analysis, and new professors were hired as full faculty members. The master-class professors included Dutilleux and Betsy Jolas for composition, Claude Helfer for piano, Igor Markevitch for conducting, Jean-Pierre Rampal for flute, Maurice Gendron for cello, Narciso Yepes and Alberto Ponce for guitar, Henryk Szeryng for violin, and Genevieve Joy for chamber music.[23] Repertoire remained constant: Fauré, Debussy, Ravel; but with the inclusion of Boulez on the guiding committee around this time, composition students appear to have been released from the limiting bonds set by Boulanger in regard to dodecaphonic and experimental forms or composition.

In August 1980, at the end of the first post-Boulanger session, the Conservatoire's pianos, music, and furnishings were moved into their new lodgings in the Henri IV wing of the Palais de Fontainebleau. The Henri IV wing, once home to the chateau's kitchens, was a step down from the airy and elegant spaciousness of the Louis XV wing. Here, on the ground floor, the ceilings were low, the walls were covered in old and poorly applied plaster, and the damp rose out of the ancient building and was absorbed by instruments. Music once housed in a proper library was filed away in cardboard boxes, and bare bulbs hung in the center of small, echoing practice rooms. Up a winding stair at the end of a dark hallway, more rooms provided lovely views of the Jardin Anglais but were marred by uneven and broken flooring, a lack of music stands, and a lively acoustic that was, if possible, worse than that in the rooms below. Alumni and administration alike were devastated by the depressing new surroundings. "It was an odd feeling," wrote Elsie Watson in the *Alumni Bulletin*, "to pass the Louis XV wing and think that it was 'ours' no longer."[24] Naoumoff described the situation further, looking past the physical properties of the school to an interpretation of the entire enterprise: "the new building [was] a disaster compared to the old building, the funding [was] not coming, the deficits [were] building, the hotels [needed] to be repaired—the whole reality of the stage of this operetta showing its backstage, the corpse. It was like the decay of it."[25]

While they caused dismay, the accommodations did not wholly deter students or faculty, and in late 1980 the Conservatoire found a musical partner with whom it seemed it could rely for support and assistance through its transition and well into the future: the Mannes College of Music. In becoming affiliated with a highly regarded New York music school, it appeared that the venerable French institution had found exactly what it needed: a stable, well-known American partner with access to funding, knowledge of publicity, and an administrative system that alleviated the strain on Fontainebleau's volunteer forces. The Mannes College also had historical ties to Fontainebleau, a fact that was not lost on Conservatoire administrators.

The Mannes College of Music had been founded by David Mannes and his wife, Clara Damrosch Mannes, the sister of Walter Damrosch, in 1916. Under the direction of their son Leopold—a Prix de Rome winner—the school became a four-year college, offering a Bachelor of Music degree. Past faculty included conductor George Szell, composers Georges Enesco and Bohuslav Martinu, and Felix Salzer, a protégé of theorist Heinrich Schenker. Since its founding, Mannes had become one of the preeminent conservatories in the United States, and had the support of countless musicians and philanthropists from its earliest days, when the Damrosch and Mannes names were frequently in print on the society pages. There was a Casadesus connection as well: the Casadesus siblings had made their early music ensemble American debut at the school in the 1920s. Philosophically, Mannes was exceptionally compatible with Boulanger's conception of the Conservatoire, stressing, as she had done, excellence in counterpoint, harmony, analysis, ear-training, and keyboard skills—integrated elements that were taught in its distinguished Techniques of Music course, developed by Salzer during his tenure as director of the college and based on the French system taught at the Paris Conservatory. Its partnership with the Conservatoire Américain would further bolster its reputation and provide a European summer program for its students and faculty. The partnership had come about through the work of James Harrison, who along with Levin was heavily involved in the restructuring and continuation of the Conservatoire during Boulanger's decline and following her death. Harrison initially approached Mannes President Charles Kaufman, whom he had met while they were colleagues at Hunter College, about a collaboration between the schools around this time. Kaufman recalls,

> At that time, [. . .] Jim Harrison got a hold of me . . . And Jim said, "Do you know about the Conservatoire?" and I said, "What am I, an idiot?" I said sure, Boulanger's gone; you lost her a couple of years ago. And he explained to me that she was what she was; we all know what a remarkable person she was and what she did. But it was sort of "après moi le deluge,"—of course it was "après *elle* le deluge"—and . . . the place was in a big mess. And he said, "would you like to get involved in this?"[26]

Kaufman had just become president of the college, following a political struggle in which the Mannes faculty had first removed its board of trustees, followed shortly by the president of the college. A music historian trained at Columbia and New York University, Kaufman had served as a professor at Mannes for four years when he was appointed president in 1979. Asking Harrison for a year's delay in his involvement in order to devote himself fully to his work at Mannes following its own internal upheavals, Kaufman joined the American board in 1980. With his acceptance of a position on the council, the Mannes College was in a position to provide stability for the Conservatoire within the United States, something it sorely lacked because of the declining health and interest of the older alumni who had for so long served as admissions committees, advertising agencies, and publicity managers all in one. In an official statement about the duties of its recent New York partner, the Fontainebleau Alumni Association wrote that, "Mannes will assist us in such areas as student recruitment, design and distribution of publicity materials, fund-raising, and the future development of curriculum."[27] In return, the American council told its members, "Fontainebleau will guarantee the admission of a number of Mannes students each year." A faculty-exchange program was also to be instituted.

The plan was a good one, and began as a success. The students and professors found Bonet to be an agreeable if not always organized director, but the influence of Mannes personnel helped to combat the inefficiencies Americans found in the French systems. "Narcis is a very capable person—a nice guy," says Kaufman. But, "he was not exactly what you call a man with natural flair for organization. So the place was sort of floating along . . . in a sea of garlic and olive oil, but there was very little coherence to what was going on."[28] The atmosphere was pleasant, but Kaufman and his Mannes colleagues found the school in need of a strong hand in bringing order to the chaos that too frequently caused problems within the Conservatoire's operating methods. The determined efforts of the New York administrators paid off as a number of celebrated performers returned to give master classes and concerts, and enrollment grew. The mayor of Fontainebleau presented the American administrators with medals and honors, and despite waning support for the school in the days of Boulanger's decline, citizens of the town turned out to concerts, and local espousal of the school, which had been flagging, gained appreciatively.

The Conservatoire was once again in the spotlight because of alumni as well. Fontainebleau pianist André-Michel Schub won the Sixth Van Cliburn International Piano Competition in May 1981, propelling his career to new heights. Singer June Anderson was, at the same time, beginning her third year a Metropolitan Opera star; and countertenor John Ferrante performed as a soloist and with Peter Schickele, recording numerous "P. D. Q. Bach" performances. Pianist Jay Gottlieb received a Rockefeller grant; violinist and composer Andreas Makris had his works premiered by Mstislav Rostropovich and the National Symphony Orchestra; and pianist Samuel Sanders performed with Itzhak Perlman, Sharon Robinson, and Mstislav Rostropovich.

The introduction of new professors and clinicians to the Conservatoire Américain in the early 1980s somewhat changed the repertoire studied and methods used in classes. Much of the new approach came straight from the United States, to the consternation of some French faculty and Conseil members. "We know what kind of programs are right for American students," the Mannes team explained, "So that what they do will be useful when they pack up and take it home with them. We are professionals at that." Kaufman recalls, "There was, of course, a kind of *résistance* on the part of the French to this, you know. It was wrong, this was Fontainebleau, [. . .] so from the very beginning there was this kind of reticence. But they sort of went along. They really sort of went along. And for a while it was terrific."[29] Composer Betsy Jolas introduced Fontainebleau composition students to the experimental media used by many French composers at the time. New sound equipment was purchased for Jolas's master classes, and students listened to recordings of works produced at IRCAM, the newly opened center for electronic and computer music in Paris. This informal association and educational partnership with IRCAM was new to the Conservatoire, and quickly became a popular and influential relationship for the composition students.

IRCAM, or, as it was formally titled, L'Institut de Recherche et Coordination Acoustique/Musique, was the creation of Pierre Boulez. In 1970 Boulez, on the invitation of Georges Pompidou, then president of France, had begun work on a center for research on new music and related technology. Located in Paris next to the Pompidou Center and extending several floors underground, the center was fully opened in 1977 with Boulez at its head. While Boulez's original plan organized the center into the areas of electro-acoustics, computer music, pedagogy, instruments, and voice, several restructurings shaped IRCAM into its present incarnation, focused on the production of and research in computer music. Along the way the center also acquired an ensemble-in-residence, the fluid and versatile Ensemble Intercontemporain, comprising virtuoso soloists from across Europe. Conservatoire students touring IRCAM's facilities took in demonstrations and received hands-on introductions to its numerous resources, including Boulez's 4X digital audio processor, originally constructed for his work *Repons*, as well as to less specialized equipment and programs. Jolas's more open approach to compositional techniques allowed for greater experimentation by the students than had Boulanger's. Consequently, student works featured in concerts in the Jeu de Paume ranged from the tonal and traditional to the extreme cutting edge, employing tape recordings, minimalist techniques, nonstandard approaches to the instruments, and other forms of sound production and interaction. In addition, members of the Ensemble Intercontemporain joined the Fontainebleau faculty rosters and performed at the Palais during the summer. The youth of the ensemble's members led to natural friendships among the student population, and provided opportunities for networking and career development in a casual but productive manner.

Other students found new freedoms as well. For the first time, pianists could hope to perform Rachmaninoff, as Boulanger's decree banning his works was no longer in effect. Repertoire representative of a greater range of nationalities than before appeared in concert programs: Symanowski, Wagner, Dowland, and Ortiz were all heard in the Jeu de Paume. Debussy, Ravel, and Fauré were given their due, but after a long hiatus, Brahms, Schumann, Schubert, and Wolf had a renewed presence in Conservatoire Américain recitals. Milhaud, Ives, Mendelssohn, Bartók, Dohnanyi, and Hindemith were other composers heard again or for the first time in the Jeu de Paume during the 1980s. The Conservatoire's history was recognized with performances of Copland and other alumni works.

The number of students grew tremendously under the affiliation with Mannes. Levin, Harrison, and Kaufman decided to broaden the faculty further by inviting musicians from all over Europe to teach at Fontainebleau. Kaufman describes the situation: "The French were not thrilled with this [hiring non-French artists as faculty] but I mean, we had people everywhere—I was in New York, Bob Levin was in Europe, at the time he was also teaching at Freiburg, and he had many contacts in European musical circles. We ended up with some of the terrific musicians from all over Europe. We had some terrific people from good orchestras in Europe—top-flight people." Enrollment increased from just a handful of pianists and composers to eighty or ninety students each summer. "They were all like lemmings," says Kaufman of the students who followed their European teachers to Fontainebleau every year.[30] Despite the climbing enrollment figures, the French Conseil had doubts about the inclusion of non-French professors. The Conservatoire Américain was, after all, intended to be a school where American musicians would study with French musicians. The doubts of the French did not deter the Americans, who were interested in creating the most successful program they could and believed that the superior musicianship training that non-French professors could offer should not be limited by national boundaries. "Then, I did something, of course, that did not exactly endear me," remembers Kaufman. He hired Mannes violin professor Shirley Givens to teach at Fontainebleau. An American, her presence—even more than that of the Europeans—stung the French. In her first year, Givens brought twenty-eight students, including prodigy Pamela Frank. In the face of such a following, and despite the disagreement over the fundamental nature of the faculty, the Conseil had to admit that the Mannes approach was succeeding and that the Conservatoire was doing well.

Bonet, as director, also thought to enlarge the Conservatoire into a more American-style summer program, choosing as his method for expansion the inclusion of an orchestra. The idea of having an orchestra and adding orchestral playing to the curriculum had been a point of contention since the opening of the school. Boulanger, not wanting to encourage the participation of instrumentalists, had flatly denied the possibility, but with the Mannes College's participation, fielding an orchestra seemed a more reasonable goal. However, the numbers were still not easy to achieve. Kaufman recalls that, while the general attitude toward having a chamber orchestra was positive, initial support was influenced by the fact that, "they were doing cockeyed transcriptions of things in which you had to use a comb and tissue paper because they didn't have enough oboes. It was ridiculous."[31] Valéry disagreed with Bonet's orchestral aspirations, promoting instead the idea of a strengthened chamber music program. It was the first of a series of conflicts in which Bonet came away as the losing party.

> The first argument [Bonet and Valéry] had was that Valéry thought the emphasis should be on chamber music, because it was perfect across the board. Not just quartets but across the board to mix and match combinations. And at that time chamber music was very much in the ascendancy in the United States, and there was a burgeoning interest in it—which hasn't really gone out of style yet. So we thought it made every good sense to do that, from every point of view. So we went that way, although Narcis was unhappy about it, the French were altogether happy.[32]

The American administrators had other problems with Bonet's direction, and as time went on, these began to increasingly chafe at the sensibilities of those exerting more control. He never learned enough English to communicate easily with American students and faculty, which, as Kaufman says wryly, "is not very helpful, when the device you are running is called the Conservatoire Américain." In addition, he was rumored to have pursued an affair with at least two students, and it became apparent that, notwithstanding his experience at the École Normale, his serious lack of organizational ability was causing rifts and strains that otherwise might not have occurred.[33] "He was a cultured gentleman, a fine musician, and he wrote excellent music," wrote Kaufman of Bonet, "but his hand was not always on the rudder."[34] The Americans began agitating for Bonet to step down, and he resigned without apparent rancor in 1986.

Once again, the issue of finding a suitable person for the job arose. Emile Naoumoff, now teaching at the school, was thought still too young to command the influence and power necessary to create a powerful entity in the school and to successfully lobby patrons and the government for funding. Betsy Jolas seemed an appropriate choice, and indeed in her brief tenure as a clinician and professor of composition she had become one of the more vocal and energetic members of the faculty, speaking on the Conservatoire's behalf at numerous meetings and functions.

Jolas grew up and was educated both in Paris and New York. At the Paris Conservatory, Jolas had studied with Messiaen and Milhaud, and had become known for a style that utilized contrapuntal writing gleaned from Renaissance polyphony combined with avant-garde techniques. The daughter of a Paris literary family (her parents founded and edited the journal *Transition*, which had published Joyce, Hemingway, and Stein), Jolas's works displayed a special ability for text-setting and vocal writing. In the 1970s she succeeded Messiaen as professor of analysis and professor of composition at the Paris Conservatory. It was because of her duties at the Paris Conservatory that she would not accept a formal position in the leadership of the Conservatoire Américain, agreeing instead to a position on the Conseil d'Administration.

Once again, Valéry and the French council found themselves searching for the right person to lead the Conservatoire into its future. Clearly someone with strong connections to the French musical establishment was needed: someone well known, someone, if at all possible, with Fontainebleau ties. After months of futile reflection, the Conseil turned to Gaby Casadesus for suggestions. Her recommendation was Jean-Pierre Marty, a pianist and conductor who had, as a prodigy, studied with and then broken away from Boulanger as a teenager at the Paris Conservatory. Later reconciling with Boulanger, Marty was known to Fontainebleau alumni through his performances and recordings, having collaborated with alumni Kenton Coe and others for various labels. A published Mozart scholar whose musicological interests centered on tempo and performance practice, fluent in several languages, and an experienced conductor and opera director, he was elected as director of the Conservatoire Américain de Fontainebleau to take office in 1987.

Notes

1. Letter, Marie Brodeur to Lucie Delécluse, March 29, 1968, CA/GA.
2. Letter, Marie Brodeur to Lucie Delécluse, March 29, 1968, CA/GA.
3. Letter, Marie Brodeur to Martha Crawford, October 21, 1970, CA/NY.
4. Letter, Marie Brodeur to Martha Crawford, July 3, 1970, CA/NY.
5. Letter, Marie Brodeur to Martha Crawford, October 10, 1968, CA/NY.
6. Letter, Marie Brodeur to Lucie Delécluse, May 16, 1971, CA/NY.
7. Elsie Watson, diaries, July 4, 1974, possession of author.
8. Watson, diaries, July 30, 1972.
9. *Fontainebleau Alumni Bulletin*, November 1972, 1.
10. Watson, diaries, July 8, 1966.
11. Programs of the Conservatoire Américain, various dates, CA/F. Also, Elsie Watson, diaries, possession of author.
12. Notes of the Conseil d'Administration, March 1972, CA/F.
13. Letter, François Valéry to Marie Brodeur, undated 1977, CA/GA.
14. Letter, François Valéry to Clarence and Marie Brodeur, February 12, 1977, CA/GA.
15. Letter, Clarence Brodeur to François Valéry, February 15, 1977, CA/GA.
16. James Harrison, interview with author, May 1, 2003, possession of author.

17. Watson, diaries.
18. Notes of the Conservatoire Américain, November 1979, CA/F.
19. Emile Naoumoff, interview with author, October 14, 2000, possession of author.
20. James Harrison, interview with author, May 1, 2003, possession of author.
21. Notes of the Conservatoire Américain, November 1979, CA/F.
22. Naoumoff, interview.
23. *Fontainebleau Alumni Bulletin*, June 1980.
24. *Fontainebleau Alumni Bulletin*, June 1981, 9.
25. Naoumoff, interview.
26. Charles Kaufman, interview with author, March 24, 1999 possession of author.
27. *Fontainebleau Alumni Bulletin*, June 1981, 1.
28. Kaufman, interview.
29. Kaufman, interview.
30. Kaufman, interview.
31. Kaufman, interview.
32. Kaufman, interview.
33. Elsie Watson, interviews with author, various dates, possession of author.
34. Letter, Charles Kaufman to author, undated October 2001, possession of author.

CHAPTER ELEVEN

~

The Schism Opens (1988–1993)

Jean-Pierre Marty became the director of the Conservatoire Américain at a time when the school was in need of determined leadership, funding, and a clear purpose. Emile Naoumoff had been correct in identifying the school's major problems, and like many associated with it, thought that it was time to move from a post-Boulanger era to a phase of reinvention and new development. Marty agreed. This was, however, one of the few issues agreed on by everyone involved. While the years of involvement with Mannes were vital and energizing ones for the school, the Americans carried a progressively heavier load while the Conseil seemed content to become involved only when it took issue with an American-led decision. A more cohesive administration was required, one in which both parties were equally responsible for the Conservatoire.

Marty had a vision that was well articulated in sweeping plans for the Conservatoire. He enlisted the help of members of the French aristocracy, just as Boulanger had done, for financial support and to lend an aura of sophistication to the conservatory. Count Jean-Charles de Moustier, Prince Alexandre Galitzine, and Baron Benoit d'Abboville were added to the Conseil d'Administration. Marty used contacts at French fashion houses Louis Vuitton and Yves Saint-Laurent to institute a corporate giving program to raise capital for the projects he hoped to undertake. The French government provided additional funds, and during his first year as director, Marty made a trip to New York to meet with the American council and Alumni Association. Relations between the American groups associated with the Conservatoire and their French counterparts had been tense throughout Boulanger's final years and those immediately following her death. The French Conseil had perceived the American council members and the alumni-newsletter publishers often to be hostile to the needs of the French administration; and the Americans had viewed their own stateside situation as one lacking in real support from fellow American alumni and supporters. The American Association also saw itself as continually antagonized by poor decisions on the part of Valéry, Bonet, and others. All of the Americans involved hoped that the meeting with Marty would lead to more supportive ties and encourage better communication and understanding between the groups.

The meeting was a disaster. Hosting the assembly at Mannes, Charles Kaufman opened by welcoming Marty and asked what plans the new director had for the Conservatoire, so that the Americans could prepare and plan their role in assisting the school. "On behalf of my colleagues," Kaufman explains, "I offered to Marty all the services of the American Council and of Mannes."[1] Rather than reciprocating the gesture, Marty responded as though the American council was impugning his capabilities as the new head of the Conservatoire, asking, "Why are you questioning my leadership?" The hostile and abrupt demand cast a pall on the event, and the meeting quite literally went no further: Marty left the room within five minutes of having entered. Kaufman was further incensed by Marty's assertion that the Conservatoire was not benefiting from its association with the Mannes College, which by all accounts was proving a fruitful partnership:

> We thought that the man had acted quite poorly from every point of view. He was hostile; he thought that it was detrimental to the school to have the office at Mannes. I said, excuse me? This is not a lower-east-side bordello. It certainly can't hurt to have an office in the place where Frederica von Stade and Murray Perahia went to school. What are you thinking about here? [Marty said,] "No, I do not want this, we will have an independent office." Where are you going to get the money? It was one of the reasons you came here in the first place.[2]

Marty brushed aside the quartet of Harrison, Kaufman, Levin, and Martin, alienating the American Council. He went instead to the Alumni Association—then still an independent group from the council—for financial and moral support, and established an office in Washington, D.C., to handle publicity, recruitment, admissions, and legal matters. Always powerful in terms of scholarship funding, the Alumni Association was frantic to keep the Conservatoire open, and had been desperately worried since Boulanger's death that closure was imminent. Following Gaby Casadesus's lead and influenced by her involvement with the new regime, the Alumni Association was initially supportive of Marty and enthusiastic about his plans.

The new director had considerable ideas for the august school. Under the direction of Marty, the Conservatoire was to become a year-round program. It would become associated with an international string quartet center, known as ProQuartet, that the town of Fontainebleau had been hoping to establish independently. Drawn by the professors and curriculum of the Conservatoire, as well as the opportunities afforded by a collaborative educational effort with the ProQuartet project, students would flock from all over the world to study in Fontainebleau—and enrollment would not be limited to Americans. Professors from the Paris Conservatory, IRCAM, and other institutions would teach the best and brightest in restored rooms of the Palais. Students would live comfortably in modernized hotels. Practice rooms within the Palais would be refitted for acoustical perfection. The Conservatoire would move back into its old haunts in the Louis XV wing, and concerts of the school's students and guest artists would no longer take place in the refurbished tennis court, but in the "forgotten theater" built by Napoleon III in 1854.

The planned refurbishment of the "forgotten theater" for use by Conservatoire Américain students, professors, and guest artists represents the projected grandeur of the Marty regime. This theater, long since closed due to unsafe flooring and other hazards, was once a jewel. It was first used in 1857 for the visit of Grand Duke Constantin of Russia to the French imperial court. Seating four hundred in two balconies, the theater's stage still holds the original nineteenth-century machinery and sets. The seats are upholstered in silk damask and the walls and ceilings are gilded and hung with tapestries. Marty estimated that to repair the theater would cost thirty million francs.[3] It would be the centerpiece of the Conservatoire Américain: a fabulously opulent setting for the reborn school, a return to the pre-Boulanger glamour of the 1920s and 1930s.

In order to accomplish his goals, Marty looked concurrently to his French sponsors, the French government, and the United States. With the Alumni Association supporting his plans, he engaged an American-style public relations firm to evaluate the Conservatoire Américain's needs. What it found and presented to the board was not surprising: the Fontainebleau locals had a negative image of the school; the school was visible enough in neither France nor the United States, much less in other countries; and there was poor communication with the French government. The firm went on to declare that the substandard student housing—which had been falling into disrepair during the 1970s and 1980s and had not been sufficiently upgraded—denoted an amateur operation, as indeed it had been run offhandedly by the French Conseil; and the school needed a stronger identity, complete with a logo and a sign on the Palais wall. In addition, the media advisers concluded, most people thought that the Conservatoire Américain was just a memory, never to be renewed.[4] Without the involvement of Mannes, the Conservatoire would have to find new means of faculty and student recruitment and accrue considerable financial strength on its own.

Marty began at once to correct these problems. He reworked the Conservatoire's publicity materials, writing the brochures himself. He hired an American development group to help raise capital. With members of the French board, he raised funds for hotel renovation and the acquisition of necessary materials including scores, stands, and recording equipment. He hired the members of IRCAM's Ensemble Intercontemporain to teach lessons, coach chamber music, give master classes, and perform. During his first session as director, Marty persuaded Leonard Bernstein, a dedicated admirer of Boulanger, to donate master classes to the Conservatoire as a commemorative act for the pedagogue. He recruited students from Eastern Europe, relying on contacts he had at the St. Petersburg Conservatory and his own fluent Russian to bring three students a year from that city to Fontainebleau on scholarships.

Implementation of a year-round program was to wait for stronger finances and visibility, and size of the enrollment for the summer session became fixed at about forty students, a shockingly small number compared to the school's earlier years and the period of Mannes's involvement that had just ended. Approximately eight composers, four pianists, eight violinists, four violists, four cellists, two flutists, two oboists, two clarinetists, two bassoonists, and two horn players were accepted for study each summer. Marty felt that it was "necessary to assure an equilibrium between the disciplines and instruments represented to guarantee a new dignity of the reputation of the Conservatoire Américain de Fontainebleau."[5] The focus was on chamber music and performances of the student composers' works. Marty, in addition to coaching small ensembles, taught a conducting class, using the amalgamated forces of the student body as a chamber orchestra.

Admission was more stringent than it had been in Boulanger's day, in order to keep the quality as high as it had been under the auspices of Mannes's involvement: performance applicants submitted a recording which was screened by Marty and the primary faculty member teaching the instrument. Composers' scores were sent to Jolas for examination, who evaluated them carefully before recommending admittance. Applicants frequently were turned down, despite their ability to pay full tuition, an event that would never have occurred under Boulanger's control. Partially as a result of the admission procedures, and partially due to administrative consensus, the student body narrowed in its age ranges during this time. Students younger than eighteen were discouraged, and none under sixteen was admitted. Most students were conservatory undergraduates in their early to mid-twenties—musicians who, while generally not prodigies, were beginning solid careers.

Concert programs by student and guest artists were unusually varied and rich under Marty's direction. The range of repertoire was expanded: French repertoire was suggested for the master classes with Gaby Casadesus and other French artists, but Britten, Bruch, Shostakovich, and other significant non-French composers, even the previously shunned Rachmaninoff, were given Fontainebleau airings during Marty's tenure. Marty's contacts brought not only Bernstein and the Ensemble Intercontemporain but soloists from the Orchestre de l'Opera de Paris and the Orchestre National de France.

The composition of the student body demonstrated the results of Marty's desire to expand the Conservatoire's recruitment base past the American-dominated field found just prior to his tenure. In addition to students from Curtis, Juilliard, Peabody, Yale, and other American institutions, students from music schools in Austria, Bulgaria, Denmark, Great Britain, Hong Kong, Korea, and Romania were accepted. The Conservatoire became more international in flavor as ideas about repertoire, technique, and interpretation were exchanged among students and faculty. With a broadened base of student recruitment, there came new venues in which the Conservatoire could become known as a premier summer academy for talented performers and composers. The inclusion of students from Eastern Europe and Asia assured that for the first time those countries would begin to feel the impact of Conservatoire Américain–trained musicians as their students returned from France to pursue highly visible careers as soloists, chamber musicians, orchestral principals, and composers. Conservatoire students of the Marty era became noted recording artists and performers around the world, surpassing the geographical spread of previous regimes at the school.

New funding meant new and bigger student prizes for performance and composition, and students eagerly worked to earn these awards at the end of each session. Cash prizes were awarded to students in several categories, changing to suit each session's range of concerts. The summer's best chamber music performance received such an award, the creator of the best new composition was given the Ravel Prize, and a prize for the best performance of a new work by a Fontainebleau composer was awarded to the interpreters of that work.

In order to further promote the Conservatoire in its local confines, contacts with the Jacques Durand estate in Avon, Bel-Ebat, which had diminished over time, were renewed, and the school began holding its end-of-summer prize-giving ceremony and concert there. Before he stepped down from his post as president in 1991, which was subsequently filled by Count de Moustier, François Valéry lauded Marty's efforts, praising the amount of work he did, the fund-raising he had accomplished, and his determination to improve the Conservatoire Américain. The local press was pleased to see the resurgence of the school, and regularly sent critics to cover the concerts in the Jeu de Paume, Salle des Colonnes, and at Bel-Ebat.

As the school stabilized and financial support returned to the Conservatoire, Marty began to sever more brutally its ties with the past. In an article in the local Fontainebleau paper, he explained that he wanted to continue the traditions of Boulanger while establishing new standards and a new identity.[6] However, some saw his outlook as spiteful and destructive of Boulanger's legacy. "He did his interview with [the paper] about visions as a new director," recalls Emile Naoumoff, "and in this article, 1987, he mentioned that Nadia Boulanger was not the great teacher that people spoke about; he had to show himself by destroying his idol."[7]

Marty explains his views of Boulanger in less psychologically fraught terms:

> I owe an immense amount to her and have always held her in great respect and affection. Yet, I am firmly convinced that, if her lessons were priceless to hundreds, her tenure as Director did not profit the school in the long run, since she managed to have herself identified with it. To this day, many people still think that without Nadia Boulanger the School was doomed, whereas I believe the opposite is true (and I am not the only one to think so).[8]

As previously discussed, much evidence suggests that while Marty's observation was difficult for Boulanger's advocates to hear, it was a correct assessment of the situation, especially as it existed toward the end of Boulanger's life. However, this view, about which Marty made no secret, upset those for whom Fontainebleau was Boulanger, and vice versa. A large and well-connected group of alumni were perfectly willing to gloss over or altogether deny Boulanger's flaws in order to preserve a rose-colored vision of how the school had been at some distant, mythical time. Conflict between the two was inevitable.

Marty's vigorous approach to running the Conservatoire Américain, despite his success in creating a stronger financial base and recruiting an excellent faculty and strong student body, gradually became unacceptable to the Alumni Association. Their members felt increasingly isolated from the actions Marty was taking, and perhaps resented his independence in taking control of Conservatoire matters without the consultation or dialogue Bonet's administration had pursued with them. On the other side of the Atlantic, the French were also unhappy, but not with Marty. The Conseil d'Administration meeting of June 1992 found general dissatisfaction with what they saw as the weaknesses of the American committee, and envisioned the possibility of a break with it. Their disappointment in the cooperation—or rather the lack thereof—of the New York–based organizations was tremendous. Not realizing that Marty's own personality and methods might have precipitated some of the friction, the Conseil placed the entire blame for the situation on the Alumni Association. In contrast, Marty, with his ability to bring in corporate funding and with his positive relationship with Fontainebleau's mayor, Juliette Bebe, was viewed by the Conseil as a savior for the Conservatoire. Its members were especially impressed by the way Marty had successfully lobbied the Ministry of Culture for more than eighty thousand dollars in 1988, a miraculous sum.[9] Seeing hope for school's future, members of the Conseil began to take the kind of proprietary interest in the Conservatoire Américain that some earlier members had: they were tired of having foreigners dictate their business to them. An internal memo written by Valéry before his resignation contains the essence of the problem: "we have never had to accede to the demands of the American committee," he wrote, not entirely accurately. He continued with his condemnation of the Alumni Association's work:

> Considering the prestige of Fontainebleau, its place in the history of American music, the number of alumni who hold faculty positions in a number of important universities or colleges in the United States, the active support given to us by Leonard Bernstein, the aid we got this year, for the first time in history, from private sources, it seems to me difficult to believe that an effort could not be made on the other side of the Atlantic, to match what we have been able to do over here.[10]

The climate of friendship and goodwill between the Conseil d'Administration and the American Alumni Association was cooling at a rapid rate, with no reconciliation in sight. Neither organization wanted to be in the wrong; neither could find the diplomacy needed to stop the spreading rift.

In New York, the Alumni Association began receiving complaints about Marty's teaching and administrative style. While some students certainly were disappointed or hurt by Marty's blunt style, few comments were as vit-riolic as those in letters castigating Boulanger just two decades earlier. Active members and officers were offended by Marty's drive to create an institution independent of Boulanger's shadow. They viewed the French Conseil as na-tionalistic and anti-American, and were outraged when Emile Naoumoff de-cided to leave the Conservatoire. This event was a final straw for many alumni, who saw Naoumoff as the last link to the Boulanger regime and could not imagine a Conservatoire Américain without him and his legacy continuing the traditions established from the 1950s.

Naoumoff had been teaching almost every subject offered—a Fontainebleau jack-of-all-trades, and well qualified to be so—when Marty arrived to take over the directorship from Bonet. Naoumoff remembers that,

> When Marty came, I realized that something evil was happening, because Marty took me aside and he told me, "I would like you to help me run this place; show me the tricks." I told him, "I did this for Narcis [Bonet]," besides, I said, "there are no tricks to this place; this place is to be reinvented," and he looked at me like I dare speak to him [in such a way]. He spoke so meanly to me about Bonet . . . that I didn't want to collaborate with somebody like this. I felt like, I'm not going to be the toy of somebody. I was willing to do a little bit of that [working for the school] when I was eighteen for Bonet after Nadia because in a way I felt like it was the [right thing] . . . I thought that in these years had passed; we had to do something else or close. That's my point of view and that's why I left.[11]

The Fontainebleau press mourned the loss of Naoumoff, who had come to represent the Conservatoire Américain's last days of Boulanger glory. *La République de Seine-et-Marne* reported that "Les Naoumoffmaniaques" deeply regretted the loss of Boulanger's "enfant cheri" and hoped for his return.[12]

The Alumni Association was deeply wounded: Naoumoff was their child prodigy, the little boy they had all seen grow up. His departure from Fontaine-bleau and apparent mistreatment by Marty, along with the student complaints about Marty's sometimes harsh critiques and a general sense of unease among the Americans about the situation at the school, sparked an investigation into the conditions there. In 1992, newly elected Alumni Association President Debra Takakjian, a piano student of 1978, visited Fontainebleau as an admin-istrative official for the purpose of evaluating Marty's directorship, the quality of students and classes, and overall operations.

Takakjian's report appeared in the April 1993 *Alumni Bulletin*, and it is clear that the Alumni Association not only wanted to retain a mythologized sense of Boulanger in perpetuity, but that it also felt the loss of power to Marty very strongly:

> The Conservatoire and Beaux-Arts Schools no longer utilize the Fontainebleau Fine Arts and Music Schools Association, Inc. (the American representatives of the school since its inception). Recruiting and processing of applications for the students are now being done by the directors of each program or through their own conduits. In addition, many of our beloved faculty of the music program have either been asked to leave or have not been invited back despite their many years of service to the Conservatoire. Many long-time patrons of the schools have stopped supporting the schools including the Fontainebleau Fine Arts and Music Schools Association, Inc., Mannes College of Music, and Les Amis de Fontainebleau, to name a few.
>
> Over the past few years, the Alumni Association has received letters and phone calls from dissatisfied students who attended the Conservatoire. Their complaints have ranged from disorganization of the program to the low caliber of the faculty, to problems with the director.
>
> In an effort to address these issues, I wrote many letters and traveled to Fontainebleau this past summer to personally meet with and discuss various issues with school officials and the directors. I am sad to say that, although most people acknowledged the above-mentioned problems, much has not changed.
>
> These issues were discussed at length at the Alumni Association's 1991 and 1992 annual meetings. It was generally agreed that the music program no longer reflects the standards and influence of Nadia Boulanger. Therefore, the Alumni Association voted *not* to give a scholarship for the 1993 session.[13]

A schism had opened. The American officers would no longer provide funding for the Conservatoire. Their fund-raising activities and grants received would go instead toward the support of the Beaux-Arts school until their problems with the music school were settled. For Takakjian, resolution would come only with Marty's resignation.

The French board was furious. Marty and Jolas immediately wrote letters refuting Takakjian's claims. Marty's response was pointed and personal. He argued that Takakjian's stay in Fontainebleau was not of sufficient length, nor did she make the kind of effort necessary there to make a thorough evaluation. "Now for what she did not say," his rebuttal began.

> She did not say that my acquaintance with Fontainebleau dates back from the fifties on Mademoiselle Boulanger's invitation when I had already been her student for several years. She did not say that mine was one of the three names considered to succeed her in 1979. She did not say that I was called by the

Board of Trustees in 1986 to save what was then a dying institution. She did not say that I was reelected in 1989 and again in 1992 on the basis of my record. She did not say that, in recognition of its role in developing international cultural links on a high level, the American Conservatory was recently granted by the French Ministry of Foreign Affairs important subsidies in a gesture without precedent since before the war. She did not say that her classmate of 1978, Joe Kerr, who was the executive secretary of the 1992 session as my closest associate, resigned last year in protest from his position as Editor of the Alumni Bulletin and that he will join me again for the success of 1993. She did not say that last September she had sent an ultimatum to our Chairman demanding my dismissal. She did not say that she had received from M. de Moustier the kind of reply she deserved together with a letter from me withdrawing recognition of the Alumni Association under the circumstances and until further notice. [. . .] Finally, she did not say what is the most important. That she is not a professional musician, but a lawyer. And this explains a lot. I have had in the past dissentions with Officers of the Alumni Association. But I know that none of these fine professional musicians would ever have made this kind of public statement at the risk of gravely undermining the future of this venerable and admirable institution, the Conservatoire Américain de Fontainebleau.[14]

Marty was correct on all of the factual points he addressed, and the Conseil and faculty agreed with him on the rest. Indeed, Betsy Jolas's letter to Takakjian was scarcely less scathing:

"It was generally agreed that the music program no longer reflects the standards and influence of Nadia Boulanger." This so-called "general agreement" is particularly shocking because it is absolutely false. [. . .] If there is anyone who has consistently kept in mind the high, severe, rigorous standards that were Nadia Boulanger's, it is the present director, Jean-Pierre Marty. [. . .] But the Music School should certainly not become a sort of Frenchified Country Club for non-professionals, gifted or not, who are looking for an excuse to go abroad!

Instead of making things difficult, an alumni association, to justify its existence, should do all it can to help the institution in question.[15]

Jolas's letter played on the fears and doubts of earlier eras of the Conservatoire Américain, when rigorous standards were threatened and not infrequently abandoned for some students in order to attract the monetarily supportive but musically untalented. Was this the kind of past policy the Alumni Association wanted to re-create? Was Boulanger, after all, a figure to be idolized without dissent? Jolas's concern at the time may have been an ugly personal jibe at Takakjian, who had chosen to go into law rather than pursue a professional music career, but was nonetheless extremely prescient: without a certain kind of leadership, the student body could well come to resemble in some aspects her dreaded "country club."

The town of Fontainebleau supported Marty. Its mayor, Juliette Bebe, gave an interview to *La République de Seine-et-Marne* in January of 1993, titled "Fontainebleau, future new Salzburg?" In the article, Bebe stressed her commitment to the arts in Fontainebleau and her desire to see it become an international artistic center through its hosting of both the Conservatoire and the ProQuartet project at the Palais.[16] Once ambivalent or even vaguely hostile toward the music school, the town now placed itself strongly in favor of the continuation of the school under Marty's direction, a welcome piece of propaganda for the beleaguered administration.

Despite its inelegant forcing of the leadership issue, the Alumni Association was not entirely wrong in its assessment of at least one aspect of the situation at the Conservatoire. Its officers and members may have carried a grudge due to their loss of control of the American operations, but it was far more difficult to dismiss so easily the Conservatoire students' criticisms of Marty. Student feedback forms were distributed at the end of each session and the anonymous comments were forwarded to the French offices. Initially, the student response to Marty was mostly positive. However, by 1990, that enthusiasm was significantly diminished. For a number of students "studying with Mr. Marty" was a highlight of the summer, but the majority of his charges in 1992 and 1993 were unhappy with his approach and temperament. "He destroys students and pieces," wrote one. "Jean-Pierre Marty has a lot of knowledge about music," conceded another, "but I hate to say that his mannerism, his attitude, and communication skills *must* be improved. The way he treats students (especially pianists) is completely unprofessional." One student's entire evaluation form was given over to condemnation of Marty:

> The teaching style of Jean-Pierre Marty impedes learning. He is knowledgeable, but absolutely unaware of the students as humans. If a student is convinced that he is bad, he will learn nothing, perform poorly, and probably quit. Is that the aim of teaching of Jean-Pierre Marty? I hope not. Although his behavior at the dress rehearsal indicated that it is. Respect for other humans must be the basis of all inter-human activities and Jean-Pierre Marty demonstrates none.[17]

The schism that had opened between the American and French councils and administrators now gaped even more widely. The American Alumni

Association, in giving its funding entirely to the Beaux-Arts division, placed a strain on the relations between Marty and the Beaux-Arts administrators, who after all, shared space in the Henri IV wing. Marty cut off all communication with the American offices; the Americans howled for Marty's resignation; the French supported their countryman.

Such an impasse could not last. The session of 1993 opened with the usual pomp and splendor, and Count de Moustier invited all of the students to his home for a banquet. Concerts were well attended, and although the Alumni Association had withheld money from the Conservatoire, several students attended on full and partial scholarships. Throughout the summer, however, Marty became more and more appalled by the machinations of the American council. At the end of the session, Marty wrote a letter to the students protesting the "slander" of Takakjian and withdrawing the participation of the music students from the final celebration, in which they were to have performed to accompany a slide show by the Beaux-Arts students.[18] For many of the students who had found fault with Marty's teaching style, this act— essentially a punishment of the students for actions outside of their control and, in many cases, their knowledge—was typically harsh and severe.

The mood at the final party that year was subdued. Students and a number of administrators felt that the end of the Conservatoire Américain had arrived, and many left thinking that its final year had come and gone. Instead of a grand fête, a buffet dinner was served in the Henri IV courtyard, and after a silent presentation of slides by the Beaux-Arts students, the music students drifted off to the Hôtel d'Albe to pack and make farewells.

Though he had seemed willing to fight for his position and the continuation of the Conservatoire, Marty's disgust with the American officers overwhelmed his desire to stay on following the session. Perhaps also fearing that the French Conseil would turn on him in light of the students' dissatisfaction, Marty preempted any termination of his position by leaving the post before he could be removed. He sent his resignation letter to de Moustier on August 12, 1993, four days before the official end of the session.

The Alumni Association, which had pushed so hard for Marty's removal, suddenly found itself in charge of a rapidly collapsing organization. Despite his many plans and actual accomplishments, such as securing funding, opening the school to non-American students, and improving some rooms of the Henri IV quarter for teaching locations, Marty had not created the Conservatoire he had set out to form. The school was not ready to open as a year-round institution, and an association with the ProQuartet center—itself still in its planning stages—was still hypothetical. The students' living quarters had not been improved, and practice rooms still lacked any kind of acoustically improved facilities. The school had not moved back into the Louis XV wing, and the Napoleon theater, held up by Marty and his associates as a symbol of the new Conservatoire, remained locked, its glory shrouded in drop-cloths. Upon Marty's resignation, de Moustier and Galitzine, Marty's aristocratic and corporate contacts, vacated their posts on the Conseil d'Administration as well. The Conservatoire was suddenly without the fund-raising powers and society connections it relied on so heavily. The Americans had accomplished what they wanted, but, like Boulanger, had made no preparations for the future.

Notes

1. Charles Kaufman, letter to author, undated October 2001, possession of author.
2. Kaufman, letter to author.
3. Roughly five million American dollars at the time.
4. Document of Jean-Pierre Marty, undated 1990s, CA/F.
5. Jean-Pierre Marty, statement on the 1990 session, undated 1990, CA/F.
6. *La République de Seine-et-Marne*, July 13, 1992, CA/F.
7. Emile Naoumoff, interview with author, October 14, 2000, possession of author.
8. Jean-Pierre Marty, letter to author, November 4, 1998, possession of author.
9. Letter, François Valéry to (first name unknown) Triggle, undated September 1988, CA/F.
10. Letter, François Valéry to (first name unknown) Triggle, undated September 1988, CA/F.
11. Naoumoff, interview.
12. *La République de Seine-et-Marne*, 13 July 1992, CA/F.
13. *Fontainebleau Alumni Bulletin*, April 1993.
14. Jean-Pierre Marty, letter to the American Council, undated 1992, CA/F.
15. Letter, Betsy Jolas to Debra Takakjian, undated 1992–1993, CA/F.
16. *La République de Seine-et-Marne*, 23 January 1993, CA/F.
17. Anonymous student evaluations, undated 1992–1993, CA/F.
18. Letter, Jean-Pierre Marty to students, August 1992, CA/F.

PART V

THE FROG RODEO

CHAPTER TWELVE

~

"The Frog Rodeo" (1994–present)

"This is the beginning of the frog rodeo."—anonymous administrator on the beginning of a new session[1]

When Jean-Pierre Marty left the Conservatoire Américain, he did so with a vengeance. The French and American councils were horrified to find that in his final summer as director, Marty had spent extravagantly, paying premium fees to guest artists and faculty members. The cumulative losses for the school were over a million and a half francs. It was suggested that Marty had intended the closure of the school, using these final, lavish expenditures as a method of forcing it to an end. "It was almost as if he said, 'If this is the end, let's have a big blowout," said one observer of Marty's final year as director.[2] Not surprisingly, the school's bank and investors were shocked by the deficit that the Conservatoire had incurred, and the Conseil d'Administration struggled to find a way to restructure its finances and stay open.

Factions disagreed as to what course of action to take. Betsy Jolas lamented the departure of Marty and pressed the Conseil to make plans for a 1994 session regardless of the lack of an elected director, while Conseil President de Moustier refused to entertain the idea of opening the school under the direction of a temporary leader or a committee. Candidates for the position of director were not as numerous as the Conseil might have expected. Charles Kaufman proposed Emile Naoumoff to de Moustier, who replied positively that despite the requirement that the director be French he "would certainly be happy and interested to meet with him, an alum of

155

the school and an eminent pianist."[3] Unfortunately for the Conservatoire, Naoumoff found no appeal in the prospect. "I'm not personally interested in a career in Fontainebleau," he said. "There is no clear vision for what I can bring there; there is no point for me to go back." Instead of trying to patch together an institution where he had been both student and faculty, celebrated and mistreated, Naoumoff created his own summer academy at Gargenville, the one-time summer home of the Boulangers. "I needed a geographical place where I could all sort of eventually connect [my students] to Boulanger; because of the symbolism of the place, Fontainebleau being one, Gargenville being the other. I just couldn't go to Fontainebleau and see what is happening; I can't walk in this place without [seeing] ghosts."[4] He had his own ideas of who should take over the Conservatoire Américain: "I don't understand why the damn council didn't give [Madame Casadesus] the directorship right away."[5] Casadesus certainly had the experience and ability to take on the job, but instead of being tapped to take up the position, she was asked by the Conseil to choose and recruit a new director.[6] In her more than seventy years, she had seen the Conservatoire through the Second World War, abandoned it in her grief over her daughter's illness there, returned to see Boulanger's rise and reputation grow, and witnessed the chaos brought on by her choices following Boulanger's death. Despite her vast knowledge of the school and its workings, Casadesus was seen by some within the administration as only a useful figurehead, representing the Conservatoire's long history rather than serving an important role in its present and future. According to Conservatoire intimates, she was guided into approving financial actions that were not to the benefit of the school, and her selection of Marty was based partially on her dealings with him as a young man and not with the adult he had become.[7]

Following Marty's resignation, Casadesus was among the first consulted. Her choice of candidate for the school's new director was Philippe Entremont, a former student and now an established pianist and conductor. Casadesus was supported in her decision by Betsy Jolas: together they believed that Entremont, with his experience in leading large organizations and his multitude of contacts in France, would be able to help the Conservatoire to its feet. He accepted the position of director late in 1993, agreeing to begin with the 1995 session, and in January, *La République de Seine-et-Marne* reported on the state of the beleaguered school.

"Will the Écoles d'Art Américaines be forced to suspend operations?" asked the paper. The article outlined the history of the school and then launched into a detailing of the current state of affairs: director Jean-Pierre Marty had been forced to resign, it reported, and the Palais de Fontainebleau was no longer as welcoming as it once had been. The Quartier Henri IV was no longer housing the school, said *La République*, implying that if the chateau was no longer interested in hosting the Conservatoire, then the end was near indeed. Supposedly the school's wing in the "Kitchen Quarter" was closed for the 1994–1995 year while repairs were made, and the Écoles d'Art Américaines would be allowed to resume their residences soon, but other issues complicating the matter soon arose. De Moustier had died and a replacement had not been named as president, weakening the school's position to lobby the Palais administrators and the French government for support. The Conservatoire had entered into an agreement to sell its historic restaurant, site of student concerts and bonhomie, but the proceedings had become enmeshed in legal complications. *La République* further explained that the school carried an enormous deficit, and despite the appointment of Entremont, sponsors and investors were nowhere to be found. Finally, where would students come from? Everyone knew, reported the paper, the Conservatoire Américain was washed up, a mockery of what it once was.[8]

As confrontational and challenging as the tone of the article was, its anonymous author was correct in many cases: the Conservatoire Américain had major problems and appeared to lack the resources necessary to do anything about them. When the Conseil met in January 1994, its main purpose was to inform Entremont of the possibly insurmountable plight of the Conservatoire Américain. The Conseil hoped to resume ties with the New York–based Alumni Association and ask it to restore its role in student recruitment and financial support. Entremont, while endorsing this plan, cautioned against suggestions that the Conservatoire return to its ties with the Mannes School of Music, saying without further explanation that it "doesn't have sufficient qualities," to partner with the Conservatoire. Although he later sought an engagement to conduct the school's orchestra and personally recruited for the Conservatoire at Mannes, Entremont was opposed to returning the school to its status as a Mannes-controlled program. His reasons for this are not clear, but since he offered for consideration potential reciprocal agreements with Indiana University at Bloomington, Yale University, the Curtis Institute, the Juilliard School, the Peabody Conservatory of Music, and other major conservatories and universities, it is likely that he saw the need for the stability and administrative acumen an American school could bring to the Conservatoire, but wanted to avoid any partnerships that could bring with them past entanglements and issues. Despite Entremont's proposals, none of these institutions ultimately accepted his proposals, likely due to the school's financial unsteadiness and lack of solid plans for retrenchment and operations.[9]

To speak to these issues and hoping to dispel the rumors of the Conservatoire's end, the Conseil met again in March 1994 with firmer resolve. The budget was revised to reflect the disastrous state of finances left by Marty, and Casadesus and Jolas divided up the responsibility of hiring a faculty and organizing a session for the coming summer.[10] However, the Conseil and its subcommittees still overlooked a major element in repositioning the school: there was no mention made of its current mission. It is unclear exactly what the Conseil was trying to accomplish. Not one member addressed the question of the purpose of the Conservatoire Américain. Of all of the musicians present, none spoke of the school's musical goals, the kinds of instruction it wanted to offer, the repertoire it wanted to teach, or the kinds of students it hoped to attract. The focus was so much on survival that the very reasons for surviving were completely disregarded.

A month later, when the Conseil met again, the logistical planning of the Conservatoire had been strengthened somewhat, although it remained concentrated on simply opening the doors for the sake of proving its continued existence. Between ten and fifteen students had committed to attend a two-week session for pianists and composers only, several returning from the disastrous 1993 session. Casadesus and Jolas would serve as the primary faculty, and Entremont would make whatever appearances he could in accordance with his performance schedule. Kerr was coaxed into reprising his role as general secretary and coordinator. Yamaha offered two grand pianos to Entremont for the session, and the school arranged to rent nine uprights. The conservator of the Palais assured the Conservatoire of its claim on the Henri IV wing and cleared the way for the school's continued use of the Jeu de Paume as a concert venue.[11] The financial situation remained bleak, however, and letters from the American board of trustees indicate that the group was at an almost total loss about funding sources.[12] Scant publicity about the continuation of the Conservatoire was circulated. Few alumni, and even fewer potential students, realized that the school was continuing to function even in a limited way.

The Alumni Association, though, was heartened by the turn of events, which it saw as the ideal situation and vehicle for a rapprochement with the Conseil, and with some grandeur it announced "with great pleasure" that it was giving five thousand dollars each to the Conservatoire Américain and the École des Beaux-Arts as part of what it called a "recapitalization fund." Alumni Association President Debra Takakjian planned a trip to the school during its two weeks of operation to make a show of support and to meet de Moustier's successor, former Ambassador to the United States Pierre Boyer.[13]

The 1994 session opened with seventeen students from the United States, Western Europe, and Asia in attendance. Solfège professor Isabelle Duha returned to teach and perform, and Gaby Casadesus's protégé, Philippe Bianconi, agreed to teach piano, increasing the small faculty to five. Entremont brought students of his own, including his assistant Xu-Zhong, with whom he performed in a duo-piano concert of French music, offering at least a small nod to the school's original intentions of promoting the literature of its native country. At Gaby Casadesus's solo concert in the Jeu de Paume, Takakjian ceremoniously presented checks from the Alumni Association to the school, symbolizing the formal return of relations between the Americans and the French.[14]

For the first time, however, the session of the Conservatoire Américain resembled a festival rather than a true summer academy. In previous years, during the months before leaving for France, students had been provided with a list of possible repertoire to bring and be ready to prepare on site. Most works were then assembled in chamber music groups or as partnerships at the Palais, and this had been part of the students' education: one of the skills students would take home with them was to be able to prepare a complete work for performance in a short time with an unfamiliar group or accompanist. By learning a piece at Fontainebleau, they would study the work with French coaches, gaining exposure to French interpretive tastes and methods. With the session shortened to a scant two weeks, this approach to preparing material for concerts hardly seemed reasonable or practical. Pianists brought music already completely learned with them, and, in some cases, had been performing the works they brought for some time prior to attending the Conservatoire. Hoping to secure a performance by a colleague, composers likewise brought completed scores, knowing that works begun or partially completed at the Conservatoire Américain would stand little chance of being heard on a student concert because of the time constraints. This departure from the preparation methods of the past gave the Conservatoire the aura of a concert series as opposed to a true learning experience.

The faculty did not discourage the students' tactics in this area. In fact, with the residence terms of faculty members and of the director himself so truncated, there would be little time to assist any student first learning a piece. Lessons would take on a more master class–like approach, in that professors expected to hear not works in progress, but pieces ready or nearly ready for performance. Only in terms of repertoire were students asked to keep with the Conservatoire's traditions, and were encouraged to bring predominantly French repertoire of the early twentieth century: Debussy and Ravel again topped the bills at student concerts.

When the small band of students and faculty departed from Fontainebleau after the two-week session in 1994, the Conseil d'Administration met again. Although the session was brief, the overall quality of students was judged to be high, and public attendance at the concerts had been good. A concrete plan to open for three weeks the following summer was made, with courses in piano, solfège, theory, composition, violin, cello, chamber music, and a course in conducting, using a chamber orchestra, much as Marty had done, which would be taught by Entremont. Gaby Casadesus's daughter, Thérèse Casadesus Rawson, would teach French-language classes. In order to boost alumni giving and awareness, Takakjian organized an "Alumni Week" as part of the publicity campaign the Conservatoire Américain would have to undertake.[15] When the Conseil met again later in the year, though, Entremont suggested radical cuts to this plan, aimed at keeping costs low. He proposed that separate classes and lessons for the string players be discontinued, but that they take part in chamber music coaching and participate in a chamber orchestra directed by him. This idea was met with considerable resistance. Students expected lessons, and the prospect of working individually with the Conservatoire's faculty members was a strong drawing point for attendees. Although it meant higher costs because of a larger faculty, the plan did not take hold, and private lessons remained part of the curriculum. Despite the failure of his plan, the episode illustrates Entremont's philosophy concerning the school: to keep it lean and easy to manage, and ultimately, to create a system in which the director did not need to directly oversee its operations.

At the time of his appointment as director of the Conservatoire Américain, Entremont was a known figure in French and American musical communities. Born in 1934 into a pianistic family—both parents were professional musicians—he had studied at the Paris Conservatoire, where he was the recipient of the *Premier Prix* in solfège, chamber music, and piano before the age of fifteen. After beginning his career as a soloist and chamber musician, Entremont turned to conducting, becoming the director of the Vienna Chamber Orchestra, the New Orleans Philharmonic, and the Colonne Orchestra of Paris. While some thought he "should stick with the piano,"[16] he nonetheless had made a reputation as a conductor. Within the structures of the Conservatoire Américain, Entremont would be a very hands-off administrator, primarily pursuing his own performance interests as a soloist, chamber musician, and conductor while making sure that he was present in Fontainebleau enough to attract enough students to the piano program and to field a chamber orchestra for his once- or twice-a-session appearance at its helm.

Having Entremont's name connected to the Conservatoire should have been a boon for the struggling school. Following Entremont's installation, though, the Conservatoire approached recruitment very poorly. Rather than launching an advertising campaign in order to promote what it felt was a new era for the school, the combined forces of the Alumni Association and the American board—now known collectively as the Fontainebleau Associations, Inc.—decided that it was preferable for potential students to learn about the school from alumni and by word of mouth. Very little of the association's annual budget was allocated for publicity, and it sent no brochures, posters, or flyers to music schools or conservatories. This lack of visibility resulted in fewer applications than at almost any other point, but the school used this situation to aggressively recruit select students, who were then provided with not only full scholarships but also airfare to and from France in order to ensure their participation in the program.[17] Other students received half-scholarships to make their attendance more likely, and a cap of approximately forty students—a far cry from the 1980s or even the 1930s—was reestablished as a guideline for admissions. This number was arrived at by financial caveat: it would enable the Conservatoire to offer large but limited scholarships to its top applicants and would also allow for a small number of full-paying but less able students to help balance things out. On the artistic side, a student body of forty allowed for a small chamber orchestra of instrumentalists and a handful of pianists and composers. The number was manageable by a staff of two or three people, and could be accommodated by the local cafeterias and restaurants providing meals. Ultimately, the lack of a proactive publicity and recruitment policy helped define the school's scope in terms of students, staff, and basic budget.

As the Conservatoire's session expanded from two weeks in 1994 to four in 1996, the need for faculty increased as well. In addition to the piano and composition professors, a group of string teachers was hired. Unlike previous years, however, during which faculty members were present for the entire session, faculty members now were hired for periods of a week at a time, and few stayed for the entire session. The makeup of the faculty changed as well. While some professors still were recruited from the Paris Conservatoire, an increasing number came from outside of France. There was no uproar from the Conseil about this mixture of faculty nationalities, as there had been when Kaufman and Levin brought American professors from Mannes to the school; in fact, the school's brochures included language indicating that the Conservatoire Américain's stance on the nationality of its professors would reflect a post–Cold War broadening of national schools and approaches. In

this regard, finally, the school was making a decision that would help determine its raison d'être for the years ahead.

The decision to formally integrate non-French faculty was a significant
departure from Francis Casadesus's original intent, but was viewed by many
involved with the Conservatoire as a reasonable accommodation to the
changes the idea of musical nationality has undergone since the 1980s. For
many years, a player's style could be characterized by the nationality of his
educational locale: in cello performance, for example, one spoke of the Russian school, the Hungarian school, or the French school. With the softening
of borders and the increased ability of musicians to travel from the East to the
West, the delineation of schools became blurred, with a new, more general
school of playing taking over from the older, more stratified ones. By the end
of the century, the faculty roster of the Conservatoire Américain boasted
professors from not only France, but the Netherlands, Italy, China, and
America as well. For the 2000 session, the performance professoriate consisted of seven French and five non-French teachers.[18] Clearly the school had
decided that while it would promote French repertoire to its students, it
would no longer uphold the goal of teaching strictly French technique and
interpretation to American students.

Other changes were effected in the mid- and late-1990s involving student life and the Conservatoire's relationship with the town and the Palais.
The Barassy Hotel, first used to house the male students and later the
Beaux-Arts students, was leased to a language school. The Hôtel d'Albe,
the nexus of student life in Fontainebleau for seventy summers, was partitioned into two sections. The grand and opulent rooms on one side of the
hotel, which during Marty's term had been the women's primary housing,
were leased to the Fontainebleau tourism bureau. The massive wardrobes,
claw-foot bathtubs, and gilt mirrors were carted away as the building was
modernized with multiple telephone lines, beige carpet, and filing cabinets.
The Albe's garden and garden enclosure, home of countless Ping-Pong
games and parties, was now made off-limits to Conservatoire students. The
Conservatoire retained only the annex of the Hôtel d'Albe, a narrow wing
adjacent to the hotel proper that had served as the men's dormitory. It had
but two showers and a handful of rooms for seventeen students, sleeping
two and three to a room. Overflow housing was obtained at the dormitory
of INSEAD, the local business school, where students shared crowded but
slightly better-appointed suites containing small kitchen units and en suite
bathrooms. Socializing took place in local cafés and bars, and in the Albe's
garden, in its kitchen, and on its roof. Attempting to lighten the mood at
the Albe after the practice rooms officially closed at night, Joe Kerr posted

the notice that "No Romantic Repertoire after 10 p.m." would be tolerated in the hotel's salon. He frequently took over the salon, the cozy front room on the ground floor of the Albe, and commandeered its upright piano himself for hugely popular impromptu jazz sessions and sing-alongs with students after hours.[19]

At the Palais, the Conservator's survey of the Henri IV wing found structural and other damages too great to ignore, and just before Entremont's appointment as director, he informed the Conservatoire that it would be required to vacate its rooms there. Music stands and office furnishings were moved into storage at the Albe, and the music library, a considerable holding, was moved into a tiny garret in the François I wing of the Palais, above some unused meeting rooms and storage spaces. Rough bookcases were erected, and workmen filled the shelves with music without regard for organization. When the shelves were full, remaining scores, recordings, and reference books went onto the floor. Scores by Naoumoff, letters of Boulanger, and rare recordings and editions of music were jumbled together in cardboard boxes and stacks, along with some materials of the École des Beaux-Arts, which fared no better in their treatment. The space was clean and dry, but it was hardly ideal for the student or professor looking for a particular work. In fact, those trying to reach the library to search for materials often were prohibited to do so by Palais staff unwilling to let Conservatoire personnel enter the upper levels of the chateau.

The foothold that the Conservatoire had in the Palais was not entirely lost, although the removal of possessions from the Henri IV wing seemed a last straw to many. The school still was permitted to use the Jeu de Paume as a concert venue, and maintained the use of several large rooms on the bottom floor of the François I wing as classrooms. The Salle des Colonnes, which for several years had gone unused as a concert hall, was reopened for use by faculty members, and Entremont convinced Palais officials to consent to the use of the visually luxuriant Chapelle de la Trinité for chamber orchestra concerts. Obtaining the use of these halls was no small feat, and, given their historical and artistic importance, the Palais's concern over their use is understandable. The Chapelle de la Trinité is a masterwork of Renaissance painting and ornamentation. Stucco angels float over the altar, supporting royal crests. Above them, the barrel-vaulted ceiling is divided into sections by gilt-covered relief work and covered with oil-on-plaster paintings depicting biblical scenes. Acoustically, the Chapelle is suitable for the kind of small-orchestra performances Entremont was interested in giving, and it had room for twenty or so orchestral musicians, two pianos, and an audience capacity of approximately ninety.

The Salle des Colonnes had been used sporadically throughout the Conservatoire Américain's history, and had hosted great performances by faculty members and guest artists. The visual impact of the Salle was almost capable of impressing audiences into not noticing its atrocious, bathroom-like acoustics. Enormous columns of smoky marble support a carved ceiling from which hang dozens of crystal chandeliers. The view of all but the first two or three rows of seats is extremely restricted, but mirrors line the walls, providing interesting perspectives for watching the musicians at the front of the hall. Smaller than the Chapelle de la Trinité, the Salle des Colonnes became established as the venue for small-ensemble and solo recitals by guests and professors of the Conservatoire Américain.

Student concerts continued to be held in the Jeu de Paume, although the Conservatoire staff had to prepare the room by laying carpet and installing seats, because the Palais, sponsoring a revival of the early form of tennis played there, had restored the hall to its original athletic-club condition, complete with an office-cum-locker room and the accompanying lingering odor of sweat. Originally a stage had been erected each year at one end of the court, but with the Conseil seeking to keep costs low, the stage was discontinued and performances took place in the center of the room with temporary seating around three sides. Artists waiting to perform stood behind the walls of mesh netting that separated the observers' area from the court, an area that became known to Conservatoire Américain students as "the Bullpen." Acoustically somewhat dry and prone to reverberate with the nearby garden-dwelling peacocks' cat-like yowling noises, as well as those produced by the performers, the Jeu de Paume also did duty as the master-class room and as a studio for lessons and rehearsals, with time slots fiercely fought over by students and faculty alike.

Thus concert spaces were assured, and although the Conservator's office promised that the Henri IV wing was reserved for the schools, the return date of the Conservatoire and of the École des Beaux-Arts to the wing was repeatedly postponed. Classes usually held in its rooms were relocated to various places: a small salon in the Hôtel d'Albe became the classroom for solfège and composition lessons; a crude tent erected behind the hotel held a handful of students during daily French classes; master classes were heard in the Albe's garden room, granted for limited use to the faculty by the tourism bureau; instrumental lessons were given in a meeting room in the business school dormitory; and practice rooms for pianists were procured from the local music school, located a fair hike from the center of activity at the Albe and the Palais. Practicing was discouraged in the INSEAD dormitory and in the Albe, but with the only other practice rooms located a

mile away, scales, Brahms, and Fauré could be heard on the Rue Royale regardless. This dispersal of students and practice rooms across the town less-
ened the school's previous tightly knit environment, and students looked for
space wherever they could find it, including local bars and hotel and dormitory recreation rooms. Scheduling practice time was an exercise in frustration; students vied for time and were required to request times on a daily
basis, rather than over the long term.

With the loss of the school's restaurant in legal and real estate complications, Conservatoire students took meals at a local restaurant several nights
a week and on other nights were given cash to eat on their own. The restaurant's staff and managers always seemed surprised to have fifty hungry music
and fine-arts students appear each evening, and dinners often lasted hours
while the cooks scrambled to feed the often impatiently waiting students.
Perhaps more important, the loss of the restaurant also meant the loss of the
informal concerts that had occurred there. Although General Secretary Joe
Kerr often entertained students at the piano in the salon of the Hôtel d'Albe
in the evenings, and other students gathered together occasionally to sight-
read, the camaraderie and professional growth provided for by the restaurant
concerts was gone forever.

The never-ending parade of classes, concerts, and official social events
that distinguished the earlier generations of Conservatoire student life was
more subdued in the school's latest incarnation. Demands on the students'
time were less stringent than in previous years. Chorus and solfège classes for
instrumentalists were optional rather than obligatory, and no one seemed to
mind if a student missed attending a concert or two. Students of the 1990s'
Conservatoire Américain returned home with none of the memories of the
social whirl that their predecessors had: there were no longer any costume
balls, no elaborately planned fêtes, no grand dinners. Students took advantage of the relaxed attendance attitudes, seemingly endorsed by the staff, and
took trips to Holland, Spain, and other countries, often without clearing
their absences with their teachers or, to its dismay, the administration. The
administration seemed incapable of setting forth rules and expectations for
students, and was inconsistent in its messages to the faculty about handling
problems, but it was quick to discipline when it deemed necessary. As a result, some students came and went without comment, but others' involvement with school activities and concerts was so notably lax that they returned from excursions to find that their scholarships had been cut and their
performances canceled.[20]

Elsie Watson, having seen fifty years of Conservatoire triumphs and
foibles, was not impressed by the new administration or by the students it

drew. "It's low class," she pronounced. The Conservatoire "had grandeur at one time and it went through M. Marty." No one knew what the school was about anymore, she said; the students treated it like just another festival in a string of such events they would attend in a single summer, hopping from full scholarship to full scholarship without any sense of commitment; the administration was disgraceful in its lack of organizational abilities and common sense.[21]

Watson's analysis of the students' attitudes was, in fact, fairly accurate; many went from Fontainebleau to other festivals, viewing their four weeks in France as just another stop on their summer program tour. Others saw the Conservatoire as a casual and relaxed program with few real obligations to meet. Yet another part of the problem was the composition of the student body: a number of nonprofessional amateurs and semiprofessional musicians were admitted to the program beginning with Entremont's tenure. Some, in the manner of returning alumni from days past, had attended the Conservatoire as young and eager artists and returned now for refresher courses and lessons. Others attended for the first time, combining playing with vacationing. Owing to this influx of "students" who attended for the first time as middle-aged adults and treated their time in Fontainebleau like a holiday with musical performances mixed in, Watson and other observers familiar with the school believed that the school had become what Betsy Jolas feared: a French country club for nonprofessionals more interested in spending time abroad than in serious work.

The younger and more sincere students also resented this policy that allowed less earnest participants to take up, as they saw it, valuable lesson, master-class, and performance time. The problem, compounded by the limited amount of time that professors spent at the school, caused intense dissatisfaction on the part of students preparing for recitals, auditions, and other important events. However, the frustrations of these students could not be expressed adequately to the administration, because some of the staff members themselves were part of the cadre of nonprofessional students. From an administrative point of view, there was no problem. Most attendees paid full tuition and often contributed in other ways as well, covering piano rentals, offering transportation in rented cars to faculty and administration members, and paying for guest artist dinners. This made their attendance very attractive to the administration.

Even more distracting and disturbing for faculty, students, and staff than the uneven mix of students was the distant position taken by Entremont after his initial plunge into directing the Conservatoire. With a busy year-round performance schedule, Entremont's residences in Fontainebleau often lasted less than a week. The director often appeared in town, stationed himself at the local five-star hotel, the Aigle Noir, gave a few classes, a concert, and just as abruptly departed. To many students and even some staff he was brusque and intimidating. Pianist Jessie Fillerup later wrote of her experiences with Entremont that, "I played for him in one master class and watched him dismantle the performances and egos of my colleagues on numerous occasions." Perhaps, she commented, "being blessed with a prodigious technique, he found it unfathomable that mere mortals like us could struggle with passages that he could dash off in his sleep. It was unfortunate for us that Entremont could never overcome his own self-importance to share with us some of the wisdom of his remarkable French pedigree."[22]

Entremont's installment did restore some semblance of normalcy to the Conservatoire, and although he was not as present as previous directors, he enabled the full-time staff to act in his absence. Office staff ran the day-to-day operations, and students, while finding the undertaking confused and disorganized, rarely went without basic needs or information for very long. However, the school had certainly lost some of its shine; its veneer of elegance was gone. "I think the school office in the squalor of the Albe annex is a disgrace," wrote Elsie Watson, who remembered the time when the director lived in the Palais, and the administrators worked there among the fine and decorative arts that were the pride of France.[23] Gaby Casadesus was alone an embodiment of the earlier Conservatoire Américain: stately and dignified in her nineties, she returned each July to give lessons and master classes in the Jeu de Paume, impeccably dressed, communicating priceless gifts to her students in words and music.

Yet all good things must end. In October 1999, after teaching all summer at Fontainebleau, Gaby Casadesus died in Paris. She was the last of the original faculty of Francis Casadesus's "institution without precedent." Without her guidance, the school became property of the "Frog Rodeo," as some jokingly termed the chaotic group of Entremont's entourage, the French board, and the Americans caught up in trying to make it all work. The proof of the school's commitment to continuation would have to be determined in the following summers.

At the beginning of July 2000, as they had for nearly eighty years, Conservatoire students made the trip from the Gare de Lyon in Paris to the small train station in Fontainebleau-Avon. They were sorted in to quarters at the Hôtel d'Albe, which had been refurbished and modernized over the winter, and into dormitories and other hotels within walking distance of the Palais. Each student listed repertoire that he or she could perform on the first concert, seven days away. Introductions were made, classes and lessons began, and the restaurant continued to appear befuddled as to why large groups of hungry Americans appeared at the door each night. Few of those hungry Americans realized that the last link to the Conservatoire Américain's foundation no longer was present. Returning students and alumni feared for the future of the school without Gaby Casadesus. She had kept the school open during the Second World War, had pushed for the continuance of the Conservatoire as a full-fledged musical academy following Boulanger's death, and had insisted that the school remain in business after the resignation of Marty.

Gaby Casadesus had been just twenty when she began teaching in the Louis XV wing at the Palais de Fontainebleau, in a brand-new, experimental school run by her husband's uncle. She and the Conservatoire Américain had a long history, inextricably entwined. The last of the original faculty, Casadesus had been a strong voice on the Conseil d'Administration and a lobbyist for the Conservatoire. Without her determined authority, many wondered how the school would fare in the coming years.

Casadesus was honored on July 15, at a concert in the Chapelle de la Trinité featuring Philippe Bianconi, Isabelle Duha, and Philippe Entremont, accompanied by the chamber orchestra of the school. Bianconi and Duha performed two movements of Debussy's *Nocturnes* arranged by Ravel for two pianos, followed by Bianconi's presentation of Robert Casadesus's *Capriccio*, op. 49, for piano and strings. After intermission, the student orchestra, directed by Entremont from the piano, played Saint-Saëns's *Carnival of the Animals*, with faculty members taking the solo roles. Recordings of Casadesus and Bianconi performing two-piano and four-hands works were given to students as mementos of the occasion.

The works chosen for the recital had special significance to those who knew the Casadesus family. In the program, Entremont explained his choices: "The work by Debussy, transcribed for two pianos by Ravel, honors she who recorded and interpreted so many works for two pianos and four hands with her husband Robert." Robert's *Capriccio*, the director wrote, was one of his crowning efforts and represented Gaby's dedication to promoting his works. Finally, Entremont wrote, the *Carnival of the Animals* was chosen because it was a work recorded by Gaby Casadesus, Entremont, and the young Yo-Yo Ma, and it commemorated Saint-Saëns's presidency of the Conservatoire Américain at its opening in 1921.[24]

Another long-time figure was missing from the Fontainebleau scene that summer as well. Betsy Jolas resigned her post as a member of the Conseil d'Administration before the session began and took a leave of absence from her position on the faculty, spending the summer instead in Berlin. While Jolas had not accepted the directorship of the Conservatoire Américain, she had willingly served on the French board and had been a strong proponent of the school's interests. She had argued on Marty's behalf for strengthening the Conservatoire's program through the development of stronger funding, attracting better students from a global pool, and working with the town of Fontainebleau to implement the ProQuartet project, which would have brought public awareness and increased recognition of the Conservatoire. Well-known in Europe, her reputation had drawn composition students to Fontainebleau year after year. Her departure from the school's faculty roster meant a loss of knowledge, experience, prestige, and advocacy for the school.

The summer proceeded much like that of any summer festival, and few present understood the changes from years prior to this one. For a few, the changes were dramatic and evident, but for most, it was a peaceful and pleasant summer spent in a little French town. Students attended classes, or skipped them; faculty came to give lessons, or went away for their own concerts; choir was an informal sight-reading session; solfège lessons were optional; students went to Paris, to Spain, to Holland, and returned to play concerts or not, as they chose; practice rooms were parceled out a day at a time; lessons and rehearsals took place in dormitory foyers, hotel rooms, and in a single concert venue in the Palais; students attended faculty and student concerts as they chose; and received diplomas issued from a laser printer at the end of the four-week session. How the Conservatoire Améri-cain had changed, a few remarked, but the changes were indelible, and the institution without precedent had become just another summer camp, just another festival, just ordinary.

Notes

1. Anonymous Conservatoire administrative staff member, conversation with author, July 2001.

2. Anonymous Conservatoire administrative staff member, interview with author, July 2000, possession of author.

3. Letter, Jean-Charles de Moustier to Charles Kaufman, undated, CA/F.

4. Emile Naoumoff, interview with author, October 24, 2000, possession of author.

5. Naoumoff, interview.

6. Notes of the Conseil d'Administration, 23 November 1993, CA/F.

7. Naoumoff, interview.

8. La République de Seine-et-Marne, January 31, 1994, CA/F.

9. Notes of the Conseil d'Administration, March 1994, CA/F.

10. Notes of the Conseil d'Administration, March 1994, CA/F.

11. Notes of the Conseil d'Administration, April 1994, CA/F.

12. Letter, Norval White to Pierre Devinoy, May 1994, CA/F.

13. Fax, Debra Takakjian to Conseil d'Administration, undated May 1994, CA/F.

14. Notes of the Conseil d'Administration, June 1994, CA/F. Also Conservatoire Américain prospectus, 1994, CA/F.

15. Notes of the Conseil d'Administration, September 1994, CA/F.

16. Charles Kaufman, interview with author, March 24, 1999, possession of author.

17. Document of the Conservatoire Américain, undated 1996, CA/F.

18. www.fontainebleauschools.org, September 14, 2000.

19. Sign on salon door, Hôtel d'Albe, July 1999.

20. As occurred in 1999.

21. Elsie Watson, interviews and letters to author, various dates 1999–2001, possession of author.

22. Jessie Fillerup, unpublished essay, possession of author.

23. Letter, Elsie Watson to author, September 8, 2000, possession of author.

24. Philippe Entremont, concert program for July 15, 2000.

EPILOGUE

~

Nutrisco et Extinguo

Throughout the Palais de Fontainebleau, as the prologue notes, visitors can find etchings, sculptures, and embossings of the salamander, the emblem of Francis I, whose vision lifted the chateau from a rough-hewn hunting lodge to the monumental edifice it is today. Several meanings are tied to the salamander, among which are patience under suffering and fortitude. Also accompanying Francis's chosen animal familiar is his motto: *Nutrisco et Extinguo*— "I nourish and I extinguish." Early in its existence, the Conservatoire Américain adopted as its own symbol this creature: the salamander, always set under a crown of France and often shown curling around an F, has appeared on the Alumni Bulletin, letterheads, and diplomas. The *nutrisco* half of its accompanying motto always seemed appropriate for a school: the unique goal of the Conservatoire Américain was to provide French musical nourishment for American musicians. Indeed, the Conservatoire, like its royal symbol, has endured patience under suffering and shown great fortitude through its lifetime. Yet today its situation is precarious at best: its history is one of artistic achievements and cultural excitement, and while threads of this past remain, they are fleeting: a singular concert that rekindles memories of the young Casadesuses, an evening of informal performances, an individual experience in a lesson. As it struggles from year to year, the school steadily diminishes from its historic greatness and role as a significant institution of artistic learning. Other programs both in Europe and America garner higher respect, enjoy greater reputations, and train greater numbers of professional and preprofessional musicians: Salzburg's Mozarteum hosts more famed European faculty and better facilities than does Fontainebleau; the Schleswig-Holstein Musik Festival in Germany offers exceptional orchestral training in the Germanic manner; and the Verbier and Menuhin Academies in Switzerland boast superstar instructors and posh surroundings in which students focus intently on chamber music. In the United States, the Aspen Festival supports five orchestras and countless pianists and singers each summer for nine full weeks; the Norfolk Festival has been midwife to a number of tremendously successful small ensembles; and Tanglewood, the Music Academy of the West, Meadowmont, the Ravinia Festival, and the Marlboro Festival all provide students with a highly structured, all-encompassing educational experience at the hands of prominent performers. What has caused the Conservatoire Américain to become such an unknown among these summer schools? Although the Conservatoire still remains open for students, employs competent professors, and enrolls a respectably sized group of students each year who are generally enthusiastic about their Fontainebleau experience, the institution today lacks the focus, energy, and status of its heyday. The school has only two options open to it: to commit to a seriously undertaken revival, or to continue on its present path of inertia to an ultimate extinction.

The reasons for the Conservatoire Américain's decline are manifold, but can essentially be distilled into three primary points: complacency and a lack of business acumen among the leadership; the decline of a coherent policy of the school's purpose and intent; and the absence of an energetic resolve through to a more clearly defined mission. Culpability must also be placed on time itself. Damrosch's comment that the Conservatoire was one of the few positive outcomes of the Great War can be analyzed in hindsight as a telling indicator of the period in which the school best flourished: as a unifying agent for cross-Atlantic artistic communities during a time when such alliances were crucial to maintaining solid popular support and respect for joint political ventures, the Conservatoire's initial founding would not be considered so today, a time in which the United States is more at odds with its European allies than any time since the 1956 Suez crisis. The national exuberance and gratitude of the French to Americans at the end of the war provided an environment ideal for the creation of intercultural partnerships such as the Conservatoire. As a result of this the school found support and patronage among the aristocracy and moneyed arts lovers of both countries. Throughout the interwar period and the immediate post–World War II era, cultural considerations again led to an anti-German backlash that, while far more tempered in terms of artistic acceptance and performance of nineteenth-century German works than that which had occurred during the First World War, was nonetheless a determining factor when it came to encouraging

American students to study abroad. France was once more the Continental location of choice for students of all disciplines, and in this atmosphere the Conservatoire flourished, both recalling the close cultural relationship between France and America during the 1920s and capitalizing on the new devotion the French displayed toward their liberators.

Nadia Boulanger's directorship continued to build on the Franco-American relationship as she solicited funding and public support from her American patrons. Even more effectively, she used the cult of personality surrounding her teaching prowess as a means for developing a hagiographic raison d'être for the school's very existence. Though this practice and Boulanger's reputation served the school well in increasing enrollment and name recognition, it has been shown that the rest of the administration—both French and American—were far too acquiescent in allowing this atmosphere of hero worship to grow into unreasonable justification solely for the promotion and continuation of the school itself; its initial purpose had, after all, been much grander than to merely showcase the abilities of a single instructor. This issue of Boulanger's mythical status is one that has largely been ignored in studies of her. Most writers, in dealing with this legend, prefer to leave her as such. In any analysis of the Conservatoire Américain, however, a critical view of Boulanger's role and the impact of her standing as the "master teacher" must be introduced as part of a greater consideration of the school's history and present existence. Boulanger, in her desire to control the school's affairs to the utmost, created a despotic system at the Conservatoire in which she became both revered as the consummate academic musician and instructor and feared as a harsh imparter of censure and dictates. Perhaps Boulanger truly believed that kindness required cruelty, or perhaps her tendencies had developed because she felt it necessary to prove that she was as strict and hard as any man in the profession. Regardless of why her temperament so developed, Boulanger's duality caused a disparity in the reactions of students. As often occurs with the perception of figures in positions of power, despite the size or natures of their empires, an amalgamation of these aspects was created, that of the stern and demanding pedagogue who sacrificed her own personal contentment for the greater good of perfecting the skills of those students whom she deemed deserving of her gifts as a mentor. This figure, the mythical "Mademoiselle" who was generous with her time and yet reserved and somehow intimidating, was a great boon to the Conservatoire during Boulanger's peak, but diminished as her decline became inevitably obvious starting in the early 1960s. To study at Fontainebleau with Boulanger meant that a student had reached the pinnacle of musical studies; that with sufficient work and self-sacrifice, an anointment of sorts was possible: the approval, at the end of the session, of the master teacher, the blessing of the virgin priestess of music. It was widely known that a Boulanger student was a real musician, one tempered by her tests and capable of great feats of the ear, eye, and hand. The pedagogical methods she used were ordinary: rote, memorization, recitation; students learned their materials and flourished; or did not and were belittled. Those who passed not only the initial tests but convinced Boulanger that they were very serious about their studies—often, those who made the commitment to stay on in Paris for further work with her after the summer had ended—could hope to be, but not rely on being, introduced to established musicians and assisted in their careers. As the Boulanger legend grew, the dissenting voices that spoke to her flaws both personally and pedagogically—including Virgil Thomson's—were crushed by the weight of her supporters, those who had believed the myth before meeting Boulanger, and who, despite evidence to the contrary, continued to believe that her methods of teaching students about music were revolutionary, inspired, and unique approaches, when in fact they were derived from her own Paris Conservatoire training with little variation.

Furthering the myth of the all-powerful teacher was the lack of attention paid to the fact that within her group of approved students, Boulanger could be fickle, withdrawing from one particular pupil or another for a perceived slight or flaw. Much of this behavior added to the cult of personality around Boulanger: that she could aid students in launching careers was well-reported, but not that she could yet be so hostile to their peers. Few who went to France to study with her realized how she had treated some of her supposedly favored students: Louise Talma remained faithful to Boulanger and her methodology all of her life, even after Boulanger had rejected Talma's work. Boulanger encouraged the perception of being the benevolent imparter of music's secrets, discussing her life's work in terms of responding to a divine gift and of wanting to do no more than help others use their equally god-given gifts in the way the Holy Spirit intended. Thus Boulanger became the conduit for celestial guidance in all things musical, the creator of a kind of musical gospel. How could any serious musician resist the lure of studying under such a figure? Countless students of the Conservatoire Américain went on to successful careers—but was it because they were guided and properly prepared for those careers through the education provided by Boulanger, or were they already exceptional talents who attended Fontainebleau because they were drawn to the myth of Boulanger? Little credit is given to any other professors of the Conservatoire during this time, but surely study with Menuhin was as influential as study with Boulanger.

The Conservatoire Américain, armed with this deified leader and a vibrant faculty beneath her, was intensely strong in its presence as a serious conservatory. The fact that end-of-session juries and exams were taken seriously by a panel of acclaimed teaching staff performers, and the fact that diplomas issued by the school carried enough weight to allow a school music teacher to be considered renewed in her credentials, or to allow a performer to be esteemed higher than a peer who had not attended, indicated that without a doubt the rest of the musical world valued the kind of study undertaken by Fontainebleau students, and equally as important, valued the assessments the school made of those students. The cult of Boulanger strengthened the Conservatoire for many years, to the point that many administrators and staff had begun to believe that their leader was not merely mostly infallible, but somehow immortal as well. Boulanger's own belief in her supremacy as the director of the school led it to the brink of closure following her death. The resulting instability put the school in a far more precarious position than it had ever experienced. Because of the succeeding administrations' inability to recall the Conservatoire Américain's initial raison d'être or to produce a renewed vision of the school's purpose without referring to Boulanger, the post-Marty years saw the school set on a murkily defined path in regard to almost every aspect of the school's operation and existence, from the student and faculty bodies to the training that would be provided and the nature of the program as a whole.

As the end of the Cold War and the resulting interaction between artists of the West and the former Soviet bloc nations became more pronounced, and as the influx of students from Asia into European conservatories grew, the blending of heretofore strictly delineated national-school styles and desire to promote the inclusion of different interpretative techniques and tastes developed. The result was the further dilution of the philosophy that American musicians—being of a country with a younger musical heritage than its Continental allies yet a nation in which the musical life was nonetheless brisk—should desire professional training administered by the most skilled musicians France had to offer.

In light of this, before further considering the matter of the effects of time and the responsibility of the Conservatoire's gatekeepers, the question must therefore be asked as to the variable nature of intent and at what point original intentions should give way to contemporary mores and cultural considerations. In its quest to become more encompassing of non-French teachers and non-American students (for a variety of reasons, discussed further below), the Conservatoire in Fontainebleau has become an institution operating, seemingly, without any premise or intent at all. The last attempt to adhere to a categorically French musical education was that of Jean-Pierre Marty, which was stunning in its complete rejection of the American professoriate that had come to serve the school. Whether Marty's outright dismissal of the administrative tactics of the Mannes-affiliated staff—not to mention the manner in which it was accomplished—was a wise decision is left for debate. In any event, the school expanded and achieved much under that program. Yet for Marty and many of the purists who had witnessed the school's pre-Boulanger incarnation, eliminating that very form was an important step in restoring the school from a chaotic existence—in which the founding principles had been set aside—to one more positively identifying with the goals of Francis Casadesus's manifesto of original intent. Marty's Conservatoire students were primarily Americans, the faculty almost exclusively French. Music was learned from scratch under the guidance of coaches intent on bringing to the fore the French aesthetics involved with each performance. Harmony, ear-training, and choral classes followed the Paris Conservatoire methods down to the solfège materials used. With Marty's resignation, the administration of the school passed to the relatively uninvolved Entremont and a cadre of Americans who have drifted away from the Paris Conservatoire—or early Conservatoire Américain, for that matter—curriculum or process of the French transmission of style and methods.

There seems to be an ambiguity as to exactly what the current administration and supporters of the Conservatoire Américain wish to accomplish. The official mission of the school is presented as follows:

> In recent years the American Conservatory at Fontainebleau has widened its mission of initiation and discovery of French music and culture to include not only the best American musicians but musicians from all parts of the globe. Courses in piano, violin, viola, cello, composition, theory and chamber music will not only provide opportunities for educational advancement, they will also set the stage for diverse cultural exchange.[1]

This statement seems to indicate that the Conservatoire retains the practice of promoting French repertoire as was initiated by Robert and Gaby Casadesus in the first years of the school's existence. However, in comparing programs of the past five years with those from before 1993, there is a clearly visible decline in the amount of French repertoire performed by both students and faculty in performances hosted by the school. The custom of holding French composer minifestivals has all but died out, save for a rare 1999 commemoration recital for Robert Casadesus in which several of his works were presented. In suggesting that the only mission of the Conservatoire is to *introduce* students to French music and culture, the statement issued by the school implies that, perhaps due to the globalization of musical style and performance, there is no longer a need or desire for American students to acquire the skills of Paris Conservatoire–trained French musicians. Certainly, the musical community is today more ecumenical in its national identifications and interpretive and performance schools, and to the administration this may be a reasonable validation of the current attitude in relation to the employment of non-French professors. Even if this rationale is received without question, there still remains a considerable fissure in the school's mission: how is it introducing students to French music and culture without a more in-depth treatment of the overlap of those arenas, the intersection of aesthetic taste and style that serves to inform performance practices. A student cannot be said to have been introduced to French music merely by hearing it, but must work within the boundaries of what constitutes French music and French compositional technique in order to assimilate that knowledge, a situation Francis Casadesus sought to promote. As for the nationality of the students, perhaps there is no compelling reason to continue the requirement of American citizenship. The political climate in the United States is one of inclusivity, and doubtless the potential for allegations of discrimination has affected this last point. Both of these are satisfactory reasons for the school to have changed from an institution focused on teaching French musicianship to Americans to one hoping for a wider musico-cultural dialogue by engaging performers and teachers from throughout the world. In making this change, the Conservatoire could have taken purposeful steps in a direction away from its initial position, but toward an equally valuable position—were it pursued vigorously enough—of advancing a curriculum and repertoire still rooted in French methods and composition. Yet this does not seem to have occurred with any authority. The curriculum is nebulously defined and the repertoire left to mere suggestion without concrete obligations. Methods in the nonperformance areas of harmony, ear-training, and analysis are offered in a course led by Isabelle Duha that is geared toward composers and pianists and often scheduled inefficiently for other students interested in attending. Despite Duha's Paris Conservatoire faculty position, the course is not offered in the format of those in years gone by—classroom instruction complete with assignments and assessment of progress—but as an informal seminar or individual coaching sessions. As for performance, students perform whatever works they have brought, be they French, German, or American works; the concerts are scheduled in advance and must be filled to certain length requirements, regardless of whether any students have French repertoire ready for performance. Thus changes have occurred more by passive allowance than thoughtfully considered actions. The current president of the Écoles d'Art Américaines, Thérèse Casadesus Rawson, indicates that she views the school more as a continuing memorial to her parents, Robert and Gaby, than a living institution in need of new energy.[2] Studying the Conservatoire Américain's uneven and haphazard path from its initial goals to its current mission statement, it is apparent that the present position was not one adopted through careful analysis and evaluation, leading to a specific and newly delineated goal.

The reasons for the shift from an organized and strongly self-deterministic organization to one shaped more by external forces to shape its policies has occurred much as water wears away stone: little by little and over much time. While today's administration cannot be faulted for negligences of the past, it must accept the necessity of clarifying and redirecting the policies of a well-established institution; of delivering it into the twenty-first century with its strengths intact and with new vigor to meet the challenges that have evolved during the last half century. New leadership—bringing with it determined objectives and vigorous, active direction—is required to prevent the Conservatoire from continuing its slide into obscurity and closure.

The Conservatoire Américain today is beset by several problems that have contributed to its decline from being an institution without precedent into one that must regain its originality. The lack of a clear agenda in teaching style and dissemination of repertoire has been discussed. Perhaps even more deadly for a school already dealing with an uncertain long-term future is the lack of an identity. In a time when "identity" and "brand" are the business world's favored catchphrases, Fontainebleau requires this ineffable and crucial characteristic. Strengthening several aspects would contribute to the school's visible identity in the musical community, consistent, creative, and energetic leadership; a visible and positive relationship with the Palais de Fontainebleau; a more competitive curriculum; rigorous public relations and active recruitment; a reassessment of the length and nature of the program; and the establishment of higher standards for levels of attainment of the students.

The Conservatoire Américain's relationship with the Palais was one of contention from its inception, when the chateau's keepers protested the manners of the Americans residing in its halls. As time has passed, the Conservatoire has been shunted from the elegant Louis XV wing to the "Kitchen Quarter" and finally into just two rooms for lesson, master-class, and performance use only. The signs that hung above the doorways even to the rooms in the Quartier Henri IV had been taken down, and today a visitor to the Palais would have no indication of the school's presence there. The Conseil is told by the Palais that as soon as the funding becomes available for renovations to be completed, the Conservatoire will be back in its lodgings, but in the ten years since the school was all but ousted from the grounds there is little indication that a full return is likely. The loss of its traditional home in the Palais has meant for the school that much of what had made it notable in the past was absent: no other summer program had been able to boast of study and performances in such a historically and artistically important venue. By having to send its students to practice at the poorly outfitted local music school and having teachers give lessons in hotel rooms, lobbies, and the Albe's pavilion, the Conservatoire Américain had been reduced to a makeshift outfit without the panache of a royal residence. Acceptable as a stopgap measure for a year or two, these conditions have persisted without any allowances by the Palais for the much needed additional space in the chateau that would help restore the school's presence in and connections with the building. The declining affiliation of the Conservatoire with the chateau weakens the school to a position where it is indistinguishable from any other summer program using borrowed buildings and materiel. As the legend holds that the Tower of London and monarchy should fall were its ravens to depart it, the inverse may be happening in Fontainebleau: the Conservatoire Américain has left the Palais and in that homeless state is prone to demise far more than were it ensconced in the chateau enjoying the support and recognition of the municipality and the public. The relationship with the Palais is indicative of the Conservatoire's state of affairs in the town as well. While Marty had worked especially diligently to enlist the support of the mayor at the time, the present civil administration of the town shows little interest in assisting, promoting, or even recognizing the school. The long-standing traditions of performing at the Hôtel de Ville (Town Hall) for Bastille Day and for the Feast of St. Louis (Fontainebleau's patron saint) have fallen away in recent years. Performing for the feast day disappeared as the session grew short and no students remained in Fontainebleau on August 16; until 2001 a traditional Bastille Day performance of the French and American national anthems, sung and played by the student body and conducted by the director, was a given. Returning students and observers were surprised when in the school's eightieth year there was no invitation to the mayoral offices for the customary singing and champagne reception. Brushed aside as a one-time administrative oversight, the same lack of an invitation was repeated in 2002, 2003, and 2004, indicating more firmly that the town was not interested in the music school bearing its name. Being unable to strongly connect with the Palais or town causes the Conservatoire Américain to take on the role of a seasonal inter-loper, more tourist than resident. Location can serve as an important factor in identification, especially when a place-name is incorporated into an en-tity's own appellation: the "London School of Economics" conjures up a very different identifying image and related recognition than does the "Madras School of Economics" or simply the "school of economics." With-out a clear connection in the present time to *Fontainebleau*—as both the town and the Palais—as a place or orientation, the Conservatoire Améri-cain loses a crucial part of its identity that was so carefully and deliberately created and had been a part of the school's historical cachet.

The issue of competing programs is one touched on earlier, but bears more thorough consideration. Other serious summer music schools— meaning those that purport to train young professionals and preprofession-als for concert careers, both in the United States and abroad—are widely disparate. Few have the lengthy artistic pedigree the Conservatoire holds, and yet many of these programs are considered more effective courses for the collegiate musicians to whom they are marketed. There are several rea-sons the Conservatoire has such difficulty competing with these younger institutions, some of which are also integral to the school's lack of identity: lack of sufficient financial means by which to attract more and better stu-dents through scholarships; the insufficient publicity and deliberately low-key recruiting protocols of the Conservatoire; and the nature of the pro-gram itself. Financially speaking, the Conservatoire Américain charges the same amount of tuition ($2,500) for its four weeks of instruction as does the Aspen Music Festival for its nine. Scholarships for Fontainebleau stu-dents are generally small, with the occasional exception for an outstanding performer already tapped by a member of the faculty or administration, whereas every student admitted to the Tanglewood Music Center and the Marlboro Festival receives a substantial if not full scholarship to attend. There is little incentive for students to travel abroad when the better value lies in staying within the United States; and the drawing power of the fes-tivals mentioned above and their faculty rosters is undeniable: the Aspen Music Festival fields several orchestras each year, and Marlboro's slots for pianists are known to be filled up to a year in advance. Should a student wish to study overseas despite the array of opportunities in the United States, there is no shortage of programs with which the Conservatoire Américain struggles to compete: the Mozarteum's Sommerakademie in Salzburg; the International Orchestral Institute Attergau, run by the Vi-enna Philharmonic Orchestra; the Schleswig-Holstein Musik Festival; and the Verbier and Menuhin academies in Switzerland. All of these younger summer schools have one distinct advantage over the Conservatoire—the presence of an ambitious and active publicity and recruitment arm.

The Conservatoire Américain's most recent position on promotion is a curious one. While during the Mannes involvement the enormous powers of that school's promotional experience served to create a high level of recognition and publicity for the school, and under Marty carefully written brochures extolling the school's history and features were likewise distributed widely, the current policy appears to take the position that in order to attract the best levels of students—as opposed to the perhaps less distinguished attendants of lower level music schools and departments—word-of-mouth advertising is the best method for attracting students to the school and letting it be known that the school is, in fact, accepting applicants for the coming summer. Today the school's existence is made known almost exclusively through its Internet site and its annual benefit recital and dinner in New York, for which it sends out invitations to alumni. This event, however, is apparently only infrequently covered by the musical or social press, the last mention being a brief review of performances of Robert Casadesus's works on the 1999 program in *The New York Times*.[3] Applications are available through those in contact with the Fontainebleau Associations and its board members and staff, but there is hardly the kind of public relations campaign one might expect from a school interested in continuing a long and important tradition of educating top-level musicians.[4] The assumption, made by members of the administration, that better students are generally referred by Fontainebleau alumni and should therefore receive information not available on a widespread basis is a difficult supposition to prove. Although it is generally agreed that the majority of students perform at a high level, it cannot be said that the school would find less adept applicants were it to promote itself more rigorously. By limiting its publicity to these scant prospects, the Conservatoire Américain denies itself an entire realm of potential students and future alumni who might in turn support the school in terms of both proffered skills and positive recommendations but also in the area of financial support, an area where the school clearly could use the monetarily expressed gratitude of satisfied alumni.

The final factor in the Conservatoire Américain's inability to truly compete with its summer conservatory rivals is the nature of the program itself. As discussed earlier, as of the current administration there is an ambiguity as to what direction the Conservatoire is attempting to take: Entremont initially proposed an end to instrumental lessons except for piano; professors, while well known on the Continent, are less recognized in the United States and come and go from the school as dictated by their own performance schedules, creating a discontinuity of study for the students; and the want of an enforced attendance policy or requirements for the students frequently leads to absences by attendees and an informal atmosphere not conducive to the intense summer of study the Conservatoire once insisted on. With its nebulous ambition and lack of communication as to what the school is seeking in applicants and for its own future, there is little surprise that the school often strives at the last moment to find enough students in one area or another so as to have an adequate balance for the session.[5]

However, recruitment problems are often offset by a tactic that is the final element in the school's decreasing reputation but that has been an unfortunate part of the Conservatoire since its inception: accepting full-paying students of lower performance levels in order to subsidize those of higher ones. Perhaps it is now time for the school's administration to decide whether it will embrace the notion of a mixed professional-amateur student body; cater more exclusively to the paying amateurs or semiprofessional students interested in attending the school as part of a musical vacation; or focus on the Conservatoire's traditional track of training young professionals serious about pursuing careers in performance. Historical precedent shows that the first option has always had a foothold, albeit grudgingly admitted in private by directors and board members. Whether this should remain the case, be ended, or be tempered into a reasonable accommodation on all fronts must be decided by an administration willing to learn from the past but to exist untied to it.

The cash-for-talent tradeoff began as far back as 1922, when the Conseil d'Administration reluctantly agreed that the less talented and less serious but more moneyed should be admitted in order to offset the costs of the talented and committed but needy. The practice continued—and flourished—during Boulanger's stint as director, and as part of this practice, older alumni of any level and professional ambition or achievement were encouraged to return for refresher courses. However, the delineation was clear: the most promising students stood out from those who were not destined for the soloist's life, and the opportunities for the younger and more viable talents were not impinged on by other attendees. As the financial situation became truly dire following Marty's resignation, it was clear that as much as the school wanted to give partial or full scholarships to every student, that would not be possible, and accepting tolerably competent students who could pay full tuition along with the more talented who could not was an attractive compromise. In comparison to the way things had been handled previously, young, collegiate musicians who could pay were accepted alongside their more talented peers, creating a more uneven level of ability within the supposedly equal ranks.

Today, there is a mixture of these practices, resulting in the acceptance of not quite as gifted but full-paying students and a number of older musicians seeking a "working vacation" experience in music. Acceptance of these students must—barring a new mission or policy of inclusion—all therefore come down to finances, and an examination of the school's economic state bears this out. Because of the low visibility that the Alumni Association—later regrouped as the Fontainebleau Associations, Inc.—had experienced (due mostly to its own lack of initiative and the fact that it had been a completely and intentionally amateur operation for many years), raising capital or immediate-use funding was more difficult than organizers had anticipated. Traditional sponsors like the Copland Foundation and the Getty Foundation stopped providing assistance, and by 2002 the largest donors were the Florence Gould Foundation ($35,000 plus) and Thérèse Casadesus Rawson ($10,000 plus) herself, with other foundations and individuals providing minute amounts compared to the annual operating costs. In 2002 just one foundation gave a grant of $5,000 or more; three groups made smaller donations, and only thirteen alumni—several of them also board members—gave gifts ranging from under $100 to $1,000.[6] Such low levels of outside funding were common through the mid- and late 1990s, and so a greater number of semiprofessional and amateur adult students were accepted who, by paying full tuition, could offset the costs of basic needs: faculty salaries, auto rentals, utilities, insurance, and so on. The Conservatoire seems to be well on the way to becoming—at least for some attendees—the "Frenchified country club" that Betsy Jolas decried ten years ago. It is clear that if the Conservatoire wishes to regain even a glimmer of its previous prestige and purpose, it will need to undergo serious reconsideration of its mission and values. While it is not the historian's place to offer prescriptive commentary, it is nonetheless obvious to all who encounter it today that the school that has nourished so many must now be nourished itself, with adept and willing leadership, or it will indeed extinguish.

Notes

1. www.fontainebleauschools.org/Pages/frameset.html (accessed January 30, 2003).
2. Thérèse Casadesus Rawson, correspondence and communication with author, various dates, possession of author.
3. Anthony Tommasini, "Little-Known Works of a Renowned French Pianist," *The New York Times*, Friday, September 24, 1999.
4. In commencing research for this book, I found available so little information on the Conservatoire Américain that initially I thought that it had, in fact, closed

for good. At that time no website existed and it was not listed in *International Musician*, *Chamber Music America*'s annual guide to summer schools, *Strings* magazine's similar annual guide, *Clavier* magazine's listings, or any other reference a student or instructor might search in order to obtain information about a given program or program opportunities.

5. Thérèse Casadesus Rawson, e-mail to author, November 27, 2000, possession of author.

6. *Fontainebleau Alumni Bulletin*, February 2002, 4.

~

A Note on the Appendixes

The archives of the Conservatoire Américain are in a precarious state. Records in France exist in the Palais de Fontainebleau, in various manners of order and condition ranging from the well preserved to the nearly destroyed. Others are stored in the school's properties in Fontainebleau, the Hôtel d'Albe and the Hôtel Barassy, in attics and basements, most of them stored in cardboard boxes roughly organized by decade. Yet other materials are held by the Fontainebleau Municipal Library, again in boxes and envelopes. Archival materials in the United States are held in a warehouse in Brooklyn; by institutions associated at one time or another with the Conservatoire; and by private individuals, some of whom have been able to properly preserve old papers and iconographic archives; others who have not. The majority of documents from the 1930s and 1940s were destroyed when a sewer line flooded the basement of the Hôtel d'Albe. Other documents have been lost to time and the deaths of record-keepers.

The information contained in the following appendixes is based on the existing records of the Conservatoire, its alumni, and others who generously opened their collections for study. Because of the conditions and document losses detailed above, some information is missing. While the information presented here is all drawn from original documents, the reader should be aware that not all of the information contained in these appendixes is complete.

APPENDIX A

~

A Timeline of the Conservatoire

1918   General Pershing requests Walter Damrosch and Francis Casadesus to establish a school for American army musicians at the Chateau of Chaumont in the Loire Valley.

1919   The École Américaine du Chef de Musique opens at Chaumont for the summer. Francis Casadesus begins planning for a permanent summer school for American musicians.

1920   In November, Casadesus, Maurice Fragnaud, and others convene to officially create the Conservatoire Américain.

1921   The Conservatoire Américain opens at the Palais de Fontainebleau on June 26. Notable students include Aaron Copland, Stanley Avery, and Zo Elliott. The Conservatoire ends its first year with performances in Paris on September 23.

1922   Francis Casadesus is named honorary director of the Conservatoire.

1923   Max d'Ollone serves as temporary music director, overseeing day-to-day affairs.

1924   Discussions begin to eliminate competitions for the *Premier Prix*. Students include David Dushkin and Ariel Gross. Charles-Marie Widor takes over as music director.

1925   The Conservatoire partially moves from the Louis XV wing to the Henri IV courtyard in the Palais. Notable students include later longtime Conservatoire supporter and pianist Beveridge Webster, Ariel Gross (Louise Lyon), Lucille Jolly, Clara Rabinowitch, and Harold Richey. The École des Beaux-Arts, the Conservatoire's sister-school for architecture, moves into the Palais.

1926   Competitions for the *Premier Prix* end in most areas, replaced by diplomas indicating Excellence in Execution or Fitness for Teaching. Louise Talma attends for the first time, beginning her long relationship with the school.

1927   Madeline Grey presents a premiere of several of Ravel's songs at a recital at the Conservatoire.

1929   The American stock market crashes; tuition for three months of study at the Conservatoire is $300.

1930   Damrosch visits the Conservatoire for an early tenth-anniversary celebration of concerts and parties. Notable students include Anita Hankwitz Kastner, Marguerite Quarles, and Virginia Quarles.

1932   The Palais insists that the Conservatoire furnish dormitories for its students, setting off a long-standing feud.

1933   Isidor Philipp begins to teach a class on memorization and stage fright to help train students to the new requirements of playing without music.

1934   Maurice Ravel is named director general of the Conservatoire, replacing Charles-Marie Widor.

1936   Robert Casadesus is appointed head of the piano department, replacing the retiring Isidor Philipp, and begins to develop a more Francophile curriculum of repertoire.

1937   Ravel dies.
         Notable students include David Diamond, who enrolls as a student of Nadia Boulanger. Composer and pianist Camille Decreus takes the position of director general.

1938   Louise Talma wins the Stovall Prize for composition for the first time.

1939   Igor Stravinsky serves as a judge on the composition competition panel, awarding the Stovall Prize to Louise Talma, her second win in two years. The Second World War begins at the end of the Conservatoire's session, sending students home early. Camille Decreus dies.

1940   Damrosch declares in April that the Conservatoire must survive the war. Gaby and Robert Casadesus operate the Conservatoire-in-exile at St. George's School in Newport, Rhode Island.

1941   The Conservatoire opens for a second year at St. George's.

1942   The Casadesuses move the Conservatoire to Great Barrington, Massachusetts, for the summer when the beaches of Rhode Island are closed for military exercises. Notable students include pianist and musicologist Charles Rosen.

1943   In France, supporters of the Conservatoire rescue music and other school possessions, hiding them in secret rooms at the Palais. Classes continue with the Casadesuses in New England.

1944   Classes continue with the Casadesuses in New England.

1945   Fontainebleau is liberated in August. Robert Casadesus is appointed director of the Conservatoire; Marcel Dupré will serve as director general.

1946   The Casadesuses return to Fontainebleau with seventeen students to reestablish the Conservatoire. Soulima Stravinsky and Nadia Boulanger perform works by Igor Stravinsky at the Conservatoire.

1947   Nadia Boulanger formally returns to the Conservatoire as professor of composition.

1948   Robert Casadesus resigns as director following the illness of his daughter Thérèse. Nadia Boulanger is appointed director of the Conservatoire. The school acquires the Hotel d'Albe for housing female students.

1949   The Pasquier Trio joins the faculty. Notable students include pianist Idil Biret, who attends as a student of Boulanger. Queen Elisabeth of Belgium attends the final student concert of the year.

1950   Kermit Moore wins the Lili Boulanger prize, and future Conservatoire director Narcis Bonet is awarded the composition prize. Other notable students include musicologist Bathia Churgin, violinist Stuart Fasovsky, and pianist Arthur Frackenpohl.

1951   Notable students include "P. D. Q. Bach" countertenor John Ferrante, Bathia Churgin, and William Battaile.

1952   Notable students include Idil Biret, Malcolm Frager, and Roger Kamien.

1953   Darius Milhaud composes student test-piece for piano competition. Notable students include Luise Vosgerchian.

1954   Concerts by Pierre Fournier, Paul Bazelaire, Jean Françaix, Doda Conrad, and Maurice Gendron are huge successes. Competition pieces are composed for the school by Aaron Copland, Henri Dutilleux, Jean Françaix, Marcelle de Manziarly, Darius Milhaud, and Michal Spisak. For the piano competition, "Mr. Darius Milhaud has accepted to compose a work to be performed for this competition. The prize winner will not only receive a money award, but M. Milhaud's work will be dedicated to him and played by him at a concert of the Radio-Diffusion Nationale Française as well as the Embassy concert." Students present the premiere of Jean Françaix's opera *Paris á Nous Deux* in the Fontainebleau Municipal Theater in honor of Yehudi Menuhin, who conducts the performances. Student Luise Vosgerchian wins the Salabert Composition Prize.

1956   The curriculum includes "master classes with Nadia Boulanger, Robert Casadesus, Clifford Curzon, Yehudi Menuhin, Pierre Bernac, & Francis Poulenc commentating and supervising the interpretation of his songs, piano, two pianos, chamber music works and concerto for organ."

1957   Boulanger turns seventy and resigns from the Paris Conservatory. The Conservatoire buys the Hôtel Barassy as lodging for male students.

1959   Alumnus Malcolm Frager wins the Leventritt Competition.

1960   Alumnus Malcolm Frager wins the Queen Elisabeth of Belgium International Competition. Notable students include Mozart scholar Robert Levin and pianist James Harrison.

1961   Notable students include Don Campbell, James Harrison, and Robert Levin.

1962   Notable students include musicologist Susan Forscher Weiss, Robert Levin, and pianist and composer Yung Shen.

1963   Notable students include Robert Levin and Yung Shen.

1964   Notable students include pianists Andre-Michel Schub, Robert Levin, and Juliana Osinchuk.

1965 Notable students include pianists Samuel Sanders, Juliana Osinchuk, and Yung Shen.

1966 Notable students include Krzysztof Meyer and Juliana Osinchuk.

1967 Notable students include pianist Jay Gottlieb and Jeremy Menuhin.

1969 Boulanger's last protégé, Emile Naoumoff, begins his summers at Fontainebleau. Other notable students include pianist Douglas Buys, cellist Pierre Djokic, theorist Donna Doyle, pianist Jay Gottlieb, composer Stefan Kozinski, and harmony student Princess Irene of Greece.

1970 Notable students include Pierre Djokic, Jay Gottlieb, Stefan Kozinski, and Emile Naoumoff.

1971 Aaron Copland attends a concert of his works presented by Conservatoire faculty and students in honor of the school's fiftieth anniversary and his own seventieth birthday. Notable students include Jay Gottlieb, Jeremy Menuhin, Emile Naoumoff, and Juliana Osinchuk.

1972 Piano professor Jean Casadesus, the son of Gaby and Robert, is killed in an automobile accident in Canada. Notable students include soprano June Anderson, Douglas Buys, Donna Doyle, Stefan Kozinski, and Emile Naoumoff.

1973 The Conservatoire's by-laws are officially changed to allow non-American students into the school in large numbers for the first time. Notable students include June Anderson, Douglas Buys, and Emile Naoumoff.

1974 Notable students include Emile Naoumoff. Alumnus Andre-Michel Schub wins the Naumberg International Piano Competition.

1975 Notable students include composer Joel Feigin, Stefan Kozinski, Emile Naoumoff, and Yuko Satoh.

1976 Notable students include musicologist Dorothy DeVal, Joel Feigin, Emile Naoumoff, and Yuko Satoh.

1977 Alumnus Andre-Michel Schub wins the Avery Fisher Recital Award.

1978 Boulanger teaches at Fontainebleau for the last time. Menuhin students Tasmin Little, Christina Thomas, and Antonio Lysy perform at a special benefit concert. Notable students include Emile Naoumoff and Christopher Zimmerman. Alumna June Anderson makes her professional debut with the New York City Opera as the Queen of the Night in *The Magic Flute*.

1979   Boulanger dies. Robert Levin begins teaching at the Conservatoire in order to keep it functioning, and James Harrison becomes president of the Board of Trustees in New York. Narcis Bonet is appointed director.

1980   The Conservatoire forms a partnership with the Mannes College of Music to provide administrative and financial support.

1981   Alumnus Andre-Michel Schub wins the Van Cliburn International Piano Competition.

1983   Notable students include Florin Parvulescu and Wendy Sutter.

1986   Bonet resigns the position of director.

1987   Jean-Pierre Marty is appointed director, cuts ties with the Mannes College of Music, and establishes a separate entity to support the school.

1988   Leonard Bernstein holds a series of concerts and master classes at the Conservatoire to benefit the school.

1992   A rift develops between the Conservatoire's French administration and the American Alumni Association.

1993   Director Jean-Pierre Marty resigns. Notable students include clarinetist Samuel Caviezel, composer Bruce Bennett, and violinist Sashka Korzenska.

1994   Pianist and conductor Philippe Entremont takes up the post of director and the Alumni Association restores its support of the Conservatoire.

1996   Notable students include composer Dalit Warshaw.

1998   Notable students include the piano duo of Jerry and Shih-Yu Wong.

1999   Gaby Casadesus, the last surviving founding member of the Conservatoire faculty, dies in Paris. Notable students include composer Hillary Zipper and pianist Elizabeth Pridgen.

2000   Betsy Jolas resigns from the Conservatoire.

2004 The American Music Research Center at the University of Colorado, Boulder, hosts "Nadia Boulanger in America: A Symposium," with keynote speakers presenting research on the Conservatoire and Boulanger.

2005 Alumni Noel Lee, Jay Gottlieb, and Régis Pasquier join the Conservatoire's faculty.

~

Curriculum Offered at the Conservatoire Américain

All courses of study were offered in both private lesson and group class formats.

Accompaniment: 1921–1939, 1947–present
Analysis: 1921–1939, 1942–1945, 1947–present (later included in "Musical Language")
Bassoon: 1984–1993
Cello: 1921–1939, 1948–present
Chamber music: 1921–present
Chromatic harp: 1921–1924
Clarinet: 1949–1993
Composition: 1921–1939, 1947–present
Conducting: 1921–1939, 1947–1993
Counterpoint: 1921–1939, 1946–present (later included in "Musical Language")
Diction: 1921–1924
Flute: 1953–1993
Fugue: 1921–present (later included in "Musical Language")
Guitar: 1984–1985
Harmony: 1921–present (later included in "Musical Language")
History: 1921–1939
Horn: 1984–1993
Instruments anciens (harpsichord): 1921–1925
Musical Language: 1921–present

Oboe: 1984–1993
Opera: 1921–1926
Opera staging: 1923–1925
Organ: 1921–1939, 1947–1979
Pedagogy: 1921–1939
Pedal harp: 1921–1939, 1953, 1984
Phonetics: 1921–1924
Piano: 1921–present
Saxophone: 1962, 1965
Sight-Reading: 1921–present (later included in "Musical Language")
Solfège: 1921–present (later included in "Musical Language")
Transposition: 1921–present (later included in "Musical Language")
Viola: 1921–1939, 1948–present
Violin: 1921–1939, 1947–present
Voice: 1921–1939, 1948–1985

~

Directors of the Conservatoire Américain

Directors

Directors—called residential directors in the school's early years—oversaw the day-to-day operations of the Conservatoire and taught classes and lessons, reporting to the Conseil d'Administration and the American Council.

1921–1922	Francis Casadesus
1922	Max d'Ollone
1923–1939	Camille Decreus
1939–1946	officially vacant; in practice Gaby and Robert Casadesus
1946–1949	Robert Casadesus
1949–1979	Nadia Boulanger
1979–1987	Narcis Bonet
1987–1993	Jean-Pierre Marty
1994–present	Philippe Entremont

Directors General/Presidents of the Conseil

Directors General—a role later primarily assumed by the President of the Conseil d'Administration—oversaw the operations of both the Conservatoire and the École des Beaux-Arts, the Conservatoire's sister-school in architecture and the fine arts.

1921–1934	Charles-Marie Widor
1934–1937	Maurice Ravel

1937–1939	Camille Decreus
1939–1946	officially vacant; in practice Gaby and Robert Casadesus and Walter Damrosch
1947–1954	Marcel Dupré
1954–1992	François Valéry (President of the Conseil)
1992–1994	Jean-Charles de Moustier (President of the Conseil)
1994–present	Pierre Boyer (President of the Conseil)

APPENDIX D

~

Selected Professors of the Conservatoire Américain

Byron Adams, analysis
Pierre Amoyal, violin
André Asselin, violin
Dalton Baldwin, accompaniment
Jean Battala, piano
André Bauchy, saxophone
Paul Bazelaire, cello
Norman Beedie, accompaniment
Pierre Bernac, voice
Hatto Beyerle, viola
Philippe Bianconi, piano
André Bloch, composition
Patrice Bocquillon, flute, chamber music
Narcis Bonet, Director of Conservatoire, 1979–1987; analysis, composition, accompaniment, orchestra
André Boucourechiliev, composition
Nadia Boulanger, Director of Conservatoire, 1949–1979; harmony, composition, solfège, piano, organ, conducting
Lucien Capet, violin
Francis Casadesus, Founder of Conservatoire; Director of Conservatoire, 1921; piano, chamber music
Gaby Casadesus, piano
Jean Casadesus, piano

Mrs. M. L. Henri Casadesus, chromatic harp
Robert Casadesus, Director of Conservatoire, 1946–1948; piano
Robert Casadesus Sr., diction
Suzanne Cesbron-Viseur, voice
Marcel Chadeigne, opera coaching
Alain Chantaraud, clarinet
Olivier Charlier, violin
Hélène Chaumont, piano
Patrice Chéreau, opera staging
Pierre Chéreau, opera staging
André Chevalet, oboe
Yvan Chiffoleau, cello
Hughes Cuenod, voice
Max d'Ollone, Director of Conservatoire, 1922
Camille Decreus, Director of Conservatoire, 1923–1939; Director General, 1937–1939; piano, composition
Daniel Deffayet, saxophone
Marcelle Demougeot, voice
Annette Dieudonné, harmony, solfège
Carlos Dourthé, cello
Isabelle Duha, analysis, sight-reading, harmony, solfège
Arnaud Dumond, guitar
Marcel Dupré, Director General, 1947–1954; organ
Henri Dutilleux, composition
Philippe Entremont, Director of Conservatoire, 1993–present; piano
Rolande Falcinelli, organ
Paul Fauchet, piano, accompaniment
Renaud Fontanarosa, cello
Jean Françaix, composition
Pascal Gallois, bassoon
André Gantiez, horn
Alice Gaultier Léon, piano
Maurice Gendron, cello
Shirley Givens, violin
Antoine Goulard, violin
Marcel Grandjany, pedal harp
Gabriel Grandmaison, bassoon
Bertrand Grenat, oboe
Louis Gromer, oboe
André Hekking, cello

Marcelle Herrenschmidt, piano
A. Landély Hettich, voice
Maurice Hewitt, violin
Gilles Honorat, clarinet
Maurice Husson, viola
Marie-Claire Jamet, harp
Pierre Jamet, harp
Marcel Jean, flute
Irène Joachim, voice
Betsy Jolas, composition
Genevieve Joy-Dutilleux, piano
Christian Larde, flute
Frédéric Laroque, violin
Gilberte Lecompte, voice, sight-reading
Noel Lee, piano
Renée Lenars, harp
Pierre Lenert, viola
Robert Levin, analysis, chamber music, solfège
Henri Libert, organ
Félia Litvinne, voice
Tamara Lubimova, child pedagogy applied to the teaching of music
Beverly Lunt, violin
Dmitry Markevitch, cello
Germaine Martinelli, voice
Louis Martinelli, solfège
Jean-Pierre Marty, Director of Conservatoire, 1986–1993; piano, chamber
    music
Georges Mauguiere, voice
Jens McManama, horn
Yehudi Menuhin, violin
Dominique Merlet, piano
Jean Morel, piano
Ferdinand Motte Lacroix, piano
Tristan Murail, composition
Lucien Muratore, voice
André Musset, flute
Emile Naoumoff, analysis, solfège, vocal ensemble
Yfrah Neaman, violin
Raphaël Oleg, violin
Jean Painchaud, piano

Charles Panzera, voice
Stéphane Part, oboe
André Pascal, violin
Jean Pasquier, violin
Nelly Pasquier, cello
Pierre Pasquier, viola, chamber music
Didier Pateau, oboe
Isidor Philipp, piano
Jacques Pillois, history, diction
Marthe Pillois, diction
Francis Poulenc, composition
Gaston Poulet, violin
Gerard Poulet, violin
Mathilde Radisse, piano
Maurice Ravel, Director General, 1934–1937
Guillaume Remy, violin
Hilda Roosevelt-Arosa, voice
Helda Rosewald, piano
Thomas Salignac, opera
Paul Silva Hérard, piano
Herre-Jan Stegenga, violoncello
Diane Stuart, voice
Henryk Szering, violin
Louise Talma, analysis, solfège
Paul Vidal, composition
Maurice Vieux, viola
Georges Viseur, voice
Charles-Marie Widor, Director General, 1921–1934, organ
Colette Wilkens-Jousse, solfège
Albert Wolfe, orchestral conducting
Richard Wolfe, viola

APPENDIX E

~

Selected Guest Artists
at the Conservatoire Américain

Guest artists usually performed with faculty members and offered a master class for students.

Pierre Bernac, voice
Leonard Bernstein, conducting
Idil Biret, piano
Doda Conrad, voice
Aaron Copland, composition
Clifford Curzon, piano
Henri Dutilleux, composition
Leon Fleisher, piano
Pierre Fournier, cello
Jean Françaix, composition
Zino Francescatti, violin
Peter Frankl, piano
Kenneth Gordon, violin
Claude Helfer, piano
Maurice Jacquemont, stage direction
Grant Johannesen, piano
Genevieve Joy, piano
Robert Levin, piano
Nikita Magaloff, piano
André Marchal, organ

Maurice Marechal, cello
Yehudi Menuhin, violin
Darius Milhaud, composition
Florica Musicesco, piano
Emile Naoumoff, piano
Yfrah Neaman, violin
Daniel Pinkham, composition
Francis Poulenc, composition
Janet Price, voice
Rafael Puyana, harpsichord
Jean-Pierre Rampal, flute
Gérard Souzay, voice
Michal Spisak, composition and piano
Igor Stravinsky, composition
Soulima Stravinsky, piano
Blanche Tarjus, violin
Christine Whittlesey, voice
Narciso Yepes, composition

APPENDIX F

~

Selected Notable Students
of the Conservatoire Américain

June Anderson, voice, 1972
George Antheil, composition, 1924
Romeo Arsenault, violin, 1935–1939
Stanley Avery, composition, 1921
Seymour Bernstein, piano, 1953
Idil Biret, piano, 1952
Frank Brieff, conducting, 1930–1932
Douglas Buys, piano, 1969, 1972–1973
Maria Pia Cafagna, voice, 1925
Don Campbell, composition, 1960–1961
Hector Campos-Parsi, composition, 1953
Elliott Carter, composition, 1921–1924
Samuel Caviezel, clarinet, 1993
Genevieve Chinn, composition, 1953
Bathia Churgin, analysis, piano, 1950–1951
Kenton Coe, composition, 1953
Leland Coon, composition, 1922
Aaron Copland, composition, 1921
Robert Crawford, voice, 1924–1926
Margaret DeGraff Herron, harp, 1927
Dorothy DeVal, analysis, 1976
David Diamond, composition, 1937
Samuel Dilworth-Leslie, piano, 1961–1962, 1964, 1974

Pierre Djokic, cello, 1969–1970
Dorothy Duckwitz Searle, piano, 1931
Yvonne DuPeyron, voice, 1933–1934
David Dushkin, piano, 1924–1926
Walter Edelstein, violin, 1926, 1929
Zo Elliott, composition, 1921
Herbert Elwell, composition, 1921
Emma Endres, piano, 1937–1938
Stuart Fastofsky, violin, 1950
Joel Feigin, composition, 1972, 1974–1976
John Ferrante, voice, 1951
Rock Ferris, piano, 1926–1927
Suzanne Fisher, voice, 1932
Susan Forscher Weiss, cello, piano, harmony, 1962
Arthur Frackenpohl, piano, 1950
Malcolm Frager, piano, 1952
Pamela Frank, violin, 1982
Virginia French Mackie, composition, 1933
Nina Geverts, violin, 1955
Jay Gottlieb, piano, 1967, 1969–1971
Ariel Gross (Louise Lyon), piano, 1924–1925
Felix Guerrero, composition, 1952
Anita Hankwitz Kastner, piano, 1930
James Harrison, analysis, piano, 1960–1961
Helen Hosmer, piano, 1925
Grant Johannesen, piano, 1947
Quincy Jones, composition, 1957
Roger Kamien, composition, 1952
Harrison Kerr, composition, 1921
John Kirkpatrick, piano, 1925–1928
Sashka Korzenska, violin, 1993
Stefan Kozinski, piano, organ, composition, 1969, 1975
Charles Kullman, voice, 1926–1927
Hannah Lefkowitz, piano, 1928
Leonard Lehrman, composition, 1969
Robert Levin, piano, composition, 1960–1964
Tasmin Little, violin, 1978
Barbara Lull Rahm, violin, 1926–1927
Antonio Lysy, cello, 1978
Quinto Maganini, composition, 1925–1927

Ozen Marsh, piano, 1938
Katherine McClintock Ellis, piano, 1924–1925
Colin McPhee, composition, 1924
Jeremy Menuhin, violin, 1967, 1971
Krzysztof Meyer, composition, 1964, 1966
James Ming, composition, 1960
David Montagu, violin, 1950
Maria Montana, voice, 1925
Dorothy Rudd Moore, composition, 1963
Kermit Moore, cello, 1953, 1957
Emile Naoumoff, piano, 1970–1979
Rosine Nocera, piano, 1951–1952
Juliana Osinchuk, piano, 1964–1966, 1968, 1971
Esther Ostroff, piano, 1930, 1932
Florin Parvulescu, violin, 1983
Julia Perry, composition, 1952
Viola Peters, piano, 1921,1925, 1930–1932
Joseph Plon, piano, 1955
Max Polikoff, violin, 1928
Victor Prahl, voice, 1921, 1924, 1926–1927
Charles Premmac, voice, 1924, 1925
Marguerite Quarles, piano, violin, 1930, 1932
Virginia Quarles, cello, 1930, 1932
Clara Rabinowitch, piano, 1924–1925
Rose Resnick, piano, 1928
Harold Richey, piano, 1924–1925
Charles Rosen, piano, 1942
Samuel Sanders, piano, ensemble, 1965
Yuko Satoh, analysis, piano, 1972, 1974–1976, 1978
Andre-Michel Schub, piano, 1964
Anna Mae Sharp, violin, 1924
Yung Shen, piano, 1962–1966
Guelda Sherman, cello, 1953
Florence Stage, piano, 1926, 1927
Barbara Stein Mallow, harmony, piano, 1952
Reginald Stewart, conducting, 1929, 1932
Wendy Sutter, cello, 1983
Gizi Szanto, piano, 1931
Louise Talma, composition, 1926–1929, 1931, 1933–1934, 1951, 1964,
    1969, 1971–1972, 1976

Augusta Read Thomas, composition, 1985
Ethel Thurston, solfège, 1930
Manuel Villet, piano, 1954
Luise Vosgerchian, piano, 1952
Dalit Warshaw, composition, 1996, 1999
Beveridge Webster, piano, 1922–1925
Frederick Werle, composition, 1937
Colette Wilkins, piano, solfège, 1976
Jerry Wong, piano, 1998
Shih-Yu Wong, piano, 1998
Charles Wuorinen, composition, 1961
Hadley Yates, composition, 1950
Christopher Zimmerman, piano, 1978
Princess Irene of Greece, piano, harmony, 1969
Princess Ululani of Hawai'i, harmony, 1932

APPENDIX G

~

Diplomas and Awards
of the Conservatoire Américain

Diplomas were sometimes issued with conditional modifiers. The designation of *degré preparatoire*, *degré elementaire*, or *degré moyen* meant that a student had prepared easier pieces than his or her peers and had not been awarded a full diploma, but was recognized for performance of those works and was encouraged to return for further study. Honors were indicated by *mention bien* and *mention très bien*. Diplomas could also be issued without comments of either type. Not all areas issued diplomas in performance or teaching each year. Since the 1980s, diplomas have been issued to all students, indicating only their attendance at the school. Awards such as the *Prix Ravel* and *Prix de Ville de Fontainebleau* have also been given sporadically without competitions, and the records are not extant.

Competitions were held irregularly throughout the history of the Conservatoire. Juries had the discretion to omit or add levels of recognition as they saw fit. During the 1950s, prize terms were changed from the previously used English "first, second, third prize," to the French hierarchy of *premier prix*, *deuxieme prix*, and so on, also allowing for *premier accessite*, an equivalent of "runner-up." Near-countless other designations were handed out, even going to the level of "second third (honorable) *mention*." The shadings between some of these levels may seem minute to today's readers, but scholarships and other prize money often hung in the balance. Jury members are listed where available, as are monetary prize amounts and other details.

Areas of study are listed in alphabetical order. Students are listed in alphabetical order using the names under which they registered (i.e., Bathia

Churgin is listed as Betty Churgin). Full names have been given as much as records permit.

1925

Cello

Diplome d'Execution *(Performance)*
    Oliver Edel, *mention bien*

Organ

Diplome d'Execution *(Performance)*
    Albert Coleman, *mention bien*
    Lawerence Cook, *mention bien*
    Emily Boekell
    Margaret Funkhouser
    Herbert Irvine
    Charles Marsh
    Hugh McAmis
    Mrs. McGinley, *mention bien*
    Alexander Schreiner, *mention très bien*
    Louise Titcomb
    Homer Witford

Diplome d'Aptitude à l'Enseignement *(Teaching)*
    Albert Coleman
    Charles Marsh
    Edward Mead
    Max Miranda, *degré preparatoire*
    Alexander Schreiner
    Louise Titcomb

Pedagogy (General Music Education)

Diplome d'Aptitude à l'Enseignement *(Teaching)*
    Robert Crawford
    David Dushkin
    Charles Hennedy Freeman
    Franklin Launer
    Hugh McAmis
    Mildred Meehan, *degré preparatoire*
    Frances Morgan, *degré preparatoire*

Leah Mynderse
Gerard Reynolds
Adrienne Sullivan
Hess Wagner, *degré preparatoire*
Elisabeth Webster, *mention bien*
William Wentzell
Gertrude Williamson, *degré preparatoire*

Piano

Diplome d'Execution *(Performance)*
Josephine Brown
Helen Ganhowsha
Ariel Gross (Louise Lyon), *degré preparatoire*
Caroline Gray
Frances C. Hall, *mention bien*
Russel B. Howe
Lucile Jolly, *degré preparatoire*
Edith Kimple
Willard MacGregor, *mention bien*
Jane Peek
Clara Rabinowitch, *mention bien*
Harold Richey
Etta Schmid, *degré preparatoire*
Beatrice Swartz, *mention bien*
Beveridge Webster, *mention très bien*
Elisabeth Webster
Ferguson Webster, *degré preparatoire*

Diplome d'Aptitude à l'Enseignement *(Teaching)*
Helen Bahn
Helen Caples, *degré preparatoire*
Jessie Crenshaw
John Starts Evans
Louise Findlay
Constance Graham, *mention bien*
Ariel Gross (Louise Lyon)
Alice Hanson
Winifred Hughes, *mention bien*
Lucile Jolly, *mention bien*
Beatrice Jones

Dorothy Leavitt
Sarah MacDonald
Catherine Ellis McClintock
Max Miranda, *degré preparatoire*
Hermine Montagne
Olivia Noël
Dorothy Okey, *degré preparatoire*
Parie Petty
Clara Rabinowitch, *mention bien*
Etta Schmid
Burnyce Stevens
Edith Woodcock, *mention bien*
Bertha Weber
Thetis Westcott
Irma de Villers

Solfège

Harriet Alford
Marion Boulette
Helen Broadwell
Deborah Brown
Violet Cassack
Rosalie Edge
Florence Fraser
Dorothy Gerry
Helen Hosmer
Eleanor Meredith
Marie Neubeiser
Gray Perry
Mildred Seaman
Henri Stewart
H. P. Sturges
Maud Wanzer
Mary Williams

Violin

Diplome d'Execution (*Performance*)
Mark Chestney
Gordon Groth
Rese Underwood

Diplome d'Aptitude à l'Enseignement *(Teaching)*
Mark Chestney, *mention bien*
Gordon Groth
Francis Morgan, *degré preparatoire*
Gertrude Bowes Peabody
Arthur Talmadge

Voice

Diplome d'Execution *(Performance)*
Gladys Burns
Grace Farrar
Helen Harrison
John Parrish
Charles Premmac
Burnyce Stevens, *degré preparatoire*
Helen White

Diplome d'Aptitude à l'Enseignement *(Teaching)*
Richmond Gardner
Muriel Izzard
John Parrish
Charles Premmac
Zelia Vaissade

1926

Organ

Diplome d'Execution *(Performance)*
Adelaide Lee
Elmer A. Tidmarsh

Diplome d'Aptitude à l'Enseignement *(Teaching)*
Walter Angell
Elmer Tidmarsh

Piano

Diplome d'Execution *(Performance)*
Julia Amolsky
Veronique Bakowska

Violet Cassack, *mention bien*
Mary R. Clifford
Claire Crawford
Florence Fraser, *mention bien*
Irene Jones, *mention bien*
Merle MacCarthy West
Margaret Malowney, *mention bien*
Sonya Mints
Mara Molenar
Margaret Morrison
Oliver Reardon
Lillian Roseland
Sister Cecelia Schwab
Hedy Spielter
Mae E. Swanscott
Louise Talma, *mention bien*
Margaret Walsh
Ferguson Webster, *mention bien*

Diplome d'Aptitude à l'Enseignement *(Teaching)*
Violet Cassack
Mary R. Clifford
Kathryn Cole, *mention bien*
Marjorie Galloway
Sister Cecelia Schwab, *mention bien*
Merle MacCarty West
Margaret Malowney
Hazel Martin
Oliver Reardon
Lillian Roseland
Mae Swancott
Margaret Walsh

Solfège
Veronique Bakowska
Verna Brachinreev
Kathryn Cole
Margaret Ferris
Eleanor Herring

Lurine Myrtle Karon
Giuseppe de Lellis
Hazel Martin
Louise Mercer
Margaret Morrison
Helen Richards
Sister Cecelia Schwab
Esther Shaier
Louise Williams

Violin

Diplome d'Execution *(Performance)*
    Mabel Deegan, *mention bien*
    Eva Geisinger, *mention bien*
    Eleanor Herring
    Walter Edelstein, *mention bien*
    François Hurley Uzes

Diplome d'Aptitude à l'Enseignement *(Teaching)*
    Eva Geisinger
    Walter Edelstein
    Lennie Lusby
    François Hurley Uzes

Voice

Diplome d'Execution *(Performance)*
    Florence Beresford
    Marion Capps
    Thamzine Cox, *mention bien*
    Marion Strouse
    Loretta Yates

Diplome d'Aptitude à l'Enseignement *(Teaching)*
    Florence Beresford
    Thamzine Cox
    Marion Pickles
    Leroy Weil
    Loretta Yates

1927

Composition

Prix Tremaine
  First Prize: Helen Roessing
  Second Prize: Hedy Spielter
  Third Prize: Margaret Kenney

Organ

Diplome d'Execution *(Performance)*
  Ruth Barrett
  Robert Cato, *mention très bien*
  Margaret Dow
  Irene Jones
  Vera Kitchner
  Talbot G. Lowe
  Wilbur Rowand
  Pearl Wolpert

Diplome d'Aptitude à l'Enseignement *(Teaching)*
  Margaret Dow
  Wilbur Rowand

Piano

Prix Erard
  Fergusson Webster

Prix Pleyel
  Louise Talma

Prix Chickering
  Florence Stage and Sidney Sukoening

Diplome d'Execution *(Performance)*
  Inez Bringgold
  Erwin Connell
  Lucia Francisco
  Horace Greenberg

Maurice Katz
John Kirkpatrick
Giuseppe de Lellis
Helen Moore, *mention très bien*
Sidney Sukoening
Gladys Olson
Helen Parrot
Kathleen Schofeld
Telesphore Severault
Florence Stage, *mention très bien*
Mildred Warner, *mention bien*
Ada Zeller, *mention bien*

Diplome d'Aptitude à l'Enseignement *(Teaching)*
Erwin Connell, *mention bien*
Fidelia Burgess Duncan, *mention bien*
Eleanor Fourtin
Lucia Francisco, *mention bien*
Helen Parrot
Mae Herbert
Nell Johnson
Albert Lafon
Catherine Margeson, *mention bien*
Helen Moore, *mention bien*
Gladys Olson, *mention bien*
Myrtle Roberts
Kathleen Schofeld
Mildred Warner
Ada Zeller, *mention bien*

Solfège Teaching
Inez Bringgold
Frederic Cardin
Lillian Fish
Eleanor Fourtin
Lucia Francisco
Mae Herbers
Frances Hipple
Charles Kullmann
Catherine Margeson

Clifford McAvoy
Wilma Nobiling
Myrtle Roberts
Mildred Warner
Ada Zeller

Violin

Diplome d'Execution *(Performance)*
Frederic Cardin
Paul Rosenblum

Diplome d'Aptitude à l'Enseignement *(Teaching)*
Harriet Alford
Clara Berovitz
Paul Rosenblum
H. Pemberton Sturges

Voice

Diplome d'Execution *(Performance)*
Louise Belcher, *mention bien*
Richard Condie, *mention très bien*
Constance King, *mention bien*
Charles Kullmann, *mention très bien*
Josephine Martin, *mention très bien*
Vilma Nobiling
Helena Yngre

Diplome d'Aptitude à l'Enseignement *(Teaching)*
Louise Belcher
Richard Condie
Lillian Fish
Eva Gary
Winifred Hopkins
Charles Kullmann
Eva Lawrence
Lucile Morley, *mention bien*
Vilma Nobiling
Helena Yngre

1928

Cello

Diplome d'Execution (*Performance*)
    Irene Hubbard
    Milton Prinz, *mention bien*

Diplome d'Aptitude à l'Enseignement (*Teaching*)
    Irene Hubbard
    Carol Niles
    Milton Prinz, *mention bien*

Organ

Prix Presser et Durand
    First Prize, 1,200 francs: Catherine Morgan
    Second Prize, 800 francs: Janet Maria Clayton
    Third Prize, 500 francs: Harold Schwab

Diplome d'Execution (*Performance*)
    Marion Clayton, *mention bien*
    Harold Schwab
    Robert Gould
    John Groth
    Helen Henshaw
    Charlotte Linsch
    Catherine Morgan, *mention très bien*
    Barbara Singer
    MarionVan Lien
    Ellen Waite

Diplome d'Aptitude à l'Enseignement (*Teaching*)
    Catherine Morgan
    Harold Schwab
    Gearle Porter Weikel

Piano

Concours Presser-Erard
Jury: Auguste de Radwan, President; Marcel Dupré; Jean Batalla; Paul Bazelaire; Marcel Grandjany

First Prize, 2,000 francs (unanimous): Louise Carpenter
Second Prize, 1,000 francs: Joseph Machlis, Hannah Lefkowitz
Third Prize, 750 francs: Louise Talma

Diplome d'Execution (*Performance*)
Louise Carpenter
Elizabeth Coots
Leola Fairchild
William Field
Alice Vernice Gay
Cassius Jolley
Willie Morris
Ellen Waite

Diplome d'Aptitude à l'Enseignement (*Teaching*)
Lillian Brunett
Louise Carpenter
Irma Combs
Elizabeth Coots
Leopoldine Damrosch
William Field
Rose Resnick
Alfred Masonheimer

Solfège
Jacqueline Tyler Bickford
Guy Booth
Leola Fairchild
James A. Gibb
Robert B Gould
Lucy D. Kolp
Kathleen Schofeld
Lois Reed MacLure
Kathleen McKitrick
Hazel Martin
Willie Morris
Martha Richardson
Marjorie Smith

Violin

Prix Theodore Presser
First Prize, 1,200 francs: Max Weiser
Second Prize, 800 francs: Milton Feher
Third Prize, 500 francs: Romeo Tata

Diplome d'Execution *(Performance)*
Milton Feher, *mention bien*
Romeo Tata
Max Weiser, *mention bien*

Diplome d'Aptitude à l'Enseignement *(Teaching)*
Milton Feher
Richard Orton
K. E. Powers
Helen Richards
Romeo Tata
Max Weiser

Voice

Diplome d'Execution *(Performance)*
Hilda Berkey
Janet Creighton
Wesley Howard
Blanche de la Fontaine Scott
Georges Magis
Rhea Massicotte
Louise McIlvain
William Clegg Monroe
Geraldine Nolan
Eugene Ramey
Gertrude Schwentker

Diplome d'Aptitude à l'Enseignement *(Teaching)*
Blanche de la Fontaine Scott
Georges Magis

1929

Organ

Diplome d'Execution *(Performance)*
  Joseph Black
  Madeleine Ernich
  George Faulkner
  Raymond Hicks
  Edward W. Jenkins
  Madelon Maclary
  Herman Ostheimer
  Ford Saunders
  Herman F. Siewart

Diplome d'Aptitude à l'Enseignement *(Teaching)*
  Raymond Hicks

Piano

Prix Steinway-Erard-Tremaine
Jury: Henri Chantavoine, President; Guillaume Remy, Marcel Dupré, Marcel
Grandjany, Paul Bazelaire, Jeanne Michèle Charbonet, Nathalie Radisse

  First Prize: Marian Kalayjian
  Second Prize: Ruth Webb
  Third Prize: Jean Kaplan and Juliette Mirova
  Fourth Prize: Oliver Koa and Florence Fraser

Diplome d'Execution *(Performance)*
  Josephine Carolin
  Ocy Downs
  Margaret Haskins
  Ada Hershfield
  Herbert Irvine
  Louise Jackson
  Marian Kalayjian
  Jean Kaplan
  Oliver Koa
  Clare Little
  Dorothy Maerklein

Theodore Schaefer
Katherin Snowden
Ruth Webb
Hermine Weisner

Diplome d'Aptitude à l'Enseignement *(Teaching)*
Alma Faust
Jeanes Helworth
Muriel Howard
Clare Little
Edythe Logan
Charles Maclary
Katherin Robertson
Louise Jackson

Solfège

Diplome d'Aptitude à l'Enseignement *(Teaching)*
Alfred Finch
Ada Hershfield
Jean Kaplan
Helen Kelly
Eugenia Lichtfield
Clara Little
Eleanor Mims
Catherine Snowden

Violin

Diplome d'Execution *(Performance)*
Edward Powers

Diplome d'Aptitude à l'Enseignement *(Teaching)*
Helen Kelly

Voice

Diplome d'Execution *(Performance)*
Donald MacGill
Louise Rock
Marceil Schwartz

Diplome d'Aptitude à l'Enseignement *(Teaching)*
  Florence Babcock
  Jacqueline Tyler Bickford
  Alfred Finch
  Donald MacGill
  May Mason Speed
  Elsie M. McDowell

1930

Cello

Diplome d'Execution *(Performance)*
  Joy Loomis
  Virginia Quarles, *mention bien*

Organ

Diplome d'Execution *(Performance)*
  Mary Duncan
  Burton Lawrence
  Eleanor Palmer
  Rachel Pierce

Diplome d'Aptitude à l'Enseignement *(Teaching)*
  Mary Duncan
  Burton Lawrence
  Rachel Pierce

Piano

Diplome d'Execution *(Performance)*
  Leah Brown, *mention bien*
  Ethel Flentye, *mention bien*
  Jeannette Giguere, *mention bien*
  Anita Hankwitz
  Suzanne Hotkine
  Esther Ostriff
  Muriel Parker, *mention bien*
  Alice Quarles, *mention bien*
  Mary Robinson

Diplome d'Aptitude à l'Enseignement (*Teaching*)
Mildred Bickett
Leah Brown
Ethel Flentye
Olive Frost, *mention bien*
Anita Hankwitz
Cecile Hindeman
Louise Hoffer
Suzanne Hotkine
Virginia Mountser
Olga Norgreen
Esther Ostroff
Mary Robinson
Elyse Rushford
Agnes Steadman
Mary Stewart
Beatrice Ward, *mention bien*

Solfège
Ethel Flentye
Dorothy Frink, *mention bien*
Anita Hankwitz, *mention bien*
Cecile Hindeman
Louise Hoffer
Suzanne Hotkine
Leonard Langlois
Marjorie Legge
Virginia Mountser
Esther Ostroff
Eleanor Palmer
John Edward Ronan
Ethel Thurston

Violin

Diplome d'Execution (*Performance*)
Frank Brieff, *mention bien*
Arthur Brown
Leonard Langlois
Margaret Quarles, *mention bien*

Diplome d'Aptitude à l'Enseignement (*Teaching*)
    Arthur Brown
    Leonard Langlois

Voice

Diplome d'Execution (*Performance*)
    Harry Blank
    Alfred Finch
    Mrs. Frank Hankinson
    Ruby Heritage
    Lucile Morley
    Martha Doehler Overstreet
    Florence Poling
    Julia Strelitz
    Florence Wilson
    Elizabeth Young

Diplome d'Aptitude à l'Enseignement (*Teaching*)
    Yvette Attinson
    Harry Blank
    Mrs. Frank Hankinson
    Ruby Heritage
    Martha Overstreet
    Elyse Rushford

1931

Cello

Diplome d'Aptitude à l'Enseignement (*Teaching*)
    Bernard Barron
    Alice Wechtell

Solfège
    Myra Conlon
    Mary Ruth Edwards
    Betty Lasley
    Virginia McCarthy
    Sibyl Nichols

Dorothy Ruskin
Gizi Szanto

Piano

Diplome d'Execution *(Performance)*
Maria Conlon
Ruth Edwards
Grace Emery
Evelyn Hansen
Walter Hinkle
Betty Leasley
Virginia McCarthy
Frances Moyer
Sibyl Nichols
Grace Rabinowitch
Gizi Szanto
Marie Van Brock
Harry Wilson

Diplome d'Aptitude à l'Enseignement *(Teaching)*
Ruth Edwards
Grace Emery
Bertha Feitner
Evelyn Hausen
Walter Hinkle
Virginia McCarthy
Frances Moyer
Mary Patterson
Grace Rabinowitch
Gizi Szanto, *mention très bien*
Marie Van Brock, *mention bien*
Edith Van Buskirk
Harry Wilson

Violin

Diplome d'Execution *(Performance)*
Sidney Greenstein
Denny Hannan, *mention bien*
Katherine Lincoln

Winifred Marie Meyer
Michaël Ostrowsky

Diplome d'Aptitude à l'Enseignement *(Teaching)*
Frank Brieff
Sidney Greenstein
Denny Hannan
Katherine Lincoln
Winifred Marie Meyer
Michaël Ostrowsky

Voice

Diplome d'Execution *(Performance)*
Alice Bogardus, *mention bien*
Thorald Croasdale
Mollie Gould
Isabelle Jones
Margherita Kuppersmith
Geraldine Marwick, *mention bien*
Cecil Mitchell
Roland Partridge, *mention bien*
Marjorie Schobel, *mention bien*

Diplome d'Aptitude à l'Enseignement *(Teaching)*
Frieda Behrens
Alice Bogardus
Roland Partridge
Marion Ross
Clet T. Silvey

1932

Organ

Diplome d'Execution *(Performance)*
Newell Guillan
Harold Raymond Thompson

Diplome d'Aptitude à l'Enseignement *(Teaching)*
   Harold Raymond Thompson

Piano

Diplome d'Execution *(Performance)*
   Lillian Brunett
   Catherine McClintock Ellis
   Gladys Heath
   Sophia Jaffe
   Florence Koletzke
   Gertrude Noll
   Carl Parrish
   Alice Payne
   Beatrice Plummer
   Louise Trebika

Diplome d'Aptitude à l'Enseignement *(Teaching)*
   Eloise Beinert
   Louise Trebicka
   Alice Gayne
   Gladys Heath
   Sophia Jaffe
   Florence Koletzke
   Gertrude Noll
   Beatrice Plummer
   Dorothy Rediker

Piano Accompaniment

Diplome d'Execution *(Performance)*
   Editha Messer

Solfège
   Howard Abell
   Carl Parrish, *mention très bien*
   Gertrude Noll

Violin

Diplome d'Execution *(Performance)*
  Simone Beck

Voice

Diplome d'Execution *(Performance)*
  Alice Mary Anderson
  Helen Chapin
  Edna Haddock
  Helen Marshall
  Aletha Stacey
  Louise Burt Wood

Diplome d'Aptitude à l'Enseignement *(Teaching)*
  Marjorie Schobel
  Louisa Burt Wood

1933

Harmony
  Virginia Mackie
  Louise Talma

Organ

Diplome d'Execution *(Performance)*
  Ralph Davis
  Robert Hufstader

Piano

Diplome d'Execution *(Performance)*
  Lela Hardy
  Polly Johnson
  Juliette Rodrigue

Diplome d'Aptitude à l'Enseignement *(Teaching)*
  Lela Hardy
  Polly Johnson

Solfège
  Margery Dykes
  Robert Hufstader, *mention très bien*
  Virginia Mackie, *mention très bien*

Violin

Diplome d'Execution *(Performance)*
  Minna Willener
  Frances Woodbury, *mention bien*

Diplome d'Aptitude à l'Enseignement *(Teaching)*
  Frances Woodbury

Voice

Diplome d'Execution *(Performance)*
  Jeannette Booth
  Katherine Metcalf, *mention bien*
  Madeleine de Morsier
  Harold Peterson
  Eugene Riese
  Evelyn Sprager
  Rhea Webb
  Helen Wilson

Diplome d'Aptitude à l'Enseignement *(Teaching)*
  Katherine Metcalf
  Helen Wilson

1934

Organ

Diplome d'Execution *(Performance)*
  Edgar Groth

Piano

Diplome d'Execution *(Performance)*
  Cinabelle Burzinsky
  Lucy Clark
  Marion Swan

Solfège
Marion Swan
Frances Woodbury

Violin

Diplome d'Execution *(Performance)*
Lucy Clark

Voice

Diplome d'Execution *(Performance)*
Anne Dyer

1935

Organ

Diplome d'Execution *(Performance)*
David Berger, *mention bien*
Edward Mead
Ruth Stockwell Melville, *mention bien*
Marcus Naylor, *mention très bien*

Diplome d'Aptitude à l'Enseignement *(Teaching)*
David Berger, *mention bien*
Ruth Stockwell Melville, *mention très bien*
Marcus Naylor

Piano

Diplome d'Execution *(Performance)*
Romeo Arsenault
Juan Nazarian
Mary Van Valkenburg, *mention bien*

Diplome d'Aptitude à l'Enseignement *(Teaching)*
Alexandra Grow, *mention bien*
Juan Nazarian, *mention très bien*
Mary Van Valkenburg, *mention très bien*

Solfège
Ruth Melville
Mary Van Valkenburg, *mention très bien*

1936

Harp

Diplome d'Execution *(Performance)*
Helen Higgins

Organ

Diplome d'Execution *(Performance)*
Lucile Hammill

Diplome d'Aptitude à l'Enseignement *(Teaching)*
Lucile Hammill

Piano

Diplome d'Execution *(Performance)*
Reginald Bedford, *mention bien*
Vesta Case
Corinne Frederick, *mention très bien*
Irene Graffuis
Margaret Rosenfeldt
Sarah Supplee

Diplome d'Aptitude à l'Enseignement *(Teaching)*
Vesta Case
Irene Graffuis
Sarane Ives
Margaret Rosenfeldt
Lucia Simmons
Sarah Supplee

Solfège
William M. Eves
Elizabeth Fretz
Lucile Hammill

John Donald Robb
Lucia Simmons
Sarah Supplee

Voice

Diplome d'Execution *(Performance)*
    Edison Harris
    Otis Holley

Diplome d'Aptitude à l'Enseignement *(Teaching)*
    A. S. Ebersole
    Annie Laura Tronsdale

1937

Cello

Diplome d'Aptitude à l'Enseignement *(Teaching)*
    Enrico Tamburini

Composition

Prix Stovall
Jury: Nadia Boulanger, Marcelle de Manziarly, Annette Dieudonné, Roger Ducasse, Jean Françaix, Lennox Berkeley, Herbert Elwell, Boleslaw Wojtwicz

    First Prize: none awarded
    Second Prize, 1,000 francs: Livingston Gearhart
    Mentions, 333 francs each: Andrew Imbrie, Floyd Morgernstern, Frederick
        Werle

Organ

Diplome d'Execution *(Performance)*
    Dora Poteet
    Cornelius Van Rees
    Margaret Work

Diplome d'Aptitude à l'Enseignement *(Teaching)*
    Dora Poteet
    Margaret Work

Piano

Diplome d'Execution *(Performance)*
　　Angela Annicharieo
　　Romeo Arsenault
　　Virginia Clotfelter, *mention bien*
　　Emma Endes, *mention très bien*
　　William Eves
　　Margaret Ferguson
　　Rita Gagen, *mention bien*
　　Helene Landry
　　Irene Leftwich, *mention bien*
　　Marjorie Lohmann
　　Ann McDougle
　　Bessie Scharff
　　Frederick Werle

Diplome d'Aptitude à l'Enseignement *(Teaching)*
　　Virginia Clotfelter
　　Ocy Downs
　　Ann Katzenstein
　　Irene Leftwich
　　Marjorie Lohman
　　Maryetta Roop
　　Katherine Schaefer

Voice

Diplome d'Execution *(Performance)*
　　Josephine Case
　　Charles Davis
　　Mildred Jenkins
　　Lucia Simmons

Diplome d'Aptitude à l'Enseignement *(Teaching)*
　　Charles Davis

1938

Cello

Diplome d'Aptitude à l'Enseignement *(Teaching)*
　　Louise Wingold, *mention bien*

Chansons regionales (Folk song)
Germaine Arosa

Composition

Prix Stovall
Jury: Nadia Boulanger, Igor Stravinsky

First Prize, 1,300 francs: Louise Talma
Mention, 400 francs: Louis O. Palmer II

Organ

Diplome d'Execution *(Performance)*
Clifford C. Loomis
Margaret McPherson

Diplome d'Aptitude à l'Enseignement *(Teaching)*
Margaret McPherson
Ethel Thurston

Piano

Diplome d'Execution *(Performance)*
Murray Baylor
Jane Boedcker
Elwood Kraft
Leo Lawless
Emmanuelina Lizzuto
Frances Loftus
Ruth McLinn, *mention bien*
Mary Shep Mann
Ozanne Marsh, *mention très bien*
Bertha Melnik, *mention bien*
J. B. Middleton
Aloysio de Alenear Pinto, *mention très bien*
Jean Seybold
Della Wilson

Diplome d'Aptitude à l'Enseignement *(Teaching)*
Jane Cleveland, *degré elementaire*
Frances Loftus

Mary Shep Mann
Sarah Marvin
Goodrich White, *degré elementaire*

Solfège
Harvey F. Armington
Bertha Melnik
Ethel Thurston

Violin

Diplome d'Execution *(Performance)*
Zoya Maximoff
William Stone, *mention très bien*

Voice

Diplome d'Execution *(Performance)*
Jane Rogers

1939

Cello

Diplome d'Execution *(Performance)*
Marie-Therese Gosset
Pierre Delvincourt

Composition

Prix Stovall
First Prize (award amount unknown): Louise Talma
Second Prize, 1,000 francs: Cecil Effinger
Third Prize, 500 francs each: Ali Fenmen, Albert Fillmore

Organ

Diplome d'Execution *(Performance)*
Alice Clement
Sally Marion
Louise Talma

Diplome d'Aptitude à l'Enseignement *(Teaching)*
  Alice Clement
  Laurence Dilsner
  Louise Talma

Piano

Diplome d'Execution *(Performance)*
  Cedric Chase Jr.
  Margaret Colson, *mention bien*
  Irene Heindl
  Marion Louise King
  Lydia Lesta
  Louise Mardiras, *mention très bien*
  Elizabeth Powell
  Constance Russell, *mention bien*
  Nathalie Tuttle, *mention bien*

Diplome d'Aptitude à l'Enseignement *(Teaching)*
  Ruth Grace, *degré moyen*
  Perle Mumma, *mention bien*
  Robert Parsons, *mention bien*
  Elizabeth Powell
  Constance Russell

Solfège
  Elizabeth Powell

Violin

Diplome d'Execution *(Performance)*
  Frances Shapiro, *mention très bien*

Diplome d'Aptitude à l'Enseignement *(Teaching)*
  Margaret Sweeney

Voice

Diplome d'Execution *(Performance)*
  Evelyn Gibson
  Joanne de Nault

Ruth Murray
Harry Thomson

Diplome d'Aptitude à l'Enseignement *(Teaching)*
Evelyn Gibson
Joanne de Nault
Ruth Murray
Harry Thomson

1946

Scholarships for the Service of Cultural Relations, 8,000 Francs Each
Anne de Ramus
Lydia Ryvicher

1947

Piano Prizes
First Prize, 10,000 francs: Deene Reece
Second Prize, 5,000 francs: Grant Johannesen

Scholarships for the Service of Cultural Relations, 4,000 Francs Each
Anne de Ramus
Lydia Ryvicher

1950

Concours de Composition
Jury: Marcel Dupré, Paul Bazelaire, Nadia Boulanger, Annette Dieudonné, Rolande Falcinelli, Paul Fievet, Jean Françaix, Marcel Jean, Roland Manuel, Nicholas Nabokoff, Leo Preger, Michael Spisak, Antoni Szalowski

Premier Prix, 3,000 francs each: Arthur Frackenpohl (*Prix Deane Reese*), Robert Moevs (*Prix Lili Boulanger*)
Premier Accessite: Allyn Ferguson, Norman Voelker
Deuxieme Accessite: Alfred Pew Brooks

Concours de Chant
Jury: Marcel Dupré, Nadia Boulanger, Annette Dieudonné, Rolande Falcinelli, Paul Fievet, Jean Françaix, Marcel Jean, Germaine Martinelli,

Roland Manuel, Nicholas Nabokoff, Leo Preger, Michael Spisak, Antoni Szalowski

Premier Prix (Prix Martinelli): Iris Fribrock, Wilbur Jones
Premier Accessite: Isabelle McClung, Donna Precht

Concours de Clarinette
Jury: Marcel Dupré, Paul Bazelaire, Nadia Boulanger, Annette Dieudonné, Rolande Falcinelli, Paul Fievet, Jean Françaix, Marcel Jean, Roland Manuel, Nicholas Nabokoff, Leo Preger, Michael Spisak, Antoni Szalowski

Premier Prix (Prix Gaston Hamelin) (unanimous), 3,000 francs: Ernest Bright
Premier Accessite (unanimous): Albert Fine

Concours de Déchiffrage
Jury: Nadia Boulanger, Annette Dieudonné, Alice Gaultier Léon, Mademoiselle Spycket, Jean Painchaud

Premiere Mention: Norman Voelker
Deuxieme Mention: James Lotze, Judith Yaeger
Troisième Mention: Richard Strasburg

Concours d'Ensemble Instrumental
Jury: Nadia Boulanger, Annette Dieudonné, Paul Bazelaire, Paul Fievet, M. Henry, Alice Gaultier Léon, M. Merckel, Jean Painchaud, Pierre Pasquier

Premier Prix: David Montagu, Norman Voelker
Deuxieme Prix: Ernest Bright, Betty Churgin, Stuart Fastofsky, Norman Voelker, J. Yaeger
Premier Accessite: Betty Churgin, Roy Christophersen, David Montagu, Calvin Sieb, R. Strasburg, Norman Voelker, Elton Young
Deuxieme Accessite: Betty Churgin, Ann Estill, Albert Fine, James Lotze

Concours d'Orgue
Jury: Marcel Dupré, Paul Bazelaire, Nadia Boulanger, Annette Dieudonné, Rolande Falcinelli, Paul Fievet, Jean Françaix, Marcel Jean, Roland Manuel, Nicholas Nabokoff, Leo Preger, Michael Spisak, Antoni Szalowski

Premier Prix, 3,000 francs: Robert Wolff
Deuxieme Prix: Thomas Brumby, David Hewlett, Augustine Plamondon

Concours de Piano

Jury: Nadia Boulanger, Robert Casadesus, Alice Gaultier Léon, Paul Baze-laire, Annette Dieudonné, Henri Dutilleux, Rolande Falcinelli, Genevieve Joy, Gilberte Lecompte, Jean Painchaud

Premier Prix, Prix Robert Casadesus, 3,000 francs: Norman Voelker
Deuxieme Prix: Richard Strasburg, Judith Yaeger
Premier Accessite: Hadley Yates
Deuxieme Accessite: Vada Easter

Concours de Solfège

Jury: Nadia Boulanger, Annette Dieudonné, Alice Gaultier Léon, Mademoi-selle Spycket, Jean Painchaud

Degré Elementaire, Premiere Mentions: Jo Anne Barr, David Hewlett
Degré Elementaire, Deuxieme Mention: Donna Precht
Degré Moyen, Premiere Mention: Allyn Ferguson
Degré Moyen, Deuxieme Mention: Linda Muschenheim
Degré Moyen, Troisième Mention: Elsie Kohlenstein
Troisième Degré, Premiere Mention: Arthur Frackenpohl, Charles Hender-son, Calvin Sieb, Norman Voelker
Troisième Degré, Deuxieme Mention: Betty Churgin, Albert Fine
Troisième Degré, Troisième Mention: Richard Strasburg

Concours de Violon

Jury: Marcel Dupré, Paul Bazelaire, Nadia Boulanger, Annette Dieudonné, Rolande Falcinelli, Paul Fievet, Jean Françaix, Marcel Jean, Roland Manuel, Nicholas Nabokoff, Leo Preger, Michael Spisak, Antoni Szalowski

Premier Prix: David Montagu, Calvin Sieb
Deuxieme Prix: Stuart Fastofsky

1951

Concours d'Analyse Harmonique

Degré Superieur
Premieres Medailles: Betty Churgin, Norman Voelker (Prix Relations Cul-turelles)
Secondes Medailles: Rosette Renshaw, Dean Witter

Troisième Medaille: Shirley Okon
Premiere Mention: Virginia Hageman (*classe preparatoire*)

Concours de Composition

Jury: Nadia Boulanger, Jean Françaix, Paul Bazelaire, Michel Spisak, Annette Dieudonné

Premiere Mention: Richard Wienhorst
Premiere Seconde Mention: Virginia Hageman
Deuxieme Seconde Mention: Dean Nuernberger
Premiere Troisième Mention: Richard Oliver
Deuxieme Troisième Mention: Dean Witter
Prix d'Excellence and *Prix du Gouvernement Français*: Louise Talma
Seconde Prix: Richard Wienhorst, Dean Nuernburger
Premier Accessite: Betty Churgin, Rosette Renshaw

Concours de Chant

Premier Prix d'Excellence: Janet Southwick
Premier Prix: Leon Grat
Seconde Prix: H. William Battaile, Donna Precht, Donna Rumsey
Premier Accessite: John Ferrante, Churchill Jackson
Seconde Accessite: Germaine Barre, Roberta Basnett, Meline Kuhlanjian

Concours de Dechiffrage

Premiere Mention and *Prix Gilbert Lecompte*, 2,000 francs: William Gant
Seconde Mention: James Darling, Louise Harwell
Troisième Mention: La Verne Dalka, John Elton

Concours Direction d'Ensemble Vocal

Prix d'Excellence and *Prix du Gouvernement Français*: Elaine Brown
Premier Prix and *Prix Lili Boulanger*: John Westmoreland
Premier Accessite: Sonya Garfinkle

Concours Interpretation de Musique Ancienne

Prix d'Excellence and *Prix des Relations Culturelles*: Janet Southwick
Premier Prix and *Prix des Relations Culturelles*: L'Ensemble Vocal, Donna Precht, Donna Rumsey
Seconde Prix: Leon Gray, William Battaile
Premier Accessite: John Ferrante

Concours de Musique d'Ensemble
Premier Prix: Stuart Fastofsky, Norman Voelker
Seconde Prix: Betty Churgin, William Gant, John Golz, Walter Harelson,
William Klentz, Norman Voelker

Individual Prizes
Premier Prix: John Elton, Thomas Borkcman,
Seconde Prix: James Darling, Joy Hazelrigg
Premier Accessite: Ann Fiore, Mary Jane Troop
Seconde Accessite: Ann McKinley

Concours de Piano

Concours "A"
Premiere Medaille: Anna Fiore
Secondes Medailles: Rosie Banaag, Ann McKinley
Troisièmes Medailles: La Verne Dalka, Elsie Kohlenstein
Mention: Rose Ane Lonier

Concours "B"
Prix d'Excellence: William Brockman
Premier Prix: John Elton, William Harelson, Louise Harwell, Joy Hazelrigg
Seconde Prix: Rosine Nocera
Premiers Accessites: James Darling, Laura King
Seconde Accessite: Raphael Valerio

Concours de Solfège

Degré Superieur
Premieres Medailles: Betty Churgin, Joy Hazelrigg, Rosette Renshaw
Deuxieme Medailles: Louise Harwell, Rose Ann Lonier, Raphael Valerio
Troisième Medailles: Rosie Banaag, John Elton, Dean Witter, Virginia
Hageman

Degré Moyen
Premiere Mention: Ann Fiore, Shirley Okon
Deuxieme Mention: Elsie Kohlenstein, Donna Precht
Encouragement: La Verne Dalka

Degré Elementaire
  Premiere Mention: William Battaile, John Westmoreland
  Deuxieme Mention: Eleanor Folwell, Mary F. Raphael
  Troisième Mention: Churchill Jackson
  Encouragements: Germaine Barre, Dorothy Dittman, J. Lewis-Comas

Concours de Violon
Jury: Nadia Boulanger, Paul Bazelaire, Maurice Gendron, Jean Françaix, Jean Pasquier

  Premier Prix: Stuart Fastofsky
  Seconde Prix: John Golz
  Seconde Accessite: Marguerite Learning

1952

Concours de Chant
  Premier Prix: Norman Farrow
  Seconde Prix: Meline Kulhanjian
  Rappel de Seconde Prix: William Battaile

Concours de Composition
  Premier Prix: Narcis Bonet, Julia Perry
  Seconde Prix: William Rogers
  Deuxiemes Accessites: Felix Guerrero, Eulia Dick
  Mention: Elizabeth Melroy
  Exceptional mention for performance of composers' works: Idil Biret

Concours de Keyboard Harmony
  Deuxieme Prix: Rosette Renshaw
  Premier Accessite: Ursula Clutterbuck, Elizabeth Melloy, Luise Vosgerchian

Concours de Piano
  Prix d'Excellence: Malcolm Frager
  Premier Prix: Rosine Nocera
  Premier Accessite: Robert Howat, Roger Kamien
  Seconde Accessite: William Rogers

1953

Concours de Composition
Premier Prix: Narcis Bonet, Eulia Dick
Premier Seconde Prix, Prix Ravel: Hector Campos-Parsi
Deuxieme Seconde Prix: Dean Witter
Premier Accessite: Kenton Coe
Deuxieme Accessite: Robert Browne, William Simon, Elliot Weisgarber
Mention: Barbara Buckley, Laila Padorr, Barbara Scholl, Francis Scott

Concours de Chant
Premier Prix and *Prix Jean-Paul Alaux*: Vivian McDowell Martin
Premier Accessite: Taudie Simon
Seconde Accessite: Sonya Can Dam, Salvador Tomas

Concours d'Ensemble Vocal
Seconde Prix: Harold Decker

Concours de Musique de Chambre
Seconde Prix: Quattor Fauré: William Bruni, Derry Deane, Frederic Grande, Kermit Moore; Trio Beethoven: Derry Deane, Earl Kelly, Guelda Sherman

Concours de Piano
Premier Prix and *Prix Salabert*: Seymour Bernstein
Seconde Prix: Genevieve Chinn

Concours de Violon
Premier Prix and *Prix Salabert*: Derry Deane
Seconde Prix: William Bruni

Concours de Violoncello
Seconde Prix: Kermit Moore, Guelda Sherman

1954

Concours de Chant
Premier Prix and *Prix Arthur Sachs*, 50,000 francs: Janice Seward
Premier Prix and *Prix Jean de Polignac*, 50,000 francs: Leah Crohn
Seconde Prix: Virginia English, William Battaile (Rappel)

Premier Accessite: Robert Wilson
Seconde Accessite: Una Field, Margot Long

Concours de Composition
Premier Prix and *Prix Francis Salabert*,100,000 francs: Luise Vosgerchian
Premier Accessite: Richard Oliver
Seconde Accessite: Barbara Buckley

Concours de Harpe
Premier Prix and *Prix Lili Boulanger*, 50,000 francs: Nina Dunkel

Concours de Musique de Chambre
Premier Prix and *Prix Dinu Lipatti*, 25,000 francs each: Kenneth Gordon,
    Murray Present
Premier Prix and *Prix Madame Psycha*, 10,000 francs: Manuel Villet
Premier Accessite: Elizabeth Potteiger, Pilar Sarracas
Seconde Accessite: Helene Blanchard, Carol Calkins, Betty Swanson

Concours d'Orgue
Seconde Prix: Jerome Rainey
Premier Accessite: Paul Thomas

Concours de Piano
Prix d'Excellence and *Prix Maurice Ravel*, 200,000 francs: Manuel Villet
Premier Prix and *Prix Jacques Durand*, 100,000 francs: Murray Present
Seconde Prix: Georgene Van Sciver
Premier Accessite: Pilar Larracas, Adele Velo
Seconde Accessite: Eugene Harsh

Concours de Violon
Premier Prix and *Prix Jacques Durand*, 100,000 francs: Kenneth Gordon
Seconde Prix: Caroline Calkins
Premier Accessite: Pierre Dessaint

Concours de Violoncello
Seconde Prix: Arthur Howard
Premiere Accessite: Elizabeth Potteiger
Seconde Accessite: Betty Swanson

1955

Concours de Composition
   Premier Prix and *Prix Jean de Polignac*, 60,000 francs: Earsley Blackwood
   Seconde Prix: Jean Miller, John Perkins
   Premier Accessite: Boyd MacDonald

Concours de Chant
   Premier Accessite: Martha Joyce Ritchey
   Seconde Accessite: Douglas Bredt

Concours de Piano
   Prix d'Excellence, Prix Arthur Sachs, 60,000 francs, and *Prix Jean de Polignac,*
   40,000 francs: Joseph Plon
   Premier Accessite: Rebecca Gresham
   Seconde Accessite: Joel Shapiro

Concours de Violon
   Seconde Prix: Nina Geverts, Carol Stein
   Premier Accessite: Mary Louise Galen

Concours de Violoncello
   Deuxieme Accessite: Barbara Stein

1956

No competitions held

1957

No competitions held

1958

No competitions held

1959

Concours de Conducting
Jury: Nadia Boulanger, Annette Dieudonné, Jean Françaix, Jean Pasquier,
Michel Spisak

Seconde Prix and *Prix Batchelder*, $100 each: Mark Anstendig, Fiora Contino
Premier Mention: Harriet Simons
Seconde Mention: Barbara Lingelback
Troisième Mention: Zenobia Martin

1960

Concours de Chant
Diplome: André Aerne, Joseph Parella, Jane Schleicher

Concours de Clarinette
Diplome cum laudes: Sherman Friedland

Concours de Composition
Hors Concours, avec felicitations: James Ming
Diplome: Laurence Taylor, Donald McAfee
Mention cum laudes: Charles Fox
Mention: Robert Levin

Concours de Conducting
Diplome hors concours cum laudes: Fiora Contino
Diplome cum laudes: Marion Vree
Diplome: John Parella, Ruth Milliken
Mention: Donald Reber

Concours d'Ensemble Instrumental
Diplome: Judith Basch, Arthur Lewis, Sophie Schultz

Concours de Flute
Diplome cum laude: Sophie Schultz

Concours d'Orgue
Diplome: Donald Reber
Mention: Helen Caruthers

Concours de Piano
Jury: Nadia Boulanger, Jean Casadesus, Gilberte Lecompte, Annette Dieudonné, Michel Spisak, Antoni Szalowski

Diplome: Raymond Jackson
Mention (in order of jury ranking): Harriet Elsom, Susan Heimbach, Robert Levin

Concours de Violon
Mention: Judith Basch

1966

Concours de Composition

Prix du Publique
Air (required composed work)
Premier Prix: Yung Chen, Krzysztof Meyer
Deuxieme Prix: Alinda Couper, Michael Flakesman, Hugh Robertson
Mention: Harold Gilmore
Recitative (required composed work)
Premier Prix: Yung Shen, Krzysztof Meyer
Seconde Prix: Alinda Couper, Harold Gilmore, Hugh Robertson

Prix de Jury
Jury: Nadia Boulanger, Annette Dieudonné, Henri Dutilleux

Air
Premier Prix: Yung Shen, Krzysztof Meyer
Seconde Prix: Hugh Robertson, Michael Flakesman
Mention: Alinda Couper, Harold Gilmore
Recitative
Premier Prix: Krzysztof Meyer
Deuxieme Prix: Yung Shen, Hugh Robertson
Mention: Alinda Couper, Harold Gilmore

1968

Concours de Composition
Premier Prix: Hugh Robertson, Mirgana Zitkovic
Seconde Prix: Christopher Bockman, Duncan Jones
Troisième Prix: Shirley Mackie, Jay Gottlieb, Philipp Wachsmann

1969

Concours de Composition
Trios: *Mention Magna cum laude*: Jay Gottlieb, Leonard Lehrman, Robert Rodriguez, Robert Shafer
Motets: *Mention Magna cum laude*: Robert Rodriguez, Robert Shafer
Mention cum laude: Stefan Kozinski
Honorable Mention: Evelyn Steinbock, Sue Wink

1970

Concours de Composition
Mention magna cum laude: Christopher Bockman
Mention cum laude: Stephan Kozinski, Almeida Prado
Mention Honorable: Robert Gage, Jean Louis Hagenauer

1973

Concours Robert et Jean Casadesus
Jury: Gaby Casadesus, Nadia Boulanger, Noel Lee, Gilberte Lecompte, Annette Dieudonné

Premier Degré and Prix Robert et Jean Casadesus (unanimous): Charles Pettaway
Mention: Dennis Pitasi
Mention: Sister Elisabeth Angilette
Seconde Degré: *Premier Mention*: Robert Kapilow
Deuxieme Mention: Emile Naoumoff
Troisième Mention: Geoffery Bond
Quatrième Mention: Judith Kogan
Cinquième Mention: Elsie Watson
Troisième Degré: *Mention*: Richard Kogan

~

Bibliography

Primary Sources

Echo de Paris. August 8, 1927. Re. Naming of swans at Palais. BMF
———. August 11, 1927. BMF
Figaro. October 28, 1922. "Est-ce le Palais de Fontainebleau un menace d'incendie?"
———. Undated, 1976. Re. Conservatoire Américain's fiftieth anniversary. BMF
Fontainebleau Alumni Bulletin. January 1929. CA/F, CA/NY, possession of author.
———. May 1930. CA/F, CA/NY, possession of author.
———. May 1931. CA/F, CA/NY, possession of author.
———. January 1932. CA/F, CA/NY, possession of author.
———. May 1932. CA/F, CA/NY, possession of author.
———. January 1933. CA/F, CA/NY, possession of author.
———. May 1933. CA/F, CA/NY, possession of author.
———. January 1934. CA/F, CA/NY, possession of author.
———. May 1934. CA/F, CA/NY, possession of author.
———. March 1935. CA/F, CA/NY, possession of author.
———. May 1939. CA/F, CA/NY, possession of author.
———. June 1940. CA/F, CA/NY, possession of author.
———. November 1945. CA/F, CA/NY, possession of author.
———. June 1947. CA/F, CA/NY, possession of author.
———. November 1954. CA/F, CA/NY, possession of author.
———. April 1955. CA/F, CA/NY, possession of author.
———. November 1955. CA/F, CA/NY, possession of author.
———. April 1956. CA/F, CA/NY, possession of author.
———. November 1956. CA/F, CA/NY, possession of author.

———. April 1957. CA/F, CA/NY, possession of author.

———. November 1957. CA/F, CA/NY, possession of author.

———. April 1958. CA/F, CA/NY, possession of author.

———. November 1958. CA/F, CA/NY, possession of author.

———. April 1959. CA/F, CA/NY, possession of author.

———. November 1959. CA/F, CA/NY, possession of author.

———. April 1960. CA/F, CA/NY, possession of author.

———. April 1961. CA/F, CA/NY, possession of author.

———. November 1963. CA/F, CA/NY, possession of author.

———. November 1965. CA/F, CA/NY, possession of author.

———. April 1966. CA/F, CA/NY, possession of author.

———. November 1966. CA/F, CA/NY, possession of author.

———. April 1967. CA/F, CA/NY, possession of author.

———. November 1967. CA/F, CA/NY, possession of author.

———. April 1968. CA/F, CA/NY, possession of author.

———. November 1968. CA/F, CA/NY, possession of author.

———. April 1969. CA/F, CA/NY, possession of author.

———. November 1969. CA/F, CA/NY, possession of author.

———. April 1970. CA/F, CA/NY, possession of author.

———. November 1970. CA/F, CA/NY, possession of author.

———. April 1971. CA/F, CA/NY, possession of author.

———. November 1971. CA/F, CA/NY, possession of author.

———. April 1972. CA/F, CA/NY, possession of author.

———. May 1974. CA/F, CA/NY, possession of author.

———. May 1976. CA/F, CA/NY, possession of author.

———. May 1977. CA/F, CA/NY, possession of author.

———. July 1978. CA/F, CA/NY, possession of author.

———. January 1979. CA/F, CA/NY, possession of author.

———. June 1980. CA/F, CA/NY, possession of author.

———. June 1981. CA/F, CA/NY, possession of author.

———. February 1997. CA/F, CA/NY, possession of author.

———. February 1998. CA/F, CA/NY, possession of author.

———. February 1999. CA/F, CA/NY, possession of author.

———. January 2000. CA/F, CA/NY, possession of author.

———. January 2001. CA/F, CA/NY, possession of author.

Le Journal. Article. June 26, 1924. BMF

La Liberte. Article. July 3, 1959. Re. Opening of Conservatoire Américain de Fontainebleau for the year. BMF

———. Article. 1962. Re. Concert to honor Jean Françaix. BMF

Musical Courier. Article. April 22, 1932, Paris. Re. Housing of Conservatoire Américain students and future of school. CA/F

Les Nouvelles Litteraires. Article. Undated, 1962. Interview with Jean Françaix. BMF

La République de Seine-et-Marne. Article. Undated. Interview with Pierre Devinoy. BMF
——. Article. June 13, 1988.
——. Article. July 13, 1992.
——. Article. January 23, 1993.
——. Article: "Écoles d'Art Américaines en sursis?" January 31, 1994.

Interviews
Casadesus, Gaby, and Thérèse Casadesus Rawson. Interview with author, July 20, 1999, Recloses, France. Tape recording.
Gottlieb, Jay. Interview with author, July 24, 2000, Fontainebleau, France. Tape recording.
Harrison, James. Telephone interview with author, May 1, 2003, Cincinnati, Ohio. Notes.
Kerr, Joe. Interviews with author, July 1999 and July 2000, Fontainebleau, France. Notes.
Kaufman, Charles. Interview with author. March 24, 1999, New York City. Tape recording.
Marty, Jean-Pierre. Telephone interview with author, July 1999, Fontainebleau, France. Notes.
Naoumoff, Emile. Interview with author, October 14, 2000, Bloomington, Indiana. Tape recording.
Takakjian, Debra. Interview with author, July 1999, Fontainebleau, France. Notes.
Watson, Elsie. Interviews with author, July 1999 and July 2000, Fontainebleau, France; Boulder, Colo., 2004. Notes and tape recordings.

Secondary Sources
Brodeur, Clarence. "Fontainebleau: A Golden Jubilee." *Music Journal* 29, no. 4 (April 1971): 31–33.
Brooks, Jeanice. "Nadia Boulanger and the Salon of the Princesse de Polignac." *Journal of the American Musicological Society* 16, no. 3 (Fall 1993): 415–468.
Brosman, Catherine Savage, ed. *French Culture 1900–1975*. Detroit: Gale Research, 1995.
Campbell, Don G. *Master Teacher: Nadia Boulanger*. Washington, D.C.: Pastoral Press, 1984.
Carter, Elliott. *Collected Essays and Lectures*. Rochester, N.Y.: University of Rochester Press, 1997.
Casadesus, Gaby. *Mes noces musicales*. Paris: Buchet/Chastel, 1989.
Copland, Aaron, and Vivian Perlis. *Copland 1900 through 1945*. New York: St. Martin's, 1984.
Crawford, Richard. *America's Musical Life: A History*. New York: Norton, 2001.

Damrosch, Walter. *My Musical Life*. New York: Scribner, 1923.

Fay, Amy. *Music-Study in Germany: The Classic Memoir of the Romantic Era, with a New Introduction by Francis Dillon*. New York: Dover, 1991.

Flanner, Janet. *Paris Was Yesterday*. New York: Harcourt Brace Jovanovich, 1972.

Gann, Kyle. *American Music in the Twentieth Century*. New York: Schirmer, 1997.

Hall, Charles J. *A Chronicle of American Music, 1700–1995*. New York: Schirmer, 1996.

Heintze, James, ed. *Perspectives on American Music since 1950*. New York: Garland, 1999.

Hitchcock, H. Wiley, ed. *The Phonograph and Our Musical Life: Proceedings of a Centennial Conference, 7–10 December 1977*. New York: Institute for Studies in American Music, University of New York, 1980.

Karnow, Stanley. *Paris in the Fifties*. New York: Times Books, 1997.

Karolyi, Otto. *Modern American Music: From Charles Ives to the Minimalists*. London: Cygnus Arts, 1996.

Kendall, Alan. *The Tender Tyrant: Nadia Boulanger: A Life Dedicated to Music*. Wilton, Conn: Lyceum Books, 1977.

Kimberling, Victoria J. *David Diamond: A Bio-Bibliography*. Metuchen, N.J.: Scarecrow Press, 1987.

Kingman, Daniel. *American Music: A Panorama*. New York: Schirmer, 1990.

Locke, Ralph P., and Cyrilla Barr. *Cultivating Music in America: Women Patrons and Patronage since 1860*. Berkeley: University of California Press, 1997.

MacLean, Helene. *There's No Place Like Paris*. New York: Doubleday and Co., 1951.

Martin, George. *The Damrosch Dynasty*. Boston: Houghton Mifflin, 1983.

McMillan, James F. *Twentieth Century France: Politics and Society 1898–1991*. London: Arnold Books, 1985.

Mellers, Wilfrid. *Music in a New-Found Land: Themes and Developments in the History of American Music*. New York: Knopf, 1965.

Mender, Mona. *Extraordinary Women in Support of Music*. Lanham, Md.: Scarecrow Press, 1997.

Montsaingeon, Bruno. *Mademoiselle: Conversations with Nadia Boulanger*. Boston: Northeastern University Press, 1985.

Nectoux, Jean-Michel. *The New Grove Twentieth-Century French Masters*. New York: Norton, 1986.

Norton Grove Concise Encyclopedia of Music. New York: Norton and Company, 1988.

Olmstead, Andrea. *Juilliard: A History*. Urbana: University of Illinois Press, 1999.

Orenstein, Arbie. *Ravel: Man and Musician*. New York: Columbia University Press, 1975.

Patorini-Casadesus, Regina. *Ma famille Casadesus: Souvenirs d'une claveciniste 1890–1955*. Paris: La Ruche Ouvriere, 1962.

Perryman, William Ray. *Walter Damrosch: An Educational Force in American Music*. MA thesis, Indiana University, 1973.

Philip, Robert. *Early Recordings and Musical Style: Changing Tastes in Instrumental Performance, 1900–1950*. Cambridge, U.K.: Cambridge University Press, 1992.

Pollack, Howard. *Aaron Copland: The Life and Work of an Uncommon Man*. New York: Henry Holt, 1999.

Price, Roger. *A Concise History of France*. Cambridge, U.K.: Cambridge University Press, 1993.

Rockwell, John. *All American Music: Composition in the Late Twentieth Century*. New York: Knopf, 1983.

Rosenstiel, Léonie. *Nadia Boulanger: A Life in Music*. New York: Norton, 1982.

Saffle, Michael, ed. *Perspectives on American Music, 1900–1950*. New York: Garland, 2000.

Slonimsky, Nicolas. *The Concise Baker's Biographical Dictionary of Musicians*. New York: Schirmer, 1994.

Spycket, Jérôme. *Nadia Boulanger*. Translated by M. M. Shriver. Stuyvesant, N.Y.: Pendragon Press, 1992.

Stevens, Elizabeth Mruk. *The Influence of Nadia Boulanger on Composition in the United States: A Study of Piano Solo Works by Her American Students*. DMA thesis: Boston University, 1975.

Stooks, Sacha. *The Art of Robert Casadesus*. London: Fortune Press, 1960.

Struble, John Warthen. *The History of American Music: MacDowell through Minimalism*. New York: Facts on File, 1995.

Thomson, Virgil. *Virgil Thomson*. New York: Dutton, 1985.

Thuillier, Jacques. *Fontainebleau*. Fontainebleau: privately printed, 1999.

Timbrell, Charles. *French Pianism*. Portland, Ore.: Amadeus Press, 1999.

Tischler, Barbara L. *An American Music: The Search for an American Musical Identity*. New York: Oxford University Press, 1986.

Tommasini, Anthony. "Little-Known Works of a Renowned French Pianist," *The New York Times*, Friday, September 24, 1999.

———. *Virgil Thomson: Composer on the Aisle*. New York: Norton, 1997.

Weber, Eugen. *The Hollow Years: France in the 1930s*. New York: Norton, 1994.

Index

155, 164, 166, 203–4; library of, 58,
64, 130, 163, 185; locations of,
xx–xxiii, 13, 52, 54, 63, 65, 128,
150, 180; restaurant of, 5, 14, 17, 20,
39–40, 54, 64, 76, 79, 100, 112, 114,
157, 161, 165, 168
Conservatoire Américain, alumni, 161,
166, 168, 181–83, 185, 205–8. *See
also* Fontainebleau Alumni
Association; Fontainebleau
Associations, Inc.
Conservatoire Américain, directors of,
12–15, 119–31, 103, 179, 182,
187–89, 192, 197–202; Bonet,
Narcis, 128, 131, 134; Boulanger,
Nadia, xii, 64–66, 68, 75, 77–81, 87,
93, 97–98, 100, 104, 125, 127–28,
173, 175, 182; Casadesus, Francis,
13; Casadesus, Robert, 63–68, 72;
Decreus, Camille, 15, 31, 60;
D'Ollone, Max, 15, 187, 197, 200;
Entremont, Philippe, 156–68, 176,
181; Marty, Jean-Pierre, 136,
139–44, 146–48, 155–56; Ravel,
Maurice, 28–31; Saint-Saëns,
Camille, 4; Widor, Charles-Marie,
15
Conservatoire Américain,
discrimination at: racial, xxvii, 117;
religious. *See also* anti-Semitism
Conservatoire Américain, faculty of,
xviii, xix–xxvi, 3–7, 9–12, 15–17,
28, 30–34, 45, 55, 59, 75–78, 80–82,
87, 92, 94, 99–98, 101–3, 106, 112,
119, 120–23, 129–31, 133, 135,
141–45, 147, 148, 155–56, 158–69,
172, 174–76, 180–81, 183, 191–93,
199–202; Bazelaire, Paul, 17, 25, 32,
81, 93, 190, 199; Boulanger, Nadia,
xi, xxiv, 7–8, 10, 16, 21, 23–25, 27,
39, 43, 63–65; Casadesus, Gaby, xi,
xxiv, xxvi, 10, 20, 60, 128, 136, 189,
192, 199, 250; Casadesus, Robert,

5–6, 10, 25, 41–43, 188–90, 197;
composition, 7, 23, 128–29, 132–36;
Dieudonné, Annette, 78, 91, 99,
102–5, 111, 126–27, 200; Dupré,
Marcel, xi, 17, 21, 24–25, 63, 89, 98,
200; Entremont, Philippe, 107,
156–68, 176, 181, 192, 197, 200;
French, xi, 51, 56, 100, 105, 125,
176; Jolas, Betsy, 132–33; Levin,
Robert, 125–27, 129, 131, 134, 140,
161, 190, 192, 203; Marty, Jean-
Pierre, 136, 139–51, 176, 179, 192,
197; Naoumoff, Emile, 128–30, 135,
139, 155–56, 201, 204; non-French,
33, 124, 126, 132, 134–35, 161–62,
176–77; Pasquier Trio, 75, 93, 147,
189, 193, 202, 240, 244; Philipp,
Isidor, xxiv–xxv, 5–6, 8, 17, 23–24,
26, 29–30, 33, 42–43, 45,188, 202;
Silva-Herard, Paul, xxiv; Talma,
Louise, 53, 94, 96–98, 100–1,
125–28; World War II, during,
52–54
Conservatoire Américain, finances of:
under direction of Boulanger, Nadia,
75–78, 80, 83, 87, 93, 97–98, 121,
126–29; during the Depression, 19,
26; under direction of Entremont,
Philippe, 156–58, 161; initial,
xix–xxii, 6, 11, 13; under direction
of Marty, Jean-Pierre, 139–40, 142,
144, 155; after World War II, 67;
during World War II, 54
Conservatoire Américain, pianism at,
xxiv, xxvi, 5–10, 12, 15, 39, 64–66,
71, 75, 80, 92–95, 102, 105, 119–22,
133, 149, 158–60, 167–68, 176–77,
181; Casadesus, Gaby, 32, 40, 42,
52–55, 143; Casadesus, Robert,
29–30, 41–43; Philipp, Isidor, 8, 17,
23–24, 26, 29–30, 42–43, 45
Conservatoire Américain, recreation
at, 19–21, 77, 83, 105–6, 163, 165;

~

About the Author

Kendra Preston Leonard is a musicologist specializing in the music and musical culture of twentieth-century America, France, and Britain; women and music; and music and film.

Trained initially as a cellist, Leonard performed throughout the United States and Europe as a soloist and chamber musician. Shifting her focus from performance to historical musicology, she did postgraduate work at the University of Cincinnati College-Conservatory of Music.

Establishing herself as an independent scholar, Leonard has presented her research regularly at conferences including those of the American Musicological Society, the Society for American Music, the International Association of Women in Music, Women in French, the British Shakespeare Association, and the Popular Culture Association/American Culture Association. She was a keynote speaker at the American Music Research Center's Fourth Annual Susan Porter Memorial Symposium on "Nadia Boulanger and American Music." She received the Yosef Wosk Award for Independent Scholarship in 2004 and in 2006 was appointed the National Coalition of Independent Scholars' representative to the American Council of Learned Societies. She is a frequent speaker and author on independent scholarship and publishing culture.